MEDIATING IDENTITIES IN
EIGHTEENTH-CENTURY ENGLAND

In memory of
Franz Meier
(1958–2011)

Mediating Identities in Eighteenth-Century England

Public Negotiations, Literary Discourses,
Topography

Edited by

ISABEL KARREMANN
Ludwig-Maximilians-Universität Munich, Germany

ANJA MÜLLER
Universität Siegen, Germany

ASHGATE

Published by
Ashgate Publishing Limited
Wey Court East
Union Road
Farnham
Surrey, GU9 7PT
England

Ashgate Publishing Company
Suite 420
101 Cherry Street
Burlington
VT 05401-4405
USA

www.ashgate.com

British Library Cataloguing in Publication Data
Mediating identities in eighteenth-century England: public negotiations, literary discourses, topography.
   1. Identity (Psychology) – England – History – 18th century. 2. Identity (Psychology) in literature. 3. Identity (Psychology) in mass media. 4. Identity (Psychology) and mass media – England – History – 18th century. 5. English literature – 18th century – History and criticism.
   I. Karremann, Isabel. II. Muller, Anja, 1969 Sept. 24–
   302.2'3'0942'09033–dc22

Library of Congress Cataloging-in-Publication Data
Mediating identities in eighteenth-century England: public negotiations, literary discourses, topography / edited by Isabel Karremann and Anja Müller.
   p. cm.
Includes bibliographical references and index.
   1. English literature—18th century—History and criticism. 2. National characteristics, English, in literature. 3. Identity (Psychology) and mass media—England. 4. Identity (Psychology) in literature. 5. Mediation—England—History. I. Karremann, Isabel. II. Müller, Anja, 1969 Sept. 24–

PR448.N38M43 2011
820.9'353—dc23

2011025511

ISBN 9781409426189 (hbk)

MIX
Paper from
responsible sources
FSC® C018575
www.fsc.org

Printed and bound in Great Britain by the
MPG Books Group, UK

Contents

List of Illustrations

List of Contributors

Isabelle Baudino is Senior Lecturer in British History and History of Art at École Normale Supérieure in Lyons. She has published mainly on British art of the eighteenth century and on the history of the Royal Academy of Arts. Her first book, *Peinture et historicité: les mutations de la peinture d'histoire en Grande-Bretagne dans la première moitié du XVIIIe siècle (1707–1768)* was published in 1999. In 2008 she co-edited, with Professor Frédéric Ogée, a new edition of *Jonathan Richardson's Complete Works* in their original French translation. In 2010 she received a fellowship from the University of Southampton, and is currently working on the gendering of art historical discourse in eighteenth-century women's travel narratives.

Uwe Böker earned his Ph.D. and his 'Habilitation' from the Universität Regensburg, Germany. He has taught at various universities in Germany and in the United States, and is now Professor Emeritus of English Literature at Technische Universität Dresden, Germany. He has co-authored a history of Old English Literature, co-edited books on medieval literature, crime, and literature during the nineteenth century, and, recently, the titles *Law/Prison/Censorship*, *Re-inventing Oscar (Wilde)*, and *The Public Sphere*. Moreover, he has written monographs on Chaucer and Graham Greene, as well as over 60 articles on various British, American, French, and German authors.

Rainer Emig is Chair of English Literature and Culture at the Leibniz Universität in Hanover, Germany. He is especially interested in the link between literature and the media and in literary, critical, and cultural theory, especially theories of identity, power, gender, and sexuality. His publications include the monographs *Modernism in Poetry* (1995), *W.H. Auden* (1999), and *Krieg als Metapher im zwanzigsten Jahrhundert* (2001). He has edited and co-edited collections on *Stereotypes in Contemporary Anglo-German Relations* (2000), *Ulysses* (2004), *Gender ↔ Religion* (2008), *Hybrid Humour* (with Graeme Dunphy 2010), *Performing Masculinity* (with Antony Rowland 2010), and *Commodifying (Post)Colonialism* (with Oliver Lindner 2010). He has recently completed a monograph entitled *Eccentricity: Culture from the Margins*, and is one of the three editors of *The Journal for the Study of British Cultures*.

Anna-Christina Giovanopoulos is a staff member at the English Department of the Technische Universität Dresden, Germany. Her main area of research is concerned with censorship in the long eighteenth century and the twentieth century, with special focus on law, politics, and literature. Her publications include articles on the reception of Faulkner, Hemingway, Updike, Kerouac, and Graham Greene in East Germany, on the role of Captain Kidd in the political struggles of early eighteenth-century England, on Jonathan Wilde, and on the public sphere in the eighteenth century.

Christoph Heyl studied English and history at the universities of Frankfurt and Reading. His Ph.D. thesis on the rise of the private sphere in eighteenth-century London (*A Passion for Privacy: Untersuchungen zur Genese der bürgerlichen Privatsphäre in London, 1650–1800*) was published in 2004; his 'Habilitation' (forthcoming) deals with the culture of collecting in seventeenth-century England. Christoph Heyl's current main research project is a study of German- and Yiddish-speaking immigrants/refugees and the literature of migration in London, 1848–1945. He is also working (as co-editor, together with Harald Mieg) on an interdisciplinary handbook of urban and metropolitan studies (*Metzler Handbuch Stadt*). He is currently teaching at the Universität Duisburg-Essen, Germany.

Christoph Houswitschka is Professor of English Literature at the Universität Bamberg, Germany. He has published on late-medieval English literature (e.g. Thomas Malory), eighteenth-century literature (e.g., 'Family, Crime, and the Public Sphere: "Incest" in Eighteenth-Century England', 'Circulating Ideas of Democracy: The Legal Culture of the High Treason Trials of 1794'), literature and science, contemporary drama, and Holocaust literature.

Christian Huck is Professor of English and American Cultural and Media Studies at the Universität Kiel, Germany. He has published on popular culture and literature, cultural and media theory, music videos, Irish poetry and nationalism, football, film, and fashion. His most recent publication is *Fashioning Society, or, The Mode of Modernity: Observing Fashion in Eighteenth-Century Britain* (2010).

Isabel Karremann is a Assistant Professor of English Literature with the Collaborative Research Group 'Pluralization and Authority in the Early Modern Age' at Ludwig-Maximilians-Universität Munich, Germany, where she is writing a book on practices of forgetting in early modern culture and Shakespearean history plays. She earned her Ph.D. for a study on concepts of masculinity in the eighteenth-century novel, published as *Männlichkeit und Körper: Inszenierungen eines geschlechtsspezifischen Unbehagens im englischen Roman des 18. und frühen 19. Jahrhunderts* (2008). A co-edited essay collection entitled *Forgetting Faith? Negotiating Confessional Conflict in Early Modern Europe* will be published in 2011, and she is currently preparing another book-length study on popular print culture in the early seventeenth century.

Franz Meier (†) studied English and German Literature and Language at the Universität Regensburg, Germany, where he taught English Literature since 1987, received his doctorate in 1990 and his 'Habilitation' in 1997. He was visiting professor at the University of Northern Iowa at Cedar Falls in 1992, taught English Literature and Culture at the Johann Wolfgang Goethe-University, Frankfurt/Main, as well as the Ludwig-Maximilians-Universität Munich, and was Chair of English Literature and Culture at the Universität Braunschweig from 2005 to 2011. His research was focussed on gender studies, popular culture, and intermediality (text/image-relationships). His publications include *Die frühe Ding-Lyrik William Carlos Williams: Genese und Poetologie* (1991) and *Sexualität und Tod: Eine Themenverknüpfung in der englischen Schauer- und Sensationsliteratur und ihrem soziokulturellen Kontext, 1764–1897* (2002), as well as articles on Gothic fiction, Victorian culture, Oscar Wilde, James Joyce, and (post-)modern English and American poetry.

Michael Meyer is Professor of English Literature in the Department of Cultural Studies at the Universität Koblenz-Landau, Campus Koblenz, Germany. He is the author of a phenomenological study of the poetry of Charles Tomlinson (1990), a study of autobiography and intertextuality in Gibbon, Mill, and Ruskin (1998), and an introduction to English and American literature (3rd ed., 2008). He has published two collections on teaching literature at university (1994, 2008) and a critical edition of Salman Rushdie's short stories *East, West* (2002), co-edited *Vertrauen und Glaubwürdigkeit* (Trust and Credibility, 2005), and edited *Word & Image in Colonial and Postcolonial Literatures and Cultures* (2009). His current research focuses on fiction, visual media, colonial, and post-colonial literature.

Anja Müller, Chair of English Literature and Culture at the Universität Siegen, Germany, has published on contemporary British drama, twentieth-century British, Irish, and Australian fiction, children's literature, intertextuality, intermediality and adaptation, and various aspects of English literature and culture of the long eighteenth century. Among her books are *Fashioning Childhood in the Eighteenth Century: Age and Identity* (ed., 2006) and *Framing Childhood in Eighteenth-Century English Periodicals and Prints, 1689–1789* (2009; Children's Literature Association Honor Book 2009). She is currently preparing collections of essays on *Adaptations of Classics in and for Children's Literature* and on *Childhood in the English Renaissance*.

Felicity Nussbaum, Distinguished Professor of English at the University of California, Los Angeles (UCLA), has published most recently *Rival Queens: Actresses, Performance, and the Eighteenth-Century British Theatre* (2010). Among her other books are *The Limits of the Human: Fictions of Anomaly, Race, and Gender in the Long Eighteenth Century* (2003) and *The Arabian Nights in Historical Context: Between East and West* (2008), co-edited with Saree Makdisi. A former president of the American Society for Eighteenth-Century Studies, she has been granted several awards including a John Simon Guggenheim Fellowship and an NEH Fellowship at the Henry E. Huntington Library.

Anette Pankratz is Professor of British Cultural Studies at Ruhr-Universität Bochum, Germany. Her research and publications focus on the long seventeenth century and contemporary British drama.

Katharina Rennhak is Professor of English Literature at Bergische Universität Wuppertal, Germany. She is especially interested in the link between literature and culture in the eighteenth, twentieth, and twenty-first centuries, in literary and critical theory, and in the relationship between British and Irish literary cultures and histories. Her publications include *Sprachkonzeptionen im metahistorischen Roman: Diskursspezifische Ausprägungen des* Linguistic Turn *in* Critical Theory, *Geschichtstheorie und Geschichtsfiktion 1970–1990* (2002), *Revolution und Emanzipation* (ed., with Virginia Richter, 2004), *Romantic Voices, Romantic Poetics* (ed., with Christoph Bode, 2005), and *Women Constructing Men: Female Novelists and Their Male Characters, 1750–2000* (ed., with

Sarah S.G. Frantz, 2010). Her second monograph on narrative cross-gendering and the construction of masculine identities in British and Irish women writers' novels around 1800 is forthcoming.

Peter Wagner is Professor of English Literature at the Universität Koblenz-Landau, Campus Landau. He has published widely on eighteenth-century literature and print culture, especially on William Hogarth. Among his monographs are *Erotica of the Enlightenment in England and America* (1988) and *Reading Iconotexts: From Swift to the French Revolution* (1995). He is the editor of the Penguin Classics edition of Cleland's *Memoirs of a Woman of Pleasure*, of *Icons – Texts – Iconotexts: Essays on Ekphrasis and Intermediality* (1996), and (together with David Bindman and Frédéric Ogée) of *Hogarth: Representing Nature's Machines* (2001). Together with Frédéric Ogée, he is the editor of the LAPASEC series (Landau Paris Studies on the Eighteenth Century), in which two volumes have appeared to date.

Preface

The present volume is based on the research undertaken by a network of young German scholars of eighteenth-century English literature and culture. The collaborative project, entitled 'Mediating Identities in Eighteenth-Century England' was funded by the German Research Foundation (DFG). For three years, the group met for workshops with distinguished experts as well as for discussing the progress of the individual research projects. In 2008, the project was concluded with a conference. The plenary lectures, papers and responses presented on that occasion form the core of this volume, which seeks to offer the results of our projects to the interested reader. The subtitle of the book, Public Negotiations, Literary Discourses, Topography, takes cognizance of the three major focal areas of the project. The book offers an assessment of the intricate and complex link between the emergence and use of various media in eighteenth-century England and the concomitant emergence of various categories of identity.

At this point, it is my pleasure to express thanks to all the various institutions and people who, each in their own way, contributed to the successful completion of both the network project and the present volume. First and foremost, I wish to thank the German Research Foundation (DFG) for their generous financing of the various meetings of our group as well as of the concluding conference. Being the coordinator of the project, I was always grateful for the support received from my Alma Mater, the Otto-Friedrich-Universität Bamberg (Germany). This support consisted in funding the initiation of the DFG proposal, administrative support for the yearly bookkeeping (special thanks go to Luise Graser), and funding the concluding conference. The workshops and meetings of our group found an ideal venue in Haus Frankenthal, next to the famous baroque basilica of Vierzehnheiligen in picturesque Franconia. While our guests provided ample food for thought, the staff members made sure that the appetites of our stomachs were satisfied as well. In organizational matters, I found valuable support from my student helpers: Anna-Maria Hartmann, Tanya Herig, Benjamin Pohl, and, especially, Johannes Weber and Nina Moritz, who both also helped with the proposal. Simone Herrmann, Seth Hulse, Mary Grace Kannapin, Maria Severin, Dominik Schäfer, Nils Wilkinson and Svenja Zenz lent a hand in formatting the manuscript and compiling the index.

The success of a research network entirely depends on the scholars contributing to it. A number of distinguished experts were generous enough to share their expertise with us in workshops: we are grateful to Ann Shteir, Udo Thiel, Oliver Jahraus and Hans-Peter Wagner (who also did not hesitate to volunteer at the last minute to contribute to our response essay). Our conference equally benefited from the plenary lectures and responses of renowned scholars in the field, some of them contributing to the present volume. It was a pleasure and an honour to have Felicity Nussbaum, Isabelle Baudino, Frédéric Ogée, Uwe Böker, Rainer Emig, Christoph Heyl and Günther Lottes share our work in the project and reflect critically on our research. Last but not least, I wish to express cordial thanks to all the members of our research group individually: first and foremost to Isabel Karremann, co-editor and author of the introduction to this volume – her sheer energy made this volume happen. The others are, in alphabetical order: Anna-Christina Giovanopoulos, Christoph Houswitschka, Christian Huck, Franz Meier, Michael Meyer, Anette Pankratz, Katharina Rennhak and Sigrid Rieuwerts. Quite congenial to the conversational culture that was so typical of eighteenth-century England, our 'salon of scholars' has amply proved that research definitely thrives if the circle of colleagues in which it is conducted turns out to become a circle of friends. The more tragic the loss if such a circle is bereaved of one of its members: while this book was in press, Franz Meier was taken from our midst by a tragic accident. He was a diligent scholar, an amiable, well-respected colleague and the best of friends. This book is for you, Franz.

Anja Müller

Siegen, February 2011

Introduction:
Mediating Identities in
Eighteenth-Century England

Isabel Karremann

> But it is a work of very great labour and difficulty to keep a journal of life, occupied in various pursuits, mingled with concomitant speculations and reflections, in so much, that I do not think it possible to do it unless one has a peculiar talent for abridging. I have tried it in that way, when it has been my good fortune to live in a multiplicity of instructive and entertaining scenes, and I have thought my notes like portable soup, of which a little bit by being dissolved in water will make a good large dish; for their substance by being expanded in words would fill a volume. Sometimes it has occurred to me that a man should not live more than he can record, as a farmer should not have a larger crop than he can gather in. And I have regretted that there is no invention for getting an immediate and exact transcript of the mind, like that instrument by which a copy of a letter is at once taken off. (Bailey, 332)

In this passage from an article 'On diaries', published in March 1783 in *The London Magazine* under the pseudonym The Hypochondriack, John Boswell analyzes the difficulties one encounters in keeping a 'journal of life'. The most troublesome problem with translating life into language seems to be that of scope: how can one hope to confine the 'multiplicity of instructive and entertaining scenes' encountered daily into words and sentences? Boswell's answer is that one needs 'a peculiar talent for abridging', for condensing life, boiling it down to the essentials, as it were. In a striking culinary metaphor he calls this extract 'portable soup', a thick, rich broth of life which can later be dissolved to provide a nourishing discursive meal. Of course Boswell himself had perfected that method, particularly for those innumerable occasions when he recorded the essentials of Dr Johnson's 'instructive and entertaining' dinner conversation in his diary. The process of dissolving these notes into the huge volume of *Life of Johnson* (1791) began when his famous friend died in 1784. In the terms of Boswell's article, this enterprise was both a success and a failure. With its mass of personal detail and dialogue, reproduced verbatim years after the event, the *Life* revolutionized biography writing. Yet it took him far too long – seven years in all, during which a flood of rival biographies managed to cash in on Johnson's fame – to serve as a convincing example of instant soup. In hindsight, Boswell's advice that 'a man should not live more than he can record' reads almost as a hidden complaint about

Johnson's extraordinary vitality and volubility. Boswell could indeed have done with an 'invention for getting an immediate and exact transcript of the mind.'

Boswell's musings on the relation between an individual's life and the means of recording it raise several questions concerning the mediation of identity in eighteenth-century England which this collection sets out to explore. How was the relationship between an individual's life and his or her sense of self conceived of? What did identity consist in, and was it consistent over time and in different contexts? What impact did 'various pursuits' in 'a multiplicity of instructive and entertaining scenes' have on one's sense and performance of self? Further, how did lived experience translate into a recorded abstract, a medium? To what extent was an identity forged from retrospective 'speculations and reflections' on one's acts, recorded in a medium? What difficulties did writers encounter in representing 'life' or 'the mind', and how did these difficulties register in the medium itself? What media were available for the construction and circulation of identities in eighteenth-century England, and how did the form of media, as well as the social and aesthetic practices of media use, influence the production and perception of identity?

Before these questions are addressed by the essays collected here, it might be useful to clarify what we mean by our key concepts, 'mediating' and 'identity'. In its broadest definition, identity is treated in terms of who we are to each other, that is, as a sense of self that is produced and communicated socially. This process entails acts of mediation: identities are constituted, implemented, negotiated, and validated through the conduit of media. While the concept of identity and identity constitution has received much critical attention, as we will see in a moment, the question of how identities are mediated has remained rather implicit. This volume of essays seeks to contribute to a more outspoken critical discussion of the connection between historically specific identities and the media available at the time. While our interest in identities in the long eighteenth century chimes in with a host of other publications in the field,[1] our focus on media and the social and aesthetic practices that regulate their use adds, we hope, a distinctly new note. Since the essays themselves explore this in historically specific constellations, this introductory chapter will recapitulate some theoretical perspectives on identity and try to extend them so as to include a perspective on media and acts of mediation.

Identity – Identification – Mediation

The theoretical debate on identity over the last 30 years or so has developed through a series of 'turns': the discursive turn, the performative turn, the spatial turn, the pictorial or visual turn. The first in this line demarcates a turn away from an interior account of identity which claimed that there is a 'real I', an inner self and its outward expressions. This essentialist notion of an internal, originary, and unified identity has been challenged at least since Freud. Nevertheless,

---

[1]   Recent publications include Wheeler, Nussbaum 2003, Harvey, Thomas King, Müller 2006, Milne, Boulukos, Straub, and Duncan.

identity is still a useful and necessary category, as Stuart Hall points out, if now in a detotalized and deconstructed form (2000, 15). This reconceptualization has been provided by the discursive account of identity which claims that who we are is accomplished, disputed, ascribed, resisted, and negotiated through discourse (Benwell and Stokoe, 4). Indeed, the very notion of an 'inner self' is itself seen as a product of discourse: an 'interiority effect', as it were, created through discourse. Interestingly, the opposition of interiority versus discursive identity is not only a phenomenon of postmodern critical debate, but can already be discerned in the long eighteenth century, which sees the emergence of both the notion of an essential, inner self and the notion of a self as a bundle of perceptions retrospectively labelled 'I'.[2]

This dichotomy also underpins the question of agency or structure. The agency view, endorsed by essentialist positions, stresses a subject's ability to construct his or her identity in any way he or she wishes. Stuart Hall argues against this view that, just like identity, 'agency' must be reconceptualized – not as a volitional act of free will carried out by an autonomous subject, but rather as discursive practices that may be performed by subjects but are preformed by social and cultural structures (2000, 16). This latter view stresses the way in which subjects are restrictively positioned within existing discourses. Again, the dualism between agency and structure is not only a phenomenon of late twentieth-century criticism but has a diachronic perspective as well. The medieval belief in the divine determination of one's place within a rigid social structure gave way to an early modern notion of identity as self-fashioning, as an internal, agentive project of the self.[3] This notion also dominated Enlightenment philosophy, with its emphasis on self-mastery through reason and reflexivity, and enabled the notion of the 'sovereign subject' or 'human agent who is able to remake himself by methodical and disciplined action' (Taylor, 143–59).[4] It reached its solipsistic climax in Romantic notions of self-fulfilment and expressive individualism. Yet all the while, as Norbert Elias (1979) and Michel Foucault have shown, this belief in autonomous agency was counter-pointed by an increasing subjection of the individual to regulative structures, both in the form of institutionalized regimes of surveillance and punishment and in that of an internalized self-discipline. Paradoxically, both the belief in individual autonomy and the reality of social regulation were underpinned by the idea of human perfectibility.

The dichotomy between agency and structure becomes important again in postmodern theory, where identity is assigned to the individual through its being subjected to discursive structures. This determining structure has been conceptualized by Lacanian psychoanalysis as well as the Derridean deconstruction of the symbolic order mediated by language; by Marxist critics, first and foremost

---

[2]   For a genealogy of the self see Taylor, and Wahrman.

[3]   This argument is developed by Greenblatt, Maus, and also by Schoenfeldt.

[4]   For an overview over the debate in eighteenth-century philosophical treatises, see Thiel, 286–318.

Antonio Gramsci and Louis Althusser, under the heading of 'interpellation'; by means of discourse analysis in the wake of Foucault, which analyzes subjects as the product of dominant discourses, practices, and institutions; and as the cultural dynamics between containment and subversion, with New Historicism pessimistically coming down on the side of containment and Cultural Materialism holding onto the idea of the resisting subject.[5]

This model of identity, in which the subject is treated as a mere effect of discourse and ideology, has been criticized and modified in the attempt to bring together the external discursive realm and the 'psychic acts of identification' (Benwell and Stokoe, 31). From this perspective, identity emerges as the meeting point or suture between

> on the one hand, the discourses and practices which attempt to 'interpellate', speak to us or hail us into places as the social subjects of particular discourses, and on the other hand, the processes which produce subjectivities which construct us as subjects which can be 'spoken'. Identities are thus points of temporary attachment to the subject positions which discursive practices construct for us. (Hall 2000, 19)

These 'temporary attachments' have been most rigorously analyzed with the help of the notion of performativity. How and why individuals as subjects identify with the 'positions' to which they are summoned; how they fashion, stylize, produce, and 'perform' these positions; why they never do so completely, for once and all time; and how they constantly struggle with, resist, and negotiate the normative rules with which they are confronted and by which they regulate themselves are central questions to which 'performativity' has yielded rich answers. The work of Judith Butler on gender and sexual identities provides a paradigmatic example of this approach. In *Gender Trouble* and *Bodies That Matter*, Butler conceptualizes identity as the result of regulatory practices which work through the principle of performativity. Identity is inscribed by social and ideological structures which can only ever be repeated or cited. Importantly, this 'forcible reiteration' also forms the material, sexed body, the ways it behaves and is perceived. Yet in the very repetition of conventionalized acts and signs of gender identity inheres the possibility of change through misquotation, ironic distancing, or resignification: 'That this reiteration is necessary', Butler maintains, is itself a sign 'that bodies never quite comply with the norms by which their materialization is impelled'. These 'instabilities' harbour 'the possibilities for rematerialization', through which 'the force of the regulatory law can be turned against itself' (Butler 1993, 2). This does not mean, however, that Butler resurrects the idea of the pre-discursive subject of resistance; on the contrary: 'Subjected to gender, but subjectivated by gender, the "I" neither precedes nor follows the process of this gendering, but emerges only within and as the matrix of gender relations themselves' (ibid., 7). The opposition between coercive interpellation and volitional or intentional

---

[5]   For a more detailed overview see Hall 2000, 19–27.

agency is here brought together in a notion of the subject's (re)articulations of and (mis)identifications with normative, institutionalized structures.

Taking the cue from this body of criticism, we regard the question of discursive structure and individual agency not as an either/or choice but rather as the two extremes of a continuum. Most essays in this volume subscribe to a reconstructed notion of agency which articulates itself within, yet is potentially able to transgress, the frame of social, cultural, aesthetic, and media structures. In other words, there are not only restrictive identity offers which interpellate the subject, but the subject can – hedged in, of course, by a host of social rules – decide which offers it will take up in what context, and which not. This notion of identification goes beyond a common-sense, naturalist understanding in terms of a mere 'recognition of some common origin or shared characteristics'. Rather, it seeks to reconceptualize identity as a 'strategic and positional' membership of and identification with particular social groups (Hall 2000, 16). This does not necessarily mean to consolidate the notion of the stable, volitional self. Identification does not always provide closure and a stable sense of self, but can also challenge it. In the words of Judith Butler, identifications also 'unsettle the I' in that they 'are the sedimentation of the "we" in the constitution of any "I", the structuring present of alterity in the very formulation of the I' (1993, 105). Hence, identification necessitates an ongoing recalibration of the relation between self and larger social groupings as well as the relation between social groupings in terms of nation, ethnicity, religion, politics, gender, and sexuality. That identification with somebody necessarily entails the exclusion of somebody else, that it requires a constitutive outside, has become a staple of postmodern critical thinking. Identification operates across difference and thus produces symbolic boundaries; as a process which operates across time it also entails a transgression and renegotiation of these boundaries as well as the individual and collective identities produced through it.[6]

Moreover, this process of identification, of simultaneous inclusion and exclusion, is interactive and intersubjective. It involves the necessity to communicate one's 'identity' and to have it recognized by others, and it does so through acts of mediation. This is the point at which our volume enters the debate on identity and identification by shifting the focus to mediation as the conduit for processes of identification. Going beyond the narrow notion of a medium as a technological vehicle, be it discursive or material, we broaden this understanding to encompass the historically specific social and aesthetic practices of media use. Hence the focus is not only on books or journals, but on reading them in specific ways; not only on the theatre, but on what happens between the performing actors and the watching audience; not only on landscape paintings, but on looking at them and walking through the countryside itself. This broader notion of the

---

[6] These processes, through which personal and collective identities are produced, are beautifully described and analyzed in Douglas, a seminal study about the concepts of pollution and taboos.

medium enables us to reconstruct processes of identification as the production of identities in specific medial forms.

The passage from Boswell's article highlights this double dimension of mediating identity: One's life needs to be 'recorded' in some kind of medium in order to yield its 'harvest', a sense of self that is communicated to and validated through recognition by others. The act of writing and reading about an individual's life is what makes it perceptible to oneself and to others as an identity. Identification as a process through which individuals identify themselves, and are in turn identified as belonging to a social group, is inconceivable without mediation. In this sense, identity is an effect of mediation.

Narrative Identities

For Boswell, identity as the essence of an individual's life is primarily a narrative reconstruction: it is a story one tells about oneself, one's own life. The connection between narrative and identity has been prominently theorized by Paul Ricoeur in volume three of his *Time and Narrative, in Oneself as Another* as well as in two essays identically entitled 'Narrative Identity'.[7] Starting from the apparent paradox that identity emerges through both change and permanence, Ricoeur resolves this aporia through the process of 'emplotment', the narrative organization of the contingencies of existence into a coherent whole. Whether the starting point is a sense of integrity or of fragmentation, self-knowledge is in both cases approached through the construction of a 'coherent and acceptable story' about oneself. That this story be acceptable to oneself as well as to others renders storytelling an eminently social practice.

Narrative identity, according to Ricoeur, is 'the sort of identity to which a human being has access thanks to the mediation of the narrative function' (1991, 73). This mediation is necessary because 'the self does not know itself immediately, but only indirectly, through the detour of cultural signs of all sorts' (ibid., 80). Narrative mediation is only one among various symbolic mediations, albeit a particularly important one: if 'knowledge of the self is an interpretation', this interpretation of the self, in turn, finds historical and fictional 'narrative, among other signs and symbols, to be a privileged mediation' (ibid., 73). The reason for this privileged status is that it 'provides precisely the "figure-able" character of the individual which has for its result that the self, narratively interpreted, is itself a figured self – a self which figures itself as this or that' (ibid., 80).

However, narrative identity is not quite as stable as Ricoeur would have it, nor is the act of storytelling quite as intentional and controllable as he makes it sound. Since the formation of narrative identity is so closely bound up with narrative form, its 'decomposition' – its relapse into the contingencies and complexities of life – necessarily prefigures the loss of a clear-cut identity of the character.

---

[7]   I am going to refer to the one published in 1991 in more detail.

Ricoeur himself admits as much in *Oneself as Another*, yet he shies away from the insight that the identity of the narrating or narrated 'I' can be systematically deconstructed by the text itself. It has been pointed out that

> though Ricoeur argues in favor of a mediation of self-understanding through texts, he subordinates the destabilizing potential of language to the principles of Aristotelian poetics, in particular the importance of composition and plot which result in the subordination of chance events to a teleological structure. Ricoeur seeks to stabilize signification and save the identity of the subject. (Crowley, 6)

Ricoeur's response, in order to stabilize his concept of identity, is to transfer his argument from narrative to the field of ethical action: if textuality cannot support the structure of the 'I' any more, ethical agency must serve as the anchor of social identity. Yet in moving from text to action,

> Ricoeur circumvents the thorny issue of a subject constituted by language. For the attempt to fix any life in words, however provisionally, is inevitably beset by the metonymic, supplemental structure of language and once inscribed or recounted each life story is subject to further interpretation. (Ibid., 8)

This is arguably the very predicament which Boswell found himself in regarding his project of capturing Johnson's life in words, and it is a predicament which I explore here in my own essay on *A Journal of the Plague Year*, the fictional autobiography of a London citizen in 1665, written by Daniel Defoe in 1722. The narrator, H.F., prefigures Boswell's recommendation that one take notes from life and then dissolve them into a substantial volume, here a guide to self-help in case of another plague epidemic. Like Boswell, H.F. is confronted with the problem of how to translate life and, indeed, death into the medium of the written and printed word, and how to 'abstract' the chaotic experience of the plague into an orderly plot. This attempt to create order and meaning out of chaos is aligned with the emergence of a middle-class urban manliness whose members are represented as the very agents of preserving order. It is challenged both on the level of the story (the manly struggle against the epidemic) and the level of narrative discourse (H.F.'s struggle for a meaningful, orderly account). The ultimate impossibility of fixing life in words arises here, too, from 'the destabilizing potential of language', which in this case is exacerbated by a rivalry between the media of oral culture and print culture.

The essays by Anja Müller, Franz Meier, and Katharina Rennhak also discuss, each in their different way, how narrative harbours opportunities for as well as challenges to identification for the writing and reading subject. Anja Müller charts the attempt at constituting an orderly narrative identity for children in the emergent genre of children's literature between 1689 and 1789. This genre negotiated the transition from oral culture to print culture and from the more 'fantastic' mode of fairy tales to the 'realistic' code of social conventions. Fusing the novel's realism with explicit didacticism, it yet departed significantly from adult literature in that it sought to render its contents unambiguous and thus fit to be consumed by children without supervision. While children's literature could be consumed in private just as the novel increasingly was, its extra- and inner-textual structures of 'monitored reading' mediated habits of self-discipline that contributed to the education of its readers into responsible citizens in the public as well as the private space.

Franz Meier discusses the connections between identity and textuality in terms of the interdependency of gender and genre. The key question here is how genre boundaries between the sentimental and the pornographic novel were conceived of in the eighteenth century and how they mediated prevailing gender boundaries, thus encouraging their readers to meditate/mediate their own gender identities along the lines constituted by literary texts. While sentimental fiction was firmly associated with femininity and pornography with masculinity, Meier's essay deconstructs these seemingly stable boundaries. His analysis of *Pamela* and *Fanny Hill* – prototypical examples of the sentimental and pornographic novel, respectively – in regard to authorship, textual features (narration, plot, characters), and reader response shows up the disconcertingly similar ways in which these texts mediate identity.

While specific media might originally pertain to specific writing or reception situations, they can also themselves become mediators between writer and reader situated in quite different spheres. The prefaces to novels by eighteenth-century women authors, which Katharina Rennhak explores in her essay, are a case in point. From the perspective of an ideology of separate spheres, which grew more rigid toward the end of the eighteenth century, female authors appeared as a moral aberration since they entered the public sphere reserved for men. Yet their prefaces did not avoid the ubiquitous language of separate spheres. On the contrary, they used it to reconstruct authorial identities and to endow them with moral authority. One strategy was to have the public world and the world of the private imagination meet in the space of the preface and to show that they abide by similar rather than different rules, thus legitimizing the woman writer's voice. Another consisted in arguing that only the printed book entered the public sphere after all, thus acting literally as a medium, a go-between, which allowed the woman to communicate beyond the order of 'her' sphere without having to leave the private realm which conferred moral authority on her.

Spatial Identities

Nor is this potential for spatial and ideological transgression restricted to printed texts alone. As Felicity Nussbaum shows, eighteenth-century star actresses like Kitty Clive (1711–1785) created for themselves a public persona of celebrity: they appropriated the roles they were famous for as their own 'theatrical property' while fusing it with what the audience would perceive as their personal, private identity. The allure of this celebrity persona was its very promise to bridge the gap between the part and the actress, between public display and personal revelation as well as between celebrated star and spell-bound audience. The celebrity part and especially the self-referential epilogue – some of which 'the Clive' wrote herself – served as the medium of this interaction. The interiority effect created thus and circulated by means of celebrity gossip had considerable value in the marketplace, which translated into salaries and gratuities. Women on stage had a 'performative property' in their public/private identities; in fact, Nussbaum argues, this performative property was the first significant property a woman could possess in her own name, and which depended upon her identity rather than her husband or her family.

Anette Pankratz's essay on eighteenth-century comedies likewise emphasizes the theatre's generically given emphasis on exteriority, which in her view highlights the faultlines of individuation and interiority. On the one hand, attending a play provides opportunities for self-reflection as well as for self-correction: the action and characters on stage not only offer an amusing spectacle, but also invite the audience to introspection, a point pushed home by often overly didactic prologues and epilogues. Observing a version of reality on stage, the spectators are enabled to observe their own lives and establish a reflective, critical relationship to their own selves. Yet this process is at the same time challenged by the fact that on stage, interiority is always mediated by words, gestures, or deeds, presenting the audience with an 'interpretable surface'. This interplay between performing and observing interiority, Pankratz claims, is often highlighted self-reflexively in eighteenth-century plays, allowing the theatre to function as a meta-medium for exploring the tensions between interiority, its mediation, and its reception on stage as well as in the auditorium.

The essays by Rennhak, Nussbaum, and Pankratz thus raise the questions of how social and symbolic spaces and the boundaries between them mediate identities, and in particular how the transgression of these boundaries constitutes an act of identification. Since several other contributions to this volume likewise engage with spatial identities and their media (for example, Boeker, Baudino, Meyer, and Houswitschka), the so-called 'spatial turn' in recent theoretical debates merits some attention.

The spatial turn, broadly speaking, signifies a recent preoccupation with space as a significant constituent of social processes and as a bearer of meaning in its own right. In addition to language practices, spatially encoded practices such as embodied movement and symbolic domains like visual representation are taken into account in the production of identity. In particular, the links between space, social action, and identity construction are at stake: who we are is inextricably linked to where we are, have been, or are going. This shift in focus has been accompanied by a shift from temporality to spatiality: space, rather than time, becomes crucial to cultural and social analysis. Before, space, place, and landscape were treated as natural givens or as abstract, neutral categories in the social sciences (if not in the humanities, where the semiotics of space always played an important role for the analysis of settings in literary texts or in paintings). The spatial turn, however, has brought about new understandings of place and space as constitutive of social meaning. Moreover, space and place are seen not as static, *a priori* phenomena but as ongoing and dynamically constructed modes of thinking, acting, and being. The interrelationship between symbolic space, discourse, and social identity can be explored from at least two different directions: on the one hand, place/space as the location for discursive identity, and on the other, place/space as produced in and as a topic of discourse (see Benwell and Stokoe, 211).

Identities in the Public Spheres

The concept of space as a location for discursive identity which has engendered productive, if highly controversial, debates about eighteenth-century culture is that of the public sphere. In his seminal study *Structural Transformation of the Public Sphere* (1962, transl. 1989), Jürgen Habermas set out to determine the social conditions for a rational-critical debate about public issues, which he saw threatened by the contemporary mass-media culture of his own day.[8] He defines the public sphere as a site where private individuals engage in rational discourse with the aim of reaching a consensus about public issues. Habermas describes the function of this 'public opinion' as 'the task of criticism and control which a public body of citizens informally […] practices *vis-à-vis* the ruling structure organized in the form of a state' (1974, 49). The public thus emerges as a cultural and political arbiter that questions the official decrees and governmental acts of the state (Melton, 2). It is important to note here that 'public' does not equal 'official politics'; rather, the public sphere is understood as an extension of the social sphere of the family.

The three developments that, historically speaking, produced the public sphere were the rise of the modern nation state, which allowed for a distinction between sovereign force and private interest; the rise of capitalism, which sought to defend private economy and consumption against state intervention; and the rise of a bourgeois conception of the family as a sphere of affection and intimacy, with the traditional judicial and proprietal functions of the *pater familias* transferred to the state and the market respectively. The innovative force of Habermas's model lay in the fact that it connected the social with the political and broadened the discursive range by investigating the public significance of private discourse and sociability (ibid., 4–10).

While both his method and the historical account of these developments have been widely acclaimed and expanded by scholars in Habermas's wake, the ideological assumptions underlying his model of the public sphere have been justly criticized. In particular, his claim that access to the public sphere was ruled by the dictates of reason only and not by the social identity of the speaker (or writer) has met with harsh criticism. For Habermas's ideal of inclusion based solely on reason,

---

[8]   For the genesis of *Structural Transformation* as an answer to particular challenges in German political and popular culture in the 1950s and 1960s, see Calhoun, 4–6 and Melton, 3, note 5.

education, and taste entirely disregards that these criteria themselves performed exclusionary functions. As Geneviève Lloyd has shown, rationality was regarded as an exclusively male attribute: while the female scholars of the eighteenth century, and especially the members of the Bluestocking Circle, claimed that both sexes have the same capacity for reason, they were the notable exception to the rule.[9] Likewise, Pierre Bourdieu's study on taste, *Distinction*, demonstrates that far from being a basis for inclusion, taste actually functions as a technique of social distinction. As Craig Calhoun points out: 'The early bourgeois public spheres were composed of narrow segments of the European population, mainly educated, propertied men, and they conducted a discourse not only exclusive of others but prejudicial to the interests of those excluded' (3).

Paradoxically, the historically factual emphasis on reason, education, and taste, with its class and gender bias, did not ensure that only members of the middling classes (or of the male gender) joined in the public sphere. For instance, while inclusion in the public sphere was undoubtedly based on property, this also brought in members of the nobility. Similarly, the professional background of participants in public debates was not only manufacturing or commerce, as Habermas would have it, but also included offices received from the crown. This fact in turn undermines the claim that the public sphere functioned as an oppositional force to the state; rather, we have to take into account that it would, to a certain extent, also have buttressed traditional institutions. The public sphere thus bridged the cultural divide between noble and non-noble, and at the same time widened the distance between propertied and plebeian (Melton, 10–13). Yet again, as the essays by Nussbaum and Pankratz in this volume show, there were also media which transgressed this divide: the theatre's oral performance rendered the question of literacy, dependent as it was on status and property, a moot point.

The chapter by Nussbaum challenges, in particular, the masculinist assumptions that underpin Habermas's model: women were not restricted to a private identity but could and did have a public persona that played with the very expectations of a difference between the two. Feminist critics have pointed out from early on that the norms of rationality and taste are intrinsically masculinist, and that the whole concept rests on a gendered distinction between a (male) public realm and a (female) private realm. Hence, the argument ran, the concept perpetuates a public/private dichotomy that sanctions women's political subordination.[10] While this critique of the gender blindness of Habermas's model was very much to the point, it exposed itself to criticism where it tended to misread the public sphere as the sphere of official political power. For Habermas, it is in fact a semi-private social realm in which women could participate as readers and authors, in theatre audiences, and in debating societies (although he perceived of their participation as, ultimately,

---

[9]   See also Pateman, who critically reassesses the gender implications of Locke's contract theory from a similar perspective.

[10]   For this body of criticism, see the essay collections edited by Meehan and by Landes, as well as Nancy Fraser's essay 'Rethinking the Public Sphere' in Calhoun, 109–42.

a symptom of degeneration). Conversely, the domestic sphere was a much more porous, semi-public realm, as Amanda Vickery has shown: the household was a place in which women read, wrote, entertained visitors, and discussed politics, religion, and literary works in salons or at dinner parties (383–414). Habermas's gender blindness thus obscures not only the gender politics underpinning the very divide of public/private; it also disregards Enlightenment voices calling for an inclusion of women as a civilizing force.[11] Of course, women's participation in the public sphere was itself authorized by a double standard: the view of women as a moral and civilizing force rested on notions of sexual difference that in turn justified their actual exclusion from the realm of politics (Melton, 13–15).

The essays by Uwe Boeker, Anna-Christina Giovanopoulos, and Christian Huck in this volume engage in a critical adaptation of Habermas's concept of the public sphere. Starting from the assumption that different discursive sites require different discursive practices and identifications, producing what he terms 'patchwork identities', Boeker examines two instances of civil society's attempts at regulating the material sites of discourse and the identities they produce. The first example is provided by the 1670 Quaker Trials and the Quakers' practice of 'bold speaking' as a means of appropriating the discursive site of the courtroom for the articulation of an oppositional political discourse. The second discusses the Societies for the Reformation of Manners as civil agents of policing aberrant behaviour. While aiming at an internalization of surveillance as a private conscience, Boeker shows that this inner self could be and was perceived as a space of withdrawal from the very attempts at policing. These cases raise the question of how those sites and their discourses were regulated, and how successful these attempts at regulation were – and could hope to be, given the inherent patchwork quality of identities.

Anna-Christina Giovanopoulos examines the public sphere as the site not only of rational debate but also of political propaganda, which did not appeal to its audience in an objective, impartial manner. Taking impeachment records and journalistic off-shoots as her example, she shows that these publications were argumentative and polemical, designed to appeal to their readers' emotions with the aim of creating an increasingly stable group identity of party supporters. This example demonstrates that personal affiliations were clearly not bracketed in the public sphere, as Habermas claimed. Instead, the identities of citizens might be regarded as 'constituted by the participatory practices, the legal discourses, or the processes of democratic activity'. The very language, for instance, that was used to discuss political issues emerged from the conflicts and relations of dominance and dependence. This perspective entails a shift of focus from consensus to contention as a source of group identity at the interface of politics, law, and journalism.

---

[11]   Emma Clery persuasively and elegantly recovers *The Feminization Debate in Eighteenth-Century England* from the luxury debates of the 1690s through the sentimental 1750s. Clery describes how the public sphere of political discourse, commerce, and consumption moved away from a misogynist model of civic humanist virtue to a cultural model in which women are seen as indexical to civilization and commercial growth.

Christian Huck's essay poses a more theoretical question: is Habermas's concept of the political public sphere an adequate tool for the analysis of popular culture? His test cases are newspapers and journals, which in Habermas's account figure as media of political communication and consensus formation. Here they are reconsidered as media of consumer culture, as becomes obvious in fashion advertisements. For Habermas, of course, fashionable consumption is the very nemesis of the rational-critical debate and, indeed, the public sphere proper. His account constructs a diachronic tale of degeneration in which he dates the shift from a 'neutral' mediating function to a commercial one in the early nineteenth century. Yet as Huck is able to show, both functions were fulfilled by the very same medium of the moral weeklies. *The Spectator*, for example, relied not only on general advertising, but also on advertisements for fashionable goods, cosmetics, and clothes in particular. Political debate and fashionable consumption were a synchronic phenomenon, even literally so: on the back-side of political criticism we find advertisements for fashionable goods of consumption.

Visual and Topographic Space as a Medium of Identity Constitution

The final three essays, by Isabelle Baudino, Michael Meyer, and Christoph Houswitschka, explore how place/space and identity are correlatively produced through aesthetic practices which, as we will see, could be appropriated as political practices. The theoretical concepts and historical insights which underpin much of this section concern the connection between identity and eighteenth-century economies of the gaze. To adopt the title of a seminal study by Peter de Bolla, the education of the eye very much amounted to an education of the I. As he points out, the various activities of seeing – looking, observing, spectating, surveying – are culturally regulated and validated activities that give 'shape or focus to a human agent' (2). Every viewer occupies a specific position in the cultural field which can be described through multiple parameters of gender, class, nation, religion, and so on. A point of view, in other words, functions as a point from which the individual can speak, think, and act – in other words, a subject position. Of course, subject positions are constituted not only in the act of looking, but also in being looked at. While de Bolla acknowledges that the scopic regimes he explores do not only produce a looking subject but also aim at making 'one's self visible' as 'an object of regard', he is concerned primarily with a specific class of visible individuals, 'a citizen in the demos of taste' (7). Looking and being looked at is here perceived as a culturally valid activity of the educated man of taste. But the eighteenth century actually offered a vast range of subjectivities in the field of vision.[12]

---

[12] In fact, as John Barrell (1989) has shown in an excellent essay, the education of the manly eye/I did not result in stable subject positions, since it could all too easily be seduced by dangerously enticing objects. On the dynamics and seductions pertaining to the gendered economy of the gaze in eighteenth-century London, see Straub 1992. The bodies

The period under consideration constitutes a particularly interesting and relevant chapter in the history of visuality. The modern era, Nicholas Mirzoeff points out, is dominated by the sense of sight in a way that sets it apart from its premodern predecessors (66). While the visual had been treated with suspicion by the iconophobic culture of the Reformation, especially in England (see O'Connell), visuality and its media reclaimed cultural authority and validity from the Restoration onwards, and by the middle of the eighteenth century flourished into what de Bolla calls a thoroughly visual culture (4). Aspects of this culture include the revivication of the public theatres; the rise of the journalistic genre of Spies, Observers, and Monitors which invests the critical gaze (most prominently embodied by Addison and Steele's Mr Spectator) with discursive authority; the conceptualization of taste as an eminently visual faculty, with all its implications for access to the public spheres and the exclusion of a broad range of individuals from its privileges; the institutionalization of tasteful painting in the Royal Academy as well as in exhibitions of art works; the increased importance of fashion, as well as fashionable places like Ranelagh or Vauxhall gardens; and scientific inventions like the telescope, the microscope, and the camera obscura, which reinforced the privilege of the visual just as technologies of social domination and disciplination relied on it (see Crary, 245–6).[13] Given these very different social places and symbolic spaces, it is necessary to recognize the variety of media as well as of the practices of media use that constituted identities in the visual field.

Such a differentiation of the practices of looking and the identities mediated through them is precisely what the three final essays in this volume are concerned with. What connects them is a focus on landscape as a symbolic space in different medial renderings, ranging from topographical and panoramic paintings to walking in the countryside, often in combination with literary texts and aesthetic treatises on the viewing of artworks, as well as the different aesthetic and political practices operative in the processes of mediation.

Isabelle Baudino explores the forging of a British identity from the visual and textual representation of the various vernacular identities of the isles. The two newly emergent genres of topography and chorography promised reliable, accurate knowledge about a country. Establishing Britain's physical identity, its very shape and place on the map, became the common denominator of otherwise disparate Welsh, English, and Scottish populations. The principle of verisimilitude – which also served to establish a national school of painting *vis-à-vis* French artificiality and dependence on convention – drew on toponomy, the depiction or mention of specific historical places in the city or countryside. Combining the deictic dimensions of space and time, the paintings discussed in this chapter provided a collective British identity based on landscape and its history: topographical painting as history lesson.

---

of other men would have been particularly dangerous objects for the male eye, charging the economy of the gaze homoerotically; this is explored in King 2004.

   [13]   For a broader discussion of scientific regimes of looking, see Ogden.

Of course, this was history as seen through eighteenth-century English eyes. Accordingly the violent colonization of Wales, Ireland, and Scotland was transfigured into idyllic views of the ancient castles which originally had served as military strongholds, as Baudino shows. A similar ideological strategy of historical or geographical verisimilitude and aestheticization underlies the representation of domestic and imperial landscapes in many topographical prospects, panoramic paintings, and travel books around 1800. Michael Meyer's essay analyzes how past and present meet in the pictorial space: domestic scenes of idyllic countryside and urban industry suggest that British identity comprises both regional tradition and national progress. The ruins of Hindu or Muslim temples in imperial scenes, for example, hint that the heyday of Oriental culture is past, and thus implicitly justify the Christian and enlightened British claim to cultural supremacy, a claim made explicit in historical battle scenes such as *The Storming of Seringapatam*. Aesthetically and ideologically informed landscape thus functions as a medium conducive to the forming of national identity in time and space.

In a still different appropriation of landscape, the radical culture of the 1790s reinvented nature as a space of democracy and participation. As Christoph Houswitschka shows, walking and rambling in the countryside gave the 'peripatetic subject' a democratic identity; writing and reading about this experience helped to establish a democratic taste. The Radicals walked from marginal places in society to the political and cultural centre, thus enacting symbolically the arrival of their political ideas in an opposing social context. In these 'topographical digressions', the body itself became a medium attributing meaning to spaces – be they literary or social – which represented alternative, democratic realities.

Taken together, the essays in this volume explore the intersection of identities and media in the long eighteenth century. Proceeding from the premise that identities are temporary affiliations or performances dependent on the social as well as medial context, rather than stable and monolithic entities, they produce new understandings of the processes of identification and mediation as interactive social practices. In so doing, they not only offer a more differentiated, complex view of eighteenth-century culture, but also contribute to an innovative conceptualization of the role that media play for our sense of self.

Chapter 1
Identifying an Age-Specific English Literature for Children

Anja Müller

Defining Children's Literature

Harvey Darton's pioneering monograph *Children's Books in England: Five Centuries of Social Life* opens with the following definition: 'By "children's books" I mean printed works produced ostensibly to give children spontaneous pleasure, and not primarily to teach them, nor solely to make them good, nor to keep them profitably quiet' (1). Darton's exclusive treatment of non-didactic material as the quintessential prototype of children's literature[1] still reverberates through most twentieth-century definitions of the genre. Sheila Egoff, for example, suggests 'that the aim of children's writing be delight not edification; that its attributes be the eternal childlike qualities of wonder; simplicity, laughter and warmth; and that in the worldwide realm of children's books, the literature be kept inside, the sociology and pedagogy out' (quoted in Lesnik-Oberstein, 25).[2] In addition to this apparent levity, Perry Nodelman also insists on the covert depths of children's literature and on its subversive potential: 'These texts can be easily and effortlessly heard or read, but once read, they continue to develop significance, importance, complexity, to echo ever outward and inward. These are texts that resonate' (2).

Despite Nodelman's emphasis on the pleasant character of children's literature, his inclusion of a didactic intention qualifies Darton's rigid split between didacticism and entertainment. For certain, children's literature is rarely merely an entertaining or aesthetic enterprise; it has always been suffused with ideologies. Definitions of

---

[1] Darton continues: 'I shall therefore exclude from this history, as a general rule, all schoolbooks, all purely moral or didactic treatises, all reflective or adult-minded descriptions of child-life and almost all alphabets, primers, and spelling books; though some works in each category will be mentioned because they purposely gave much latitude to amusement, or because they contained elements which have passed into a less austere legacy. The definition is given as a broad principle liable to perpetual exception' (1). This specification with a caveat already indicates the pitfalls of Darton's definition, which can only sustain its clear distinctions if it negates the existence of mixed forms or, more importantly, a mixed usage or reception of children's literature. It is therefore hardly surprising that, in the course of Darton's book, the text types he excludes so rigorously at the beginning tend to resurface again and again.

[2] Lesnik-Oberstein's article includes a number of further comparable definitions.

children's literature insisting on the genre's appeal to children's playfulness or on their capability of subversive readings can be referred to a liberal humanist concept of the child that can hardly betray its debts to Romanticism. Obviously, definitions of children's literature depend on concepts of childhood. Hence, if twentieth-century definitions of children's literature take the concept of the child evolving in the wake of Romanticism for granted, this entails considerable problems for an appropriate assessment of any literature for children that was published at a time when the category of childhood was conceptualized differently. Percy Muir's monograph *English Children's Books, 1600 to 1900* accordingly entitles the chapters on children's literature before the eighteenth century the 'pre-historic' age, and he only has disparaging and dismissive comments for those writers whose works do not correspond to the pleasure principle.[3]

However, childhood is no 'invention' or discovery of the late eighteenth century, even if studies written in the wake of Philippe Ariès's seminal *History of Childhood* tend to continue this myth. Numerous historians of childhood have meanwhile assessed the varying notions of the concept from antiquity to the present.[4] In my own *Framing Childhood*, I argue that during the eighteenth century different competing concepts of childhood existed side by side. Emerging as a literary genre during precisely this period, children's literature was one of the sites where competing notions of childhood were negotiated. Rather than merely reflecting existing notions of childhood, I suggest that children's literature functions as a mediating instance, presenting, negotiating, and proliferating concepts of childhood by claiming to represent the character and needs of a particular age group. As a consequence, both 'children' and 'literature' are regarded as contingent categories; both are cultural constructs, the conceptualizations of which have undergone significant changes in the course of history.

A very influential portion of eighteenth-century concepts of childhood were closely linked with the values and needs of the rising middle class.[5] Childhood, accordingly, was constructed around the need for forming future English middle-class citizens and their spouses. Conceiving children as blank pages and as

---

[3]   Especially the products from Puritan pens meet with Muir's indignation and disapproval. Opposing this disparaging of Puritan children's writers, Charles John Sommerville takes great pains in his various writings to rescue the Puritan writers for children from their bleak image of producing nothing but scary, threatening, and pleasure-forbidding texts.

[4]   Within the scope of this paper, I can only list a small selection of studies in this field, among them, for instance, Nicholas Orme's *Medieval Children* or Charles John Sommerville's *The Discovery of Childhood in Puritan England*. Among the more encompassing histories of childhood I should certainly mention the standard – if not uncontested – works by Lloyd de Mause and Linda Pollock, as well as Hugh Cunningham's *Children and Childhood in Western Society since 1500* and Colin Heywood's *History of Childhood*. A more comprehensive assessment of these studies is given in the introductory chapter to Müller 2009.

[5]   See Andrew O'Malley's excellent monograph *The Making of the Modern Child*.

potentially reasonable beings in need of cognitive and, especially, moral formation so as to render them capable of forming their own judgements, eighteenth-century discourses of childhood said less about what children were and more about what kind of children were needed to reproduce a certain set of values. Besides, the insistence on various lacks of childhood (for example, a lack of physical strength, rational judgement, power, or insight) simultaneously demarcated the borderlines to a middle-class, middle-age adult norm, which disposed of all the qualities childhood was said to lack. In other words, concepts of childhood were deployed to define an adult norm *ex negativo*.

In order to examine children's literature before 1789, it is useful to start from more general definitions of children's literature than those mentioned above, and to consider that such definitions may vary depending on whether one looks at the market, at the intended readership, at aesthetic qualities, or at the function of the texts. Murray Knowles and Kirsten Malmkjaer's suggestion – to declare as children's literature what is put on the list as such by the publisher (1) – may appear simplistic, yet it takes into account the important eighteenth-century development that children's literature became part of a burgeoning business and a flourishing literary market. In a similar vein, I shall embark from the very general assumption that children's literature is any literature written and published for children. I shall assume that, by targeting a particular age group through a certain choice of topic and form, children's literature contributes to the identification of this age group, distinguishing it from others and mediating the concomitant concept of childhood at the same time.

In order to assess the construction of an age-specific literature for children, it is important to scrutinize where children's literature was positioned and how it positioned itself within the field of eighteenth-century literature. Gauging the distinction of children's literature from other genres will help to assess the age-specific features attributed to children's literature.[6] In this context, my essay is indebted to Christoph Reinfandt, who uses a systems theory approach to reconsider the emergence of the novel in the eighteenth century. According to Reinfandt, the eighteenth-century novel employs a literary code that distinguishes between texts that are 'entertaining' or 'not entertaining', or – this is Reinfandt's preferred binary opposition – between texts that are 'interesting' or 'not interesting'. Reinfandt explains very convincingly that it was crucial for the development of the novel that the genre increasingly insisted on its freedom from extra-literary legitimation (such as purposefulness or didacticism), accentuating instead inner-literary or intra-systemic references (for example, to literary tradition) as well as expressive functions.

In what follows, I will explore the encoding of children's literature that established the identity of this emerging genre within the field of eighteenth-century literature. By tracing the distinctions of children's literature from other

---

[6]   Such an approach is also taken in Zohar Shavit's work on the distinction between children's literature and chapbooks, which focuses mainly on nineteenth-century texts.

literary genres that had been given to children as reading matter, I shall examine the features that came to be treated as age-specific and will relate them to concomitant eighteenth-century concepts of childhood. By doing so, I intend to show how changing conceptualizations of identity categories (here, the age group 'children') occur in interdependence with changes in the traditional modes of mediation, sometimes resulting in the formation of new genres or in redefinitions of old ones.

Excluding and Transforming the Supernatural: Fables, Chapbooks, and Fairy Tales

When Isaac Bickerstaff tells the readers of *The Tatler* that he 'perceived [his godson] a great historian in Aesop's Fables', but that the boy 'frankly declared [...] his mind, "that he did not delight in that learning, because he did not believe that [the Fables] were true"' (*Tatler* 95, 17 November 1709, in Steele 1987, II.93), he hints at two important aspects concerning the relationship of fables, children, and children's literature in the eighteenth century. For one thing, fables were perceived as the quintessential reading material for children, perhaps the only appropriate reading matter for this age group available at the time (see, for instance, Locke 2000, 212–13).[7] Eleanor Fenn's *The Female Guardian* (1784) praises the fable for its moral reformatory effects that result from direct interaction between the child reader and the text (10). Other texts for children adapt the structural conventions of the fable; for example, *The History of Little Goody Two-Shoes* (1766), where some episodes are followed by a 'Reflection', interrupting the narrative flow to address the reader directly. For Percy Muir, the almost effortless integration of the fable into the genre of children's literature results from children's cognitive capacities as well as from the fact that fables apparently appealed to the adults who bought the books to educate their offspring.

> Fables are ideal reading for small children, whose solemn anthropomorphism meets the talking animals half way [...]. Above all, fables have the indispensable feature of make-believe [...]. Finally, the intensely moral nature of these fables should not be overlooked. Whether the moral tale is repugnant to children or not it has been a persistent feature of books intended for their reading until well into our own day, and the stories of one of the most prolific and popular writers for children to-day exude morals in every line. (24)

This changed, however, when the unrealistic convention of talking animals caused fables to be ranked with the fairy tale and the chapbook. By the final decades of the eighteenth century, these genres had come to be regarded as highly problematic

---

[7]   Editions of *Aesop's Fables* were produced that were especially targeted at children, including an interlinear textbook attributed to John Locke (c. 1703), whose suggestions of presenting fables to children it followed. There are also the volumes produced by Samuel Richardson (1740) and John Newbery, and Dodsley's *Select Fables by Esop and Other Fabulists* (1761ff); see Jackson, 49–50.

for young readers because they were deemed incompatible with the goal to raise children rationally. Zohar Shavit perceives 'the beginning of official books for children' (416) in a distinctive generic opposition between chapbooks and children's literature. According to Mary Jackson, this opposition found support in the notoriously bad moral reputation of the chapbooks being associated with 'smut' or 'profligate and shiftless conduct' (67). Andrew O'Malley relates this distinction to middle-class ideology, yet, drawing on Raymond Williams, he also reveals a 'residue of plebeian [chapbook] culture' (19) in the children's literature of the mid-eighteenth century, especially in the publications of John Newbery. In the appearance of the new children's books, duodecimo volumes that were produced rather cheaply and often with recycled woodcuts, material traces of the chapbook are readily visible. Most authors remained anonymous, and title pages sometimes alluded to chapbook characters. These children's books thus pretended to belong to a communal tradition, simultaneously trying to establish a new, distinct, age-specific reader community. The rags-to-riches stories of poor but virtuous children like Goody Two-Shoes or her brother Tommy (who, through their moral virtues and economic skills, are rewarded with the notorious coach-and-six) reflect plebeian and middle-class fantasies of social mobility, projecting them onto the generation that might be able to fulfil these wishes. Under the impact of the French Revolution, such messages were frequently perceived as threats. Accordingly, Hannah More's *Cheap Repository Tracts* emulated chapbooks in their material appearance, but, while striving to reform plebeian moral economy, they also favoured a fixed social structure. In all these hybrid forms, the identity of children's literature as a genre in relation or opposition to the chapbook was defined through extra-literary references to what were supposed to be essential features of childhood. Hence, the inclusion of the chapbook format in children's literature necessitated a transformation of the genre according to its usefulness for moral instruction and socialization corresponding to the norms and conventions of a particular class.

As far as fairy tales are concerned, Jack Zipes describes the transformation of the folk tale, which was inclusive of all ages and classes, into the literary fairy tale by endowing the latter with 'mores, values, and manners so that children and adults would become civilized according to the social code of that time' (3). This process was partly an import from France, where standards for civility were set for the most of Europe and where this transformation had already taken place in the tales of the Countess d'Aulnoy and Charles and Pierre Perrault (see Muir, 36 and Zipes, 9). Acceptable literary 'fairy tales for children were no different from the rest of the literature (fables, primers, picture books, sermons, didactic stories, etc.) that conveyed a model of the exemplary child that was to be borne in mind while reading' (Zipes, 9). In originally English texts (for example, Sarah Fielding's *The Governess* of 1749), this transformation was achieved by adding a moral and/or by apologizing in the preface for telling such an ostensibly 'untrue' work of fiction. The fairy tale could therefore only become a legitimate part of children's literature by asserting extra-literary references, such as a moral message or a reflection on its own fictional character.

Returning to the fable, one notices that, after a long period of untroubled inclusion as legitimate reading matter for children, the fable's status as a subgenre of children's literature was challenged in the eighteenth century. It is interesting to note that both the legitimation and the exclusion of the fable were indicated by references to the literary system. While a lack of realism was used as an argument for exclusion, the venerable canonical Aesopian tradition was belaboured to legitimate at least fable elements in children's literature of the 1780s and 1790s.[8] The result is a tension between a legitimate didactic function (that is, legitimation through extra-literary reference) and an illegitimate literary form, which creates paradoxical situations in the writings of authors like Eleanor Fenn, Sarah Trimmer, and Anna Laetitia Barbauld: all advocate a simultaneously truthful and moral literature for children, and yet all frequently refer to fable traditions (for instance, in Trimmer's *Fabulous Histories* [1786]). Mary Jackson explains the reservations of these authors about fabulous fictions by citing their own Puritan or Evangelical backgrounds, which may account for their suspicion 'of all fictions and metaphors. Because they confused the literal with the Truth they profoundly mistrusted the imagination, a fear magnified where children were concerned' (Jackson, 137). This religiously motivated resentment found additional support from educational discourses based on Rousseauan principles.[9] If the fable was eventually not discarded – as is witnessed, for instance, in the popular *Fabulous Histories* by Sarah Trimmer, a stout advocate of the 'truth under fiction' precept – this inclusion was justified by referring to the function of the texts, their purposefulness and didacticism.

The temporary exclusion of the fable, the chapbook, and the fairy tale from the legitimate reading matter for children in the eighteenth century owes much to the concept of the rational child, who was supposed to learn to distinguish truth from falsity in order to be educated into a responsible citizen capable of rational judgements. According to Henry Home, Lord Kames, fascination of the supernatural belongs to an 'infancy of taste' (I.115) and thus to an inferior state of development. By expelling supernatural elements from children's books or accommodating them for didactic purposes, eighteenth-century children's

---

[8]   See, for example, the apologetic introduction to Mary Ann Kilner's *Adventures of a Whipping Top* (c. 1785): 'Tommy Clearsight looked over a few more pages, and pausing a while, asked the company, if they thought it possible for a Whipping-Top to see, hear, or write its own life? A grave gentleman, who sat at one corner of the table, addressed Tommy in the following words, "[…] Your observation is very just with regard to the Whipping-Top; and had I not read of things equally miraculous, should be inducted to suppose the Author was insulting the understanding of his readers; but every one in this company must have read the fables of the wise Athenian Aesop"' (8–10).

[9]   In his famous critique of La Fontaine's 'Le corbeau et le rénard' in *Émile*, Rousseau rejects fables because they present – among other things – a world that does not correspond to the world of the child's experience.

literature mediates the concept of the rational child, presenting and proposing it to child readers while asserting to the adult world that it does not intend to keep its young readers on an infantile level of taste.[10]

Negotiations with the Novel

The relationship of children's literature and the novel is ambiguous in the eighteenth century. On the one hand, novels like *Robinson Crusoe*, *Gulliver's Travels*, *Moll Flanders*, *Pamela*, *Clarissa*, and *Sir Charles Grandison* did not only enjoy a dual readership; soon after the first editions of these novels had appeared, publishers produced abridged or chapbook versions that were (also) intended for child readers (for example, *The Paths of Virtue Delineated* [1756], a sampler of abridged versions of Richardson's novels). These children's versions usually played down the sexual elements of the novels, while emphasizing their 'adventurous or psychologically thrilling aspects' (Jackson, 66). Otto Brunken asserts that, despite these adaptations, the novel was a highly controversial reading matter for eighteenth-century children and was neither easily nor unanimously contained in the genre of children's literature. On the one hand, the realism of the novel corresponded to the claim for 'truth under fiction' that was deemed essential for a literature suited to the concept of the rational child. A didactic purpose could further enhance the suitability of a novel and could even accommodate love plots. In his preface to *The Virtuous Novelist* (1750), a collection of stories for children, Jefferies accordingly defines the suitable 'novel' for children as follows:

> A Novel, properly so called, is a Fiction of some Love-Adventure, artfully formed, either in Prose or Verse, for the Instruction, as well as the Entertainment of the Reader. A Novel is called a Fiction, in order to distinguish it from Real History; and a Fiction of some Love-Adventure; because Love ought to be its principal Subject. [...] Delight, which the ingenious Novelist seems to make his main Design, is, in reality, no other than a Medium, subordinate to that End, namely, the Instruction of the Mind and Reformation of the Manners. (i–ii)

---

[10] This exclusion of supernatural elements has proved to be a transitional period in the history of children's literature, which was to a certain extent motivated by Puritan moralists, who very actively participated in the writing of children's literature. The most notorious example is perhaps Mrs Sherwood's revised edition of Sarah Fielding's *The Governess* (1749), a book that had actually distinguished itself from the fairy tales it related; yet the very presence of these tales in a children's book was apparently a problem to Sherwood. Contrary to such a position, William Godwin reportedly lamented that, by the turn of the century, the market for children's literature was dominated by dry, realistic narratives without imaginative elements. (One should not forget, however, that the books Godwin missed, for example *Goody Two-Shoes*, had, in their own time, professed to be realistic.)

Without these functional elements, the novel is believed to be a rather dangerous reading matter for children. The preface to Sarah Maese's *The School* (1766) outlines the problem most cogently:

> To find books that will innocently amuse, is not the least difficult part of her [a teacher's] task. The most decent novels can not be ranked in this number; for the least evil that can be said of them is, that they soften the heart, probably of itself too tender; teach the readers to see most circumstances in life in false lights; and to think, that all the colour of their future days must spring from the good or bad success of a passion, which it is desirable few of them should feel. Besides, as the heroine's virtue rises in proportion to the dangers to which it has been exposed, these sorts of productions familiarize the mind with scenes of vice, at an age when one would wish to have them totally ignorant of depravity. (n.p.)[11]

Behind such considerations lies, of course, the concept of the child as blank paper: innocent, yet highly susceptible to first impressions and thus endangered by corruption. In order to safeguard children's assumed innocence, one needed to supply a literary genre for children that neither over-stimulated their senses nor unduly incited their emotions. Sarah Maese apparently perceives in this age-specific quality of children's literature an advantage over the more complex, but also morally more ambiguous novels. Referring to Richardson's *Pamela*, *Little Master's Miscellany* similarly considers the novel's complexity or moral ambiguity to be problematic.

> [T]he Person, or rather the Virtues, of honest old Joseph Andrews was the Subject I was Reflecting on; there's something Exceeding Beautiful in the Sentiments and Conduct of his Daughter Pamela, but the Author has drawn in some Triffling [sic] things, and spun out the Story to such an Intollerable length, that I can by no means approve of the whole [...]. (50)

A later children's book, *The Renowned History of Primrose Prettyface* (1782), therefore corrects the 'defects' of Richardson's novel by providing its younger readers with a version of the *Pamela* story that leaves no doubt about the virtuous intentions of its heroine, as she gives no opportunity to be blamed for calculating falsehood.

Children's literature thus adapted novels to integrate them into its age-specific system. Brunken comments on some of these integrative processes, for example the adaptation of characters by turning the protagonists into children: 'No longer is the novel supposed to prepare one for the "big world". Rather it should aid the child in its orientation by offering models in their actual social setting that are worth emulating' (46). I would suggest, however, that this restriction of scope in

---

[11]   Maese's preface combines age with gender issues, as she emphasizes these concerns are most pertinent to young female readers: 'The purity and delicacy, which constitute the beauty of a female mind, cannot be too long nor too carefully preserved; and in some degree, must suffer by the knowlege [sic] of vice, however free from the guilt of participation.'

novels adapted for children rather maps out a restricted space for childhood, which it then represents as pertaining 'naturally' to this age group.

This also corresponds to the many hints for 'correct' reading in literature for children. James Janeway, for instance, recommended repeated readings of individual passages. Thomas White's *A Little Book for Children* (1702) encourages its readers to take notes. By explicitly instructing the child reader in how to handle and understand the book, children's literature mediates in its own structure a 'monitored reading', controlling its reception. In the absence of the parents or other adults, the children's book itself comes to embody or to reflect the tutor/monitor.[12] The child readers are not left to their own devices, but they are controlled in various ways: by the parents, by the texts themselves via instruction, and through the exemplary stories narrated in the books. As children are considered to be not yet able to judge for themselves, this control is supposed to render the content of children's literature unambiguous. This disambiguation can be seen as an age-specific feature, which children's literature acquires in opposition to the novel, the literary and aesthetic value of which is increased by complexity. In children's literature, on the other hand, complexity represents a dangerous opacity and is morally dubious. The precept of controlling children's reading finds additional support in the writings of educational theorists in the wake of Rousseau, who had fervently advocated strictly limited and monitored reading. Mediating these educational positions, eighteenth-century children's literature sometimes ends up, rather paradoxically, recommending not to read too extensively.[13]

A further reason for fearing ambiguity in eighteenth-century children's literature may consist in the yet indistinct boundaries of the genre. Since children's literature had to distinguish and identify itself in the first place, its reception was yet uncontrolled and open. At the same time, the distinctive didacticism of children's literature necessitated clearly defined interpretations, because different interpretations could destabilize the educational claim of children's literature and thus undermine the panoptical function of the genre. Insecurity or ambiguities of reception, as in the *Pamela* controversy, would have been antagonistic to these functions. Eighteenth-century children's literature therefore had to identify and present itself as a distinct genre with undisputable boundaries if it intended to mediate to its readers clear categories of a childhood identity to be socialized into a stratified society – even if the genre, in fact, was still far from having either such distinct borderlines or homogenous features.

---

[12]   See, for instance, Fenn's *School Occurrences*, where the girls relate stories of correct, monitored reading (67–74).

[13]   Mary and Charles Lamb's *Mrs Leicester's School* (1809) reflects this prohibitive yet also paradoxical attitude towards untutored children's reading, as it presents numerous occasions of socialization through reading in the cases of young girls, some of whom had to endure the debilitating and psychologically damaging effects of unmonitored reading.

Residues of Orality

The various directions in which children's literature negotiates its genre boundaries hint at the mixed character of eighteenth-century children's literature – despite the professed clear theoretical distinctions that are put forward in the prefaces of children's books. To some extent, this is also reflected in the handling of plot in eighteenth-century children's literature, which characteristically consists of an episodic structure without clearly motivated links between its individual elements. Often enough, a sequence of reading exercises or moral sermons is embedded into a crude frame that more or less convincingly provides occasions for telling the respective embedded stories. Only from the 1780s on do individual episodes tend to be integrated into a more coherent plot. One can argue that this episodic structure positions children's literature somewhere between the novel, the romance, and the periodical.

In addition to this, the lack of a coherent plot structure in eighteenth-century children's literature can be seen as a remainder of more archaic traditions[14] that testify to an affinity in children's literature with an 'infancy of taste', as it were – contrary to the more 'mature' novel. Numerous apologetic prefaces attribute the genre's alleged inferior aesthetic value to its age-specific readership. William Ronksley's *The Child's Weeks-work* (1712), for instance, even excludes aesthetic considerations from literature for children altogether:

> If any shall say, that the Matter of it is trivial and childish, they plead for it, since it is intended for Children, who can't so well relish grave and serious Discourses, nor are capable of observing Elegancy of Speech, and quick Turns of Wit; as soon as they can read perfectly, we have great store of Useful Books, they may take their Choice. (n.p.)

The supposed simplicity and primitiveness of children's tastes need not necessarily be derogatory; it can also signify the concept of children's innocence. Safeguarding this innocence requires a careful selection of content matter in children's literature, as well as certain formal elements. The Romantic appreciation of childhood as a model uncorrupted state of innocence has a particularly strong impact on the revaluation of literary forms of expression that are associated with children. Both William Blake and William Wordsworth intrinsically connect childhood with the oral or pre-literary sphere as opposed or complementary to writing (see McLane). Pursuing this strain of conceptualization, one may wonder how far eighteenth-century children's literature came to mediate such a view of the child, as well.

---

[14] Such a view would comply with Monika Fludernik's account of the archaic character of episodic narrative structures. According to Fludernik, 'the episodic pattern of narrative structure breaks down in sixteenth-century prose writing as a consequence of the pressure from the themes and the requirements of length' (129).

Indeed, the formal characteristic features of children's literature mentioned so far all appear in the catalogue of characteristics of orally based thought and expression that is listed by Walter Ong in his seminal *Orality and Literacy*. The repetition of themes, topics, and phrases (for example, recurring moralizing) takes cognizance of the child's cognitive capacities and supports the didactic function to instil moral precepts into the child's mind. Illustrations, by visually repeating passages from the verbal text, can be seen as graphic markers of redundancy, creating a surplus of information which, in turn, facilitates memorizing and remembrance. The content of children's literature is generally supposed to be close to the experiential world of children; hence the popular settings of family, home, or school. The exemplary children in the texts – originally mainly religious models, but later increasingly secularized – are types rather than individuals. Names like Billy Friendly or Jemima Placid hint at the affinity of these characters to allegorical figures.[15] The conventional motifs and the often comparable conventional plotlines illustrate the traditionally conservative character of eighteenth-century children's literature. Although children's fascination for novelties was acknowledged, children's literature of the eighteenth century did not demand originality and novelty as the novel did. Some texts even included warnings that an insistence on novelty and originality might over-strain children's susceptibility and ultimately turn out to be detrimental to the child's nerves.[16]

As far as literary quality is concerned, the initial absence of a demand for originality may account for the formulaic character of eighteenth-century children's literature. Besides, the fact that many books produced before the 1780s had been published either anonymously or pseudonymously insinuates that the disinterest in originality also entailed a decreased interest in authorship.[17] Last but not least, Ong mentions as a characteristic feature of orality the lack of a linear plotline in favour of an episodic structure, with the plot often beginning *in medias res*. This is precisely a description of the plot handling that can be traced in eighteenth-century children's texts, with their loose plotting, episodic structures, and only implicit expository hints.

With regard to these features, eighteenth-century children's literature does not only adapt previously existing literary genres to render them suitable for existing notions of childhood. It also retains many idiosyncrasies of orality. This residual

---

[15]   The same holds true, of course, for the deviant children – the Master Headstrongs or Patty Prouds – who, rather than reflecting exemplary behaviour, indicated the need for perfectibility and reform.

[16]   See, for instance, the stories in *Mrs Leicester's School*, in which uncontrolled reading of highly stimulating material even produces pathological conditions among some of the young female readers. This caveat, of course, is also to be seen in the wake of Rousseau's admonitions against untutored reading.

[17]   Quite apart from the question of whether it would have been prestigious enough for an author to have his name published on the front page of a children's book, children's books seem to have been associated with publishers rather than authors in the first two thirds of the eighteenth century.

function can be explained on the one hand by the affinity of children's literature with other pre-literary genres (for example, the fairy tale), and on the other hand by the yet incomplete or still to be developed literacy of the potential readers. Besides, I would argue that, contrary to romance, which Ong describes as a written genre heavily relying on oral modes without consciously imitating them, the affinities between eighteenth-century children's literature and orality are more consciously deployed. While the child is envisaged as a pre-literate being by the Romantic poets, conceptualizations of childhood during the eighteenth century generally support the notion of childhood as a preparatory, preliminary state of man. Accordingly, eighteenth-century literature for children mediates a sense of not (yet) being fully included in adult society, and this applies to the child readers as well as to the genre itself.

Encoding the Genre of Children's Literature

To conclude, one can say that eighteenth-century children's literature is identified as a new, age-specific subsystem in the literary field that appears to be more conservative than the novel. Contrary to the novel, children's literature foregrounds its mimetic and pragmatic dimensions. With its precept of 'truth under fiction', the reference to experiential reality serves as a legitimation for the genre. This reference to extra-literary reality also fulfils the function of a viable distinction from other literary genres, such as the fairy tale, fable, or chapbook. Once the generic boundaries of children's literature towards these initial competitors have been consolidated, fantastic elements can more easily be accommodated again into children's literature at a later time.

Emphasizing its didactic, moralizing, and socializing function, eighteenth-century children's literature orients itself towards other, extra-literary social systems, such as education, religion, or the family. Unlike the novel, which comes to legitimate itself through references to the literary tradition,[18] eighteenth-century children's literature frequently accentuates precisely these functional characteristics in order to identify itself as a genre. While mediating concepts of childhood that perceive children as yet imperfect and hence necessarily submitted to superior adults, children's literature appears to reflect a similar dependence insofar as it does not propose its generic independence from extra-literary demands like the novel (Reinfandt, 146). Instead, eighteenth-century children's literature eschews the purposeless pursuit of pleasure and entertainment that is postulated in twentieth-century definitions of the genre. Quite on the contrary, eighteenth-century children's literature comes to define itself almost entirely through extra-literary legitimation. Whereas the eighteenth-century novel gradually develops into a genre for the constitution and expression of the subject, the mimetic-pragmatic dimension prevails in the children's literature of the period. The novel's

---

[18]   Reinfandt quotes Henry Fielding as an example (144).

expressive function (hence its emphasis on the passions) and, particularly, its potential ambiguity, differ strongly from the age-specific function of children's literature to offer clear and meaningful examples of instruction.

These sets of references and distinctions that are operative in eighteenth-century children's literature offer sufficient evidence that the twentieth-century definitions of the genre mentioned above are hardly adequate for assessing the systemic processes in eighteenth-century children's literature. In particular, the insistence on 'pleasure' as the essential feature is a code that was not functionalized for children's literature in the eighteenth century. Whereas twentieth-century definitions of children's literature deploy the code 'entertaining/ pleasing' versus 'purposeful/didactic', these two categories were not perceived as binary opposites in eighteenth-century children's literature but as necessarily complementary. One can thus argue that eighteenth-century children's literature displays a quintessential double-coding for its identification, namely 'entertaining and didactic' (that is, the Horatian *utile dulci*). With this double-coding, children's literature is differentiated from unilaterally/single-coded genres such as the novel, and from merely functional genres such as sermons, schoolbooks, and conduct books. Relating these processes of differentiation within the literary field to socio-cultural concepts of age-specific identities, one can perceive an analogy between the double-coding of children's literature and conceptualizations of childhood in the eighteenth century. The discourses of childhood innocence and perfectibility, together with the notion of the child's incompleteness, lack of judgment, and yet imperfect development as a subject, necessarily entail a primary emphasis on didacticism. Addressed to child readers who are, in turn, identified through the lack of these things, children's literature needs to refer to the extra-literary systems that define its readers.

Last but not least, it is important to note that the double-coding of eighteenth-century children's literature also results from the fact that the emerging genre of children's literature is not intrinsically embedded in the literary field, especially not in the field of written literature. Instead, the genre of children's literature distinguishes itself by extrapolating and transforming existing literary forms as well as preserving features of orality. Perceiving the latter as especially adequate for its age-specific readership, children's literature assumes a special status within a literary field that is predominantly defined by written culture and literacy.[19] Therefore, I would argue that eighteenth-century children's literature pursues a strategy of identifying itself as a genre that can be compared to Rousseau's model of individuation as opposed to Locke's. According to Niklas Luhmann (1989), Rousseau's model extrapolates the child first from society, in order to enable it to

---

[19]   This identification through extra-literary references and characteristics finds further support in the insistence on the thingness of the children's book, its quality as an object or a commodity to be possessed and not chiefly coveted for its literary, aesthetic merits (see Grenby).

develop an identity, before it is reintegrated into society.[20] In analogy, the genre of children's literature initially defines itself not only through its distinction from other existing literary genres, but also by withdrawing itself strategically from the field of written literature as such. Eighteenth-century children's literature thus not only mediates age-specific identities, it also defines its own identity as a genre in a way that is similar to contemporary conceptualizations of childhood. After that, having gained momentum and having consolidated its boundaries by the beginning of the nineteenth century, children's literature will then redefine itself as literary, developing into the genre that becomes identifiable as 'children's literature' according to twentieth-century concepts.

---

[20]   In the Lockean model, on the contrary, identification occurs through integration and incorporation into society.

Chapter 2
Found and Lost in Mediation: Manly Identity in Defoe's *A Journal of the Plague Year*

Isabel Karremann

Late twentieth-century criticism of Daniel Defoe's *A Journal of the Plague Year* (1722), his fictionalized account of the 1665 plague in London, can be divided into two camps. One reads the text in terms of its didactic purpose and its reassuring message that it is possible to fight misery with charity, to manage the plague effectively and to impose order and sense onto the material world. This line of interpretation sees the *Journal* as an exercise in the ordering powers of man, with the plague serving as a kind of stage on which the cultural techniques of ordering – surveillance, distinction, meaning-making language – are successfully displayed.[1] Alternatively, it has been argued that the text foregrounds the material experience of the plague year – pain, illness, death – as an irreducible chaos that frustrates all attempts at keeping order or making sense of the epidemic. This affects the textual representation of the plague as well: the heterogeneous, contradictory narrative ultimately obscures meaning. The impossibility of explaining and containing the plague in narrative problematizes the possibility of interpreting and mastering the world.[2]

While this division does indeed reflect an inherent ambivalence of the *Journal*, it is an artificial one which mainly results from the individual readings of scholars who ignore large parts of Defoe's text as well as each other's scholarship. On the one hand, the 'order from confusion sprung' reading habitually suppresses all mention of the masses of corpses that clutter the London streets as well as the contradictory discourses which continually frustrate the vision of a unified civic and epistemological order. On the other hand, readings which acknowledge the impossibility of imposing sense and order onto the plague usually neglect to historicize their findings, thus ascribing a universal status to the dynamics of meaning-making and subject-constitution at work in this early

---

[1]   Among these are Richetti, Novak 1977 and 1992, Wainwright, Brodsley, Leavy, Hentzi, and Gregg 1999 and 2009. This list does not claim to be comprehensive, but rather reflects my reading for critical assessments of those aspects of the *Journal* which are central to my discussion here.

[2]   See Zimmerman, Rambuss, Flynn, Brooks, Benjamin Moore, Juengel, and Cynthia Wall's introduction to the *Journal* in Defoe 2003.

eighteenth-century text.[3] This ahistoric tendency is insensitive toward questions of gender and class in the formation of identity.

In this essay, I will bring these two divergent reading traditions together (and with them, seemingly incompatible aspects of Defoe's text) by seeking an answer to the question of what identity offer is articulated in the *Journal* and how it is mediated. The answer to the first part of this question is relatively straightforward: the *Journal* articulates an ideal of middle-class urban manliness which figures as the guarantor for its vision of civic order. The expression 'the ordering powers of man' may be taken quite literally here, since what is at stake in this text, though unacknowledged in almost all readings, are the ordering powers of early eighteenth-century manliness *vis-à-vis* the unruly, dangerous materiality of plague bodies. From this perspective, critical assessments of the narrator-protagonist, H.F., can be retrospectively identified as drawing on a repertoire of culturally male attributes, such as his rationality, his 'pure and disinterested intelligence', or his 'powerful apartness' from the scenes of physical suffering (Richetti, 299). The description of the plague as 'as powerful an enemy of modern man as monsters were for the heroes of old' (Steel, 88) even casts him in that stereotypical role of manliness, the valiant hero. To my knowledge, Stephen Gregg is the first to have explicitly identified manliness as a central issue of the *Journal*; yet he reads it exclusively in terms of a successful ordering principle, ignoring all textual evidence which challenges this success story (Gregg 1999, 142).

This brings me to the rather vexed second part of my question, which concerns mediation. The ideal of manliness is mediated by a set of plot elements and narrative strategies which at the same time undermine this ideal. For example, the effective plague management carried out by exemplary figures functions as the touchstone of manliness; however, by the same token, the very uncontrollability of the epidemic implies that the performance of this manliness is far from qualifying it as the conquering hero of this story. In taking such contradictory aspects of the text into account and placing them into historical context, my double reading shows that the *Journal*'s ideal of manliness is a precarious quality which is simultaneously found and lost in the fight against unruly matter – be it the physical matter of the plague bodies or the textual matter assembled in the text.[4] For disorder is not just thematized on the level of plot, it is also enacted by the text as an effect of the plurality of media represented in the *Journal*, which produces a plurality of viewpoints that defies all attempts at discursive authority, including that of the manly identity supposed to embody it.

---

[3]   A case in point is Rambuss, who focuses on problems of genre, narrative, and interpretation, or Juengel, who employs Kristeva's notion of the abject to explain how H.F.'s encounters with plague bodies both trigger and jeopardize the narrative as an ongoing process of self-constitution.

[4]   Benjamin Moore provides a similar double reading but focuses entirely on the narrative tension between perspectival unity and informational multiplicity engendered by the opposition between official government discourse and unofficial popular discourses.

It is the specific mediality of the *Journal* itself, then, that compromises its cultural function as a vehicle of order and identity. In his groundbreaking essay 'Culture, the Media and the "Ideological Effect"', Stuart Hall postulated that media are not only vehicles of a message but themselves the site of 'the provision and selective construction of social knowledge, of a social imaginary, through which we perceive the "worlds", the "lived realities" of others, and imaginarily reconstruct their lives and ours into some intelligible [world]' (Hall 1979, 340). The function of media is to produce common-sense knowledge about the world we live in, in terms of social hierarchies and order. This intelligible world is accepted on the basis of a consensus, which is reached through a process of conflict between 'varieties of life-patterns', through 'establishing the "rules" of each domain, actively ruling in and ruling out certain realities, offering maps and codes which mark out territories and assign problematic events and relations to explanatory contexts, helping us not simply to know more about "the world" but to make sense of it' (ibid., 340–41). A medium, then, structures the world by producing meaning about it; it will be most successful when it succeeds in covering the widest scope of 'the world' and presenting its version of reality as truth.

This reality effect is precisely what Defoe's text aspires to and, at least according to the 'order from confusion sprung' reading, succeeds in producing. Yet in order to function as a reliable map to the world, the *Journal* must necessarily aim at a degree of verisimilitude which in the end causes its failure: by assembling all information available about the plague – bills of mortality, medical advice, official orders, eyewitness accounts and anecdotes, to name but a few – the *Journal* turns from being the medium of a single, comprehensive view of reality into an incomprehensible assemblage of a plurality of media, each of which carries its own explanatory context, its own truth about the plague. As a novel, the *Journal* constitutes a medium in the sense that the genre actuates certain meanings, expectations, and narrative strategies that collaborate in mediating identity as a valid (in fact, the only) viewpoint from which the world emerges as common-sense reality. Its specific mediality, however, upstages this reality effect.

Marshall McLuhan once famously stated that the medium is the message. For the purposes of my essay, I take this to mean not that the message can be entirely neglected but rather that the message is so deeply inscribed in the medium (and vice versa) that it is extremely difficult to separate the one from the other. Therefore, my analysis of the manly identity articulated in the *Journal* goes hand in hand with an analysis of the specific strategies employed in its articulation. Nevertheless, in the pages that follow, the focus lies on the message, that is, on the ideal of manliness as a point of identification offered to contemporary readers and a consensus about the world they lived in, in terms of social hierarchies and order. In the second part of my essay the emphasis will be more on the different media of communication assembled in the text and the effect of this plural mediality on the ideal of manliness.

1.

Reading the *Journal* in terms of its ideological structure means to reconstruct what identity it offers, what meaningful map of 1665 plague-ridden London life it provides, what point of view it embraces – reading it, that is, in terms of its mediated message. That such a message exists is stated explicitly from the start: the narrator, H.F., repeatedly points out the didactic purpose of his memoirs as a 'story [which] may have its uses' (Defoe 2003, 58), the most immediate use being a guide-book in times of plague, a renewed threat in the early 1720s (ibid., 75).[5] Critical assessments of the novel have sought to identify the aim as well as the target audience of the *Journal*'s didactic impetus beyond such immediate uses, asking what else contemporary readers could learn from this text and what view of themselves and of the world they were offered.

Earlier readings suggest a metaphysical belief in and desire for order that emerges from the ordeal of living/reading through the chaos of the plague (see Richetti, 299–300). A more mundane view is taken by Laurel Brodsley, who sees the novel as an exercise in public health education, much along the lines of medical advice literature, with its didactic effects, however, infinitely enhanced through a mobilization of affect. The presence of an individualized narrator, the touching scenes of loyalty and farewell as well as the detailed, circumstantial narrative appeal to the readers' feelings and legitimize the at times drastic public measures against the plague (Brodsley, 11–22). The affective appeal of the *Journal*'s rhetoric is also foregrounded by V.L. Wainwright. What is at stake in his account is civil life in times of crisis, and the lesson to be learned is one of commiseration and charity. By contrasting the detrimental effects of egoistic care for oneself with pious charity, the novel appeals not only to the readers' pity but quite literally to their common sense: their sense of a communal identity as responsible, civic-minded citizens. Stephen Gregg reads the *Journal*'s attempts at providing a meaningful map of self and other not only in terms of class, but also in terms of middle-class manliness. Situating Defoe's novel in the context of the early eighteenth-century reformation of manners and comparing its rhetoric with that of reform sermons, he identifies it as a guide-book to exemplary manly conduct – 'a very good pattern for all men to follow' (Defoe 2003, 57) – and its target audience as the urban merchant and artisan classes, from whose ranks the followers of the Societies for the Reformation of Manners were recruited.[6]

What does this ideal of a middle-class 'godly manliness', as Gregg calls it (1999, 141), look like and how is it mediated in the *Journal*? In order to answer

---

[5]   Further relevant passages can be found on pages 10, 72, 89, 91, 118, 183, or 236.

[6]   Gregg argues that the historical backdrop of the 1665 plague epidemic and the reform movement of the 1680s/1690s interconnect in the *Journal* and provide both a narrative and a rationale for the manly virtues Defoe sought to promote in his own time (Gregg 1999, 145–50, and 2009, 94–9). While his identification of a double temporality at work in the text is convincing, it goes not beyond a one-sided reading in terms of social order, a shortcoming I hope to redress by focussing on the novel's contradictory double mediality.

this question, it is helpful to focus on three aspects which recur in the 'order from confusion sprung' paradigm: the issue of plague management, the figure of the narrator, and his narrative. On the level of plot, one's behaviour in the face of the epidemic serves as a touchstone of manliness. The ability and willingness to carry out an effective plague management is what distinguishes the urban middle classes from the egoistic, irresponsible nobility on the one hand and the dangerously reckless poor on the other. In this way, the plot of the *Journal* offers a twofold vision of social order: the ideal of godly manliness not only promises the preservation of civil order in the plague-ridden city, but enables a more general vision of a new order under the moral and political leadership of the middle classes beyond the immediate crisis. The qualities that allow for such a role of leadership and, by the token of their absence, disqualify the nobility for it are an unswerving religious faith, an active courage, and a rational world view (Gregg 1999, 142). These are demonstrated by exemplary individual characters, as well as collectives such as the magistrate, the clergy, and the physicians who help to sustain the moral and social order. Their rational world-view is repeatedly presented as a safeguard against the dangerous superstition and headless panic of those who fall prey to quacks, charlatans, and their useless remedies, and who thus, in fact, contribute to the speedy spread of the epidemic. Similarly, their firm belief that the sufferings of this life are to be rewarded in the next and an almost stoical endurance of the hardships of the plague are contrasted with the religious and moral apostasy shown by both the nobility and the poor. This, however, does not mean that one should suffer passively; rather, the manly ideal embraces an active courage and an ethos of self-help. A longer episode about three men from Wapping, who take their fate into their own hands and leave London in search for safety, presents active self-help coupled with piety and care for others as an exemplary behaviour: 'Their story has a Moral in every part of it, and their whole Conduct [...] is a Patern [sic] for all poor Men to follow,' the narrator concludes (Defoe 2003, 117).

Given its dissipated, luxurious lifestyle, which is incompatible with such manly attributes, the nobility as the traditional bearer of political power is not only criticized, but held morally and factually responsible for the outbreak of the plague. The Restoration court's appetite for 'Fashion and Finery [...] drew, by consequence, a great Number of Work-Men, Manufacturers, and the like, being mostly Poor People' (ibid., 17) to London so that the epidemic is aggravated by over-population. The plague itself is seen as God's punishment for the 'crying Vices' of this 'youthful and gay Court' (ibid., 20). Instead of fulfilling its political and moral duty, the court deserts the population of London shamefully. Consequently, the narrator tells us, all successful countermeasures must be attributed to the exemplary conduct of the urban middle classes alone: it is people like the mayor, 'a very sober and religious Gentleman' (ibid., 35), and such members of the clergy, the physicians, as well as those 'useful People [...] whose Business it was to take Charge of the Poor, [and who] did their Duties in general with as much Courage as any, and perhaps with more' (ibid., 227–8), that preserve 'excellent order' (ibid., 149) and save the day.[7] In contrast to the egoistic indifference of the court, responsibility, duty, usefulness, and – to use a fitting term anachronistically – civil courage emerge clearly as middle-class virtues.[8]

The relation between this middle-class manliness and the urban poor is altogether less straightforward, more ambiguous. The *Journal* finds different explanations for why the poor are affected worst by the plague and accordingly adopts different attitudes toward the lower classes. On the one hand it is argued that these people simply have no money for medicine or for stocking up on provisions, which would allow them to stay at home and out of harm's way (Defoe 2003, 76–7 and 83). Several of the characters who embody the attributes of godly manliness come from the ranks of the unpropertied masses. The barge-man Robert, for example, keeps his faith in divine providence even as his whole family is infected, and he diligently cares for them (ibid., 103–8). The consensus sought by the novel from this perspective is that charity must be extended to the 'deserving poor', even if it is only in those cases when their values are basically the same as those of the dominant class (Wainwright, 70). There is considerable symbolic capital to be reaped from charity: the knowledge of one's own prosperity, which in the Protestant world-view is a sure material sign of one's being deserving in the eyes of God (Colley 1996, 45–6 and 388–9). Hence charity does not so much blur the distinction between the classes as function here as a *perpetuum mobile* of middle-class self-esteem. On the other hand, the majority of the poor are regarded as 'ignorant and stupid in their Reflections' (Defoe 2003, 30), 'brutishly wicked' (ibid., 31), 'foolhardy and obstinate' (ibid., 201). Wasting the little money they have on useless charms or pills, falling into extremes of apostasy or religious fanaticism and recklessly moving about the city, the behaviour of the poor serves as another foil for the virtues of middle-class godly manliness: 'the Plague was chiefly among the Poor; yet were the Poor the most Venturous and Fearless of it, and went about their Employment, with a Sort of Brutal Courage; I must call it so, for it was founded neither on Religion or Prudence' (ibid., 87).

This vision of a social and moral hierarchy is presented by H.F., who is not only himself among the exemplary manly characters and even acts at a time as an official agent of the magistrate (ibid., 153–4), but as narrator-focalizer explains the events from a distinctly middle-class point of view.[9] H.F. can be positioned topographically and socially as a member of the well-to-do urban merchant class:

---

[7]   For a similar argument, see Leavy, 28–9.

[8]   These manly attributes are not only part of the discourse of moral reform, but also loom large in the republican discourse of civic humanism. Jeremy Gregory suggests that we think of this overlap in terms of Christian humanism, as a legacy of the early modern period. The centrality of civic virtue, be it of the secularized or the religious kind, to eighteenth-century debates about manliness can hardly be overestimated. The best articles on manliness and civic virtue are still Pocock 1985, 103–23, and Barrell 1989, 101–31.

[9]   As Wainwright remarks: 'The story might indeed be told differently by one of London's masses of poor citizens, or even by a member of the nobility' (28–9). See also Leavy, 23, 28, and 37–8.

he lives in the east of London, 'without Aldgate about mid-way between Aldgate Church and White-Chappel-Bars, on the left Hand or Northside of the Street'. This location allows him to distance himself explicitly from 'the richer Sort of People, especially the Nobility and Gentry' who live at the other end of the town. He is a saddler and merchant who trades with the North American colonies, and he possesses 'a House, Shop, and Ware-houses fill'd with Goods' for which he is just as concerned as for his own health or that of his 'Family of Servants'. To lose his property means to him not only the loss of his trade, but indeed of his position in society and 'of all I had in the World' (Defoe 2003, 9–11).

This emphasis on property is another cornerstone of middle-class manliness and goes some way to explain H.F.'s anxiety about a possible riot of the poor, as well as his insistent calls to charity. For as Defoe points out quite cynically, charity serves not only to display one's property but also to protect it: 'had not the Sums of Money, contributed in Charity by well disposed People […] been prodigiously great, it had not been in the Power of the Lord Mayor and Sherrifs, to have kept Publick Peace; nor were they without Apprehensions as it was, that Desperation should push the People upon Tumults, and cause them to rifle the Houses of rich Men […]' (ibid., 94). Only superficially motivated by the Christian virtue of compassion, as Gregg and others would claim, charity was a measure of godly manliness contaminated by economic interest, which emerged as the true measure of middle-class identity.[10]

Writing his memoirs in retrospect and editing his notes carefully, H.F. presents himself repeatedly as a detached observer. He rejects 'preaching a sermon instead of writing a history', and promises a reliable, objective account instead of an impassioned, partial view (Defoe 2003, 236).[11] This is taken up by critics who correctly interpret H.F.'s 'powerful apartness' as a 'privilege' and rather admiringly cast him in the role of 'a private observer […], a reporter and commentator', an 'accountant', 'a measuring intelligence', 'a dispassionate historian of contemporary life', and, in his capacity as a narrator, as an actively 'ordering principle'.[12] His narrative, confusing and digressive as it might seem, they argue, is unified and mediated through his 'univocal standpoint' and can thus be ultimately regarded as the reassuring outcome of a process of ordering and meaning-making: 'his prose creates patterns and hence suggests order, or purpose' (Wainwright, 61). Giving an explanation for the experience of the plague year, it

---

[10] As David Brooks shows, the sums raised for charity were in fact never sufficient to prevent mass riots. This suggests that Defoe's account of the amount of money and its beneficent effects were less in tune with historical fact than with the desire to present the middle classes as morally and politically responsible leaders (Defoe 2003, 176–82). That a riot is most effectually prevented by the severity of the plague among the poor adds a rather sarcastic note to the claim that good order was preserved by the prudence of the magistrate and the charity of the middling people (Defoe 2003, 95).

[11] Further relevant passages on pages 10, 72, 75, 89, 91, 100, 118, 165, and 183.

[12] See Richetti, 299; Brodsley, 11; Steel, 93; and Wainwright, 61.

explains the world in terms of middle-class godly manliness; in providing a map of the plague-ridden London, it also provides a meaningful map of the city in terms of its social structure. And by presenting this map of London society as a reliable one, claiming for it the authenticity of an eyewitness testimony, H.F.'s particular view of his world claims the status of a truth, a factual world-view. In other words: it operates as an ideology.

Reading the novel as a medium for the production of ideological structures (also known as 'common sense'), however, tells only half of the story. To see the *Journal* as unequivocally producing order and consensus means to subscribe to the same narrative strategies and ideological structures the text itself employs. In order to read the text as a successful vision of social order, one has to keep an unswerving faith in the ordering and meaning-making powers of man and of language; the problem, however, is that this is precisely what the *Journal* does not permit. For the other half of the story problematizes the very processes of keeping order and making sense on which the vision of godly manliness is staked. The key to this other story lies in the disorderly materiality and textual mediality that composes the *Journal*.

2.

What, then, does this other story tell us and how is it mediated? It is a story about failure, both of the plague management and of the narrative pattern woven by H.F. in order to make sense of it. This curiously emerges if one looks, albeit from a different angle, at the very same aspects of the text which are made to bear the evidence of the success story.

On the plot level of plague management, the epidemic figures not so much as a challenge in which the representatives of the middle classes have to prove themselves as manly leaders, but as a deeply unsettling experience that threatens the very basis of this identity. The plague management is in fact doomed to failure from the very start and so, by the *Journal*'s own rules, are the social order and manly identity premised on it. The reason for and the sign of this failure are the bodies of those who died of the plague. Early on in his narrative, H.F. reports that 'some [people] heard Voices warning them […] that there would be such a Plague in London, so that the Living would not be able to bury the Dead […]. There they saw Herses and Coffins in the Air, carrying to be buried. And there again, Heaps of Bodies lying unburied' (Defoe 2003, 23). Heaps of bodies lying unburied – this is the recurrent catchphrase which signals the failure of 'preserving good order'.

The plague management depends on the ability to distinguish the sick from the sound, to keep the infected in quarantine, and to bury the plague bodies quickly in order to prevent the fatal spread of the epidemic – in other words, on the ability to exert a controlling gaze and to render bodies 'docile'.[13] These measures, however,

---

[13] On early modern plague measures as prototype of a disciplinary society, see Foucault.

are continually frustrated. More often than not, the physical 'tokens' of the plague remain invisible until it is too late, so that 'such as had received the Contagion, and had it really upon them, yet did not shew the Consequences of it in their Countenances' and had 'very little Notice of their being infected at all, till the Gangreen was spread thro' their whole Body' (Defoe 2003, 184 and 80). Those who are infected hide their affliction in order to escape being shut up in their own houses, often without provisions or help. They lie about their illness or that of their relatives, thus rendering the official figures on the bills of mortality moot.[14] More dangerously, they 'run out of their Houses at all Hazards, and with the Plague visibly upon them, not knowing either whither to go, or what to do, or indeed what they did; and many that did so [...] drop't down by the raging violence of the Fever upon them' (ibid., 53). The narrator's repeated assurance that these plague bodies are immediately dealt with and that 'there was not the least Signal of the calamity to be seen or heard of' are contradicted by the material evidence of the corpses cluttering the streets or drifting on the river (ibid., 167–8, 171, and 178). Given what is at stake – the immediate survival of the city as well as the claim to moral and political leadership of middle-class godly men – the nervous, even hysterical tone of the following passage becomes understandable:

> This last Article [that no Bodies lay unburied or uncovered] perhaps will hardly be believ'd, when some Accounts which others have published since that shall be seen, wherein they say, that the Dead lay unburied, which I am assured was utterly false; *at least, if it had been anywhere so*, it must ha' been in Houses where [...] no Notice was given to the Officers: *All which amounts to nothing at all in the Case in Hand*; [...] I say, I am sure that there were *no dead Bodies* remain'd unburied; *that is to say, none that the proper Officers knew of; none for want of People to carry them off*, and Buriers to put them into the Ground and cover them; and this is sufficient to the Argument; *for what might lie in Houses and Holes in* Moses *and* Aaron Ally *is nothing*; for it is most certain, they were buried as soon as they were found. (Ibid., 173–4, my emphases)

This even by H.F.'s standards extremely convoluted sentence is meant to assure us of the good order kept in London, yet the impression it creates through the rhetorical gestures of evasion and denial is quite the opposite (Flynn, 29).[15]

The passage also strongly suggests that as much as H.F. enjoys presenting himself as an ordering principle, he is in fact a rather unreliable and self-contradictory narrator. While he claims for his narrative the status of an authentic eyewitness account and draws attention to his written 'Memorandums [sic] of

---

[14]   On the unreliability of the bills of mortality and other official documents, see McDowell 2006 and Benjamin Moore.

[15]   Readings that insist on a finally successful vision of order usually employ a similar strategy of denial and evasion. In fact, if these interpretations are to be consistent, they have to ignore this problem of the plague bodies. Where they are mentioned at all, they are treated as an annoying by-product of the plague, perhaps not easily but reliably dealt with by the representatives of the ordering powers.

what occurred to me every Day', on which it is based, he also suffers curious gaps of memory and could not care less: 'As to the poor Man whether he liv'd or dy'd I don't remember.' Despite positioning himself as an objective observer who looks down at and reflects on the world of plague from a window seat of his house, one can hardly say that he has a 'fundamentally superior' perspective that sets him apart from it (Richetti, 297). Rather, H.F. continually finds himself immersed in the experience of the plague and keeps looking for valid, meaningful explanations without being able to settle for one.

A case in point are the two dominant yet incompatible explanatory contexts for the plague, religion and science. The one describes the plague in terms of divine punishment and seeks to resolve the arbitrariness of health or infection, of survival or death into a providential pattern.[16] The other explanatory context accounts for the epidemic in terms of natural causes, revealing ways of infection as well as the best means of diagnosis, therapy, and prevention.[17] Neither can claim the status of a master narrative that explains the experience of the plague year in all its aspects – as individual tragedy, spiritual and social crisis, and moral as well as medical problem. The visions of a material world ordered by God on the one hand, and by Locke and Newton on the other, are simply too antagonistic (Flynn, 16). This contradiction has ramifications for the ideal of godly manliness, too, in that H.F.'s account of the plague keeps oscillating between discourses. This not only calls his status as a reliable 'ordering principle' into question but also suggests that the attributes of unswerving faith in God's providence and a rational world-view are not easily reconcilable, thus putting the manly ideal on a rather precarious basis. Add to that the discourse of economic interest that informs many of H.F.'s decisions and assessments of events, and neither the ideal of godly manliness nor the narrative maintain the stability ascribed to them in the 'order from confusion' reading.

In fact, the very choice of explanatory contexts depends on how well they serve H.F.'s interests. A telling example is his own advice that 'the best Preparation for the Plague was to run away from it' (Defoe 2003, 11). Instead of taking it, he decides to remain in town against all odds for the sake of his business, which, in the middle-class tradesmen's scale of priorities, obviously outweighs considerations of health and life. He also repeatedly urges his readers to lay up provisions and stay shut up in their own houses, yet he himself keeps venturing into the plague-infested streets, and on one memorable occasion even visits a plague-pit, despite this being highly dangerous and expressly forbidden by 'strict Order' (ibid., 59–62). Once there, his description of the experience shifts between the discourses of science and religion, contradicting itself all the time. He initially approaches the pit as something measurable, a mere hole in the ground, able to hold so many bodies; yet leaving the Enlightenment paradigm of empirical science behind, he moves on to acknowledge the uncanny fascination of the 'dreadful gulph' by night.

---

[16]   Defoe 2003, 64–7, 165, 186, 201, 234, and 236.

[17]   Ibid., 186–90, 196–200, and 216 following.

Then again, he rejects the sexton's warnings along with his pious explanation of the pit as 'an Instructing Sight [...] to call us all to repentance' (ibid., 60). Repentance, as well as the moral orientation it entails, is wiped from his mind when he watches how a cart-load of dead bodies is thrown 'promiscuously' into the grave. This horrifying erasure of social differences and personal identity is mirrored by the figure of a lonely survivor, whose admirably stoical 'Masculine Grief' gives way to incoherent cries and a fainting fit. Similarly shocked at the sheer meaninglessness of illness, death, and grief, H.F. is 'almost overwhelm'd, [...] with my Heart most afflicted and full of the afflicting Thoughts, such as I cannot describe' (ibid., 62). The material experience of the plague defies description and explanation. Only later, safely distanced from the pit, does H.F. recover the certainty that the plague's meaning is 'the terrible Judgment of God' (ibid., 64) for man's vices. Significantly, this position helps him to enact a pose of godly manliness when he upbraids a group of rakish, impious young men for their ungodly behaviour.

H.F. embraces piety and religious faith as an explanatory context here for the sake of distinguishing himself from a failed style of middle-class manliness. On other occasions, however, he scoffs at the religious enthusiasm of the poor, whose ignorance and superstition turn them into 'old women' while his reasonable, scientific view marks him as a member of the manly middling sort (ibid., 23). Especially their reliance on protection spells – 'Charms, Philters, Amulets, [...] Papers tied with so many Knots; and certain Words or Figures written on them, as particularly the Word *Abracadabra*, form'd in a Triangle, or Pyramid' (ibid., 33) – elicits his censure and contempt. Yet while the dangerous faith of the poor is dismissively exoticized as 'a kind of Turkish Predestinarianism' (ibid., 185), the good Englishman H.F. himself adopts a similar attitude when he willingly misreads a passage from the Bible to spell out a guarantee of safety in the midst of the plague, thus turning the text of the Bible itself into a protection spell of his own making.[18]

The convenient, if disorienting multiplicity of explanatory contexts for the plague thus helps to shape the *Journal's* ideal of manliness at the same time as it undermines its status as a clear-cut, reliable 'pattern for all men to follow'. The plurality of discourses itself can be explained by the plurality of media assembled in the *Journal*: collecting personal reminiscences, anecdotes, parish records, gossip, official decrees, magical diagrams, medical opinions, verses, and even a dramatic episode, the *Journal* is made up of a heterogeneous mass of textual material produced by the plague. 'Order' readings tend to ignore this plural mediality and effectively treat the printed text as a unified medium of a single, authoritative viewpoint. This simplistic view needs to be modified in at least two respects. First, much of the textual material is not derived from printed sources but belongs to the realm of oral culture (although represented here in print); this will be discussed further on. Second, the way it is assembled into a narrative emphasizes medial differences: sources such as the bills of mortality,

---

[18] On H.F.'s bibliomancy, see Zimmerman, 287–8.

official orders, and advertisements for cures or direct speech are typographically set apart, often with only minimal attempts at integrating them into the narrative flow. Usually the formula 'and were as follows, (*viz.*)' (38), or a simple 'thus' (33) serve to mark a medial insertion, while the phrase 'But I must go back again' (20) bluntly announces the return to H.F.'s narrative.

Different media are not only graphically and verbally highlighted; they also prefigure the structure of the narrative (or absence thereof). A case in point is an optical medium that was a relatively new invention at the time: the microscope. The principles of the microscope, which was invented in the late seventeenth century, were spread by scientific works such as Robert Hooke's *Micrographia* (1665). Already by the early eighteenth century, Londoners could buy simple microscopes, along with samples of insects, skin, and hair. The very fact that these early instruments showed an average distortion of 19 per cent rendered their use, or rather its results, a matter of speculation and intuition. Indeed an incentive to the imagination, the microscopic view was exploited as an aesthetic technique in several literary texts, most notably *Gulliver's Travels* (1726).[19] Defoe's *Journal* also makes use of this, and in one episode explicitly introduces the new optical medium as a means of diagnosis. In the absence of the optical instrument itself ('we had no Microscope at that Time'), H.F. imagines the enlarged sight of infectious matter, blurring the explanatory contexts of science and belief or myth in the process: 'there might living Creatures be seen by a Microscope of strange monstrous and frightful Shapes, such as Dragons, Snakes, Serpents, and Devils, horrible to behold' (Defoe 2003, 195). By analogy, the composition principle of the *Journal* could be described as taking a close look at the plague through a microscope with different lenses. Depending on which lens is chosen – the religious, the moral, the scientific, or the economic – different 'shapes' emerge. The narrative keeps shifting between lenses in an attempt to capture all the aspects of the plague and make sense of it. Yet what this shift between optical media produces is not a sense of order but rather a sense of vertigo, even more so because it also enacts a shift in terms of scale: the narrative zooms into scenes of individual suffering, retreats into wide-angle views of how the plague carries off 'heaps' of people, then returns to an intimate close-up view of one particular body, only to jump back to the impersonal figures of the bills of mortality.

This disorienting state is exacerbated by the medial difference between printed text and oral culture that is negotiated in Defoe's text. As Paula McDowell (2006) argues convincingly, the *Journal* models the media shift from early modern oral culture to modern print culture in the early eighteenth century. Her analysis shows how the new authority of the printed text (the bills of mortality, official orders) is challenged throughout by rivalling acts of oral street culture such as gossip, anecdotes, or folklore. That the printed matter is issued by the magistrate, whose supposedly successful plague management associates it with

---

[19]   On the influence of the microscope on the collective imagination, see the still authoritative study by Nicholson, especially Chapter 6, or Flynn, 17–18.

middle-class manliness, and the oral medium is part of a female culture of 'old wives' tales', renders this medial difference as a difference in class and gender. This distinction, however, is complicated by the text. Especially in the case of the bills of mortality, so-called 'Women-Searchers', poor parishioners who were sent into infected houses, were the actual source of these written statistics, which claimed to be accurate but were themselves 'infected', as it were, by the often unreliable information provided by illiterate women. This severely compromised the reliability of the bills, which the citizens used as a map to safety in the changed landscape of the plague city (McDowell 2006, 92). Moreover, print culture did not always bear the imprint of order, whereas oral culture – sermons, for example – could speak with the voice of authority. A case in point is the flood of printed texts which feed (and feed on) 'The Apprehensions of the people': 'this unhappy temper was originally raised by the Follies of some People who got Money by it; that is to say, by printing Predictions, and Prognostications I know not; but certain it is, Book's [sic] frightened them terribly' (Defoe 2003, 22). Almanacs and religious prophecies move into the suspicious vicinity of 'Oral Predictions' by 'Enthusiastics [running] about the Streets', just as advertisements and 'Doctor's Bills, and Papers of ignorant Fellows' (ibid., 31) replace the offices of the mountebank.

Apart from the fact that oral culture introduces a multitude of often jarring, contradictory voices into the printed text, thus undermining its claims to mediate a single, unified standpoint, the written account proves all too often unable to represent the oral and aural experience of the plague. Significantly, it is again the encounter with plague bodies which provokes a failure of attempts at (narrative) ordering and meaning-making: 'I had many dismal Scenes before my Eyes, as particularly of Persons falling dead in the Streets, terrible Shrieks and Skreekings of Women, who in their Agonies would throw open their Chamber Windows, and cry out in a dismal Surprising Manner' (Defoe 2003, 78); 'It is impossible to describe the most horrible Cries and Noise [...]' (ibid., 171); 'I wish I could repeat the very Sound of those Groans and of those Exclamations that I heard from some poor dying Creatures, when in the Hight [sic] of their Agonies and Distress; and that I could make him that *read* this *hear* [...]' (ibid., 101). It is not only that the written text fails as a medium, but that the soundscape of the plague is in itself 'void of all Sense', a 'dreadful Clamour, mixt or Compoundet of Skreetches, Cryings and Calling one another, that we could not conceive what to make of it' (ibid., 171). Paradoxically, the moments when the narrative acknowledges the limits of the written word as a medium of conveying and making sense, it mediates most effectively the disorienting, meaningless experience of the plague year and the failure of the manly attempts at managing it.

3.

What does this mean for the mediation of manly identity? The *Journal*'s attempts at comprehensiveness and reliability through verisimilitude produce an inherent tension in the text that undermines its cultural function as 'a pattern for all good men to follow'.[20] The very fact that contemporary readers accepted H.F.'s memoirs as a truthful account and authentic historical record (see Mayer) only renders the subject positions offered as points of identification more precarious. This affects especially the figure of the narrator, whose unifying perspective falls apart along with his pose of exemplary manliness. It is this falling apart, this failure of mediating a coherent narrative identity and stable subject position, that allows insights into its specific historical set-up. As David Brooks helpfully points out, 'the more verisimilitude Defoe gives his *Journal*, the more it exposes tensions, oppositions and contradictions in the texture of H.F.'s "lived experience", both as the citizen of 1665, and as the subsequent memorialist. In this way, H.F.'s whole mentality as a seventeenth-century bourgeois citizen and the ideologies that he espouses are brought into question' (168). However, the ideologies of the 'seventeenth-century bourgeois citizen', as well as the 'subsequent memoralist' of 1722, remain a convenient *chiffre* in his account when it comes to gender. My own reading of the *Journal* has attempted to flesh out this *chiffre* as the figure of middle-class manliness and to show how it is both articulated and challenged in the act of mediation: the same strategies which were employed to mediate this identity along with a vision of civic order as a valid, meaningful perspective – the plot of plague management as a touchstone for inclusion and exclusion, the figure of the narrator and his narrative as a meaningful pattern – become points of resistance to the authority of this ideal once the heterogeneous mediality of the text is acknowledged. In the same text that mediates middle-class manliness, the constitutive ideologies and enactments of this identity are challenged and undermined through the plural mediality employed to represent it: manliness is found and lost in mediation.

---

[20]   See, for example, Zimmerman, 286, and Benjamin Moore, 143.

Chapter 3
Gender Identity in Sentimental and Pornographic Fiction: *Pamela* and *Fanny Hill*

Franz Meier

Sentimental and Pornographic Novels: Genre and Gender

The seemingly antagonistic genres of sentimental[1] and pornographic fiction[2] were both developed within the same period, somewhat misleadingly labelled as the Age of Reason, and in connection with some of its dominant cultural developments. Together they participated in the 'rise of the novel' and its conventions of 'formal realism' (cf. Watt). Thus they both profited from the broadening of the reading public as well as the increasing individualism and privacy of reading. Furthermore, they also converge in their joint connection to eighteenth-century discourses like

---

[1]   Sentimental fiction is the literary manifestation of a larger cultural movement known as the 'Culture of Sensibility' (cf. Barker-Benfield) and it dates back to somewhere between the 1740s and the 1760s. Amongst the genres emerging from it, the sentimental novel has usually been regarded as the leading one, with Samuel Richardson's *Pamela* (1740) and *Clarissa* (1747) as the first and foremost examples. Using *Pamela* as the English prototype of the genre, I temporarily suspend (for the purposes of this essay) the more subtle distinction, suggested by Janet Todd (8, *passim*) between the novel of sentiment and the novel of sensibility, since all the features she lists for the latter (and later) subtype can already be found in Richardson's *Pamela* as well. My quotations from Richardson's *Pamela* refer to the 1980 Penguin edition of the novel, edited by Peter Sabor, and are henceforth given as *P*, followed by page numbers in the text.

[2]   Pornography in its literal sense (that is 'writing about prostitutes') is almost as old as literature itself. In its current understanding, however, as '[t]he explicit description or exhibition of sexual subjects or activity in literature, painting, films etc., in a manner intended to stimulate erotic rather than aesthetic feelings' (*SOED*), pornographic, just as sentimental fiction, can be largely seen as an innovation of the eighteenth century (cf. for example Peakman, 6; Wagner 1990, 231–2). I again suspend the problem of subtle subdivisions here, my aim rather being to point out the differences and similarities of sentimental and pornographic literature at large. Also, I have chosen to concentrate on the English prototypes of the two genres; and if *Pamela* is widely accepted to take this position in the former, the first full-fledged pornographic novel in England is John Cleland's *Memoirs of a Woman of Pleasure* (1749), better known under the name of its narrator-protagonist as *Fanny Hill*. My quotations from this novel refer to Peter Wagner's Penguin edition of the text and are henceforth given as *FH*, followed by page numbers in the text.

Moral Sense Theory and the Cult of Sensibility, but also French Materialism, Sensational Psychology, the ideal of politeness, and eighteenth-century economy. The influence of some of these phenomena has been found even in unlikely places,[3] and in the light of these discoveries, obvious differences between the sentimental and the pornographic novel with respect to thematic interest (soul versus body, virtue versus pleasure) or stylistic forms of representation soon turn out to be similarities in disguise. The same is true for the seemingly oppositional gendering of the two genres, which will be the starting point of my argument here, and which is based on common developments in the eighteenth-century discourse of sexuality. This paper, however, will focus less on the two genres' joint participation in general scientific and philosophical contexts,[4] and more specifically on the question of how such novels as *Pamela* and *Fanny Hill* mediate prevailing gender boundaries and thus encourage their readers to mediate their own gender identities.

It is no accident that from the beginning, the sentimental novel was generally connoted as feminine, the pornographic novel as masculine;[5] rather, it perfectly fits a period when, according to Laqueur, the discourse of gender was beginning to be reshaped from a 'one-sex' to a 'two-sex model'. Woman's body, which had formerly been seen as 'a lesser version of the male's', was now increasingly considered man's 'incommensurable opposite' (see Laqueur, vii–viii, *passim*).[6]

---

[3]   To give some examples: The influence of French Materialism on *Fanny Hill* has been pointed out by Braudy; cf. Wagner's introduction to *Fanny Hill*, 22–3, as well as his notes 30 and 38 to *FH*. Connections between the Cult of Sensibility and Sensational Psychology have been pointed out by Rousseau, 137–57; cf. Barker-Benfield, 3–7 and Van Sant, esp. 1, n2. The importance of the ideal of politeness for eighteenth-century erotic culture has been noted by Harvey, 68–76, 223, *passim*; cf. Roy Porter, esp. 18. The economic contexts of eighteenth-century sentimentalism and pornography have been stressed by Kibbie, 561–77.

[4]   I also largely exclude the complex intertextual connections of sentimental to erotic literature, which have been hinted at from the very birth of the former genre, the most famous instance being the so-called *Pamela* Controversy ensuing the publication of Richardson's novel and producing Fielding's parody *Shamela* (1741) as well as many other intertexts, now available in a collection edited by Thomas Keymer and Peter Sabor. Reverse intertextual relations are mentioned by Wagner in Chapter 7 of his *Eros Revived*, where he describes sentimental traits in eighteenth-century pornographic fiction, and in particular calls Cleland's *Fanny Hill* 'an Anti-*Pamela* and a libertine novel [which] attempts to combine the sensual with the sentimental' (220; cf. ibid., 237–47). Peter Sabor sees Fanny Hill as a character who combines traits of Richardson's Pamela and Fielding's Shamela (Samuel Richardson 1980, xii–xxvi). Copeland lists, in a lengthy footnote, about a dozen parallels between the characters and plots of *Pamela* and *Fanny Hill*, though he states that they 'may or may not be deliberate'. (351, n4; cf. 343–4.)

[5]   On the gendering of language and writing in the eighteenth century, see, for example, Harvey, 57–60.

[6]   Laqueur's theory of a change between a *one-sex* and a *two-sex model* has not remained undisputed (for a short summary of critical responses see, recently, Karremann, 35, n22.) Nevertheless, despite necessary historical readjustments and additions, his model

Considering the impact of French Materialism on eighteenth-century thought, it was of course to be expected that this gender differentiation also encompassed the fields of emotion and intellect. The consequences thereof for eighteenth-century women have been most famously described by Mary Wollstonecraft in her *Vindication of the Rights of Woman* (1792). She pointed out how strongly the cult of sensibility, by then already declining, was linked to notions of femininity – and complained that, starting from the implication that 'the sexes ought not to be compared' (that is the two-sex model), it was generally concluded that 'man was made to reason, woman to feel' (see Barker-Benfield, 1). Utilizing theories of sensational psychology, this was proven on the grounds of their different nervous systems. In the words of Barker-Benfield, 'women's subordination was naturalized on the basis of their finer sensibility' (ibid., 3).

This ideological constellation, however, has its moral pitfalls if seen in connection with sexuality, because not only were women now thought to be endowed with a more refined moral sense (woman as saint), they also were suspected of being more easily seduced into the quite immoral abyss of sensuality (woman as sinner). As for the two literary genres under investigation here, sentimental fiction is generally taken to be based on the first assumption, the pornographic novel on the second. The intricate consequences of this binary constellation shall be investigated in the following chapters with regard to (in increasing detail) authorship, text (narration, plot, characters), and reader response.

Authorship and Publication

Beginning with the 'amatory fiction' of Aphra Behn, Delarivier Manley, and Eliza Haywood, a considerable number of eighteenth-century novels (particularly popular ones) was written by women, and 'the balance between male and female authors [even] shifted in women's favour ... after 1779' (Harvey, 44). Nevertheless, for the greater part of the century, the much-despised 'Amazons of the pen', as Dr Johnson called them (quoted in Todd, 21), had to expect considerable resistance in the male-dominated public sphere of publication. Within the gender model sketched by Wollstonecraft, writing was generally considered to belong to the realm of reason, thus pens in the hands of men. Even in the (supposedly feminine) field of sentimental fiction, women writers had to face considerable resistance in a male-dominated market – though authors like Charlotte Lennox, Fanny Burney, and Jane Austen considerably contributed to its development and, interestingly enough, even more to the genre's parodistic deconstruction.[7]

---

still provides a useful tool for the description of prevalent structures and developments in the gender discourse of the eighteenth century.

[7]   Note also the substantial influence of female collaborators like Catherine Talbot or Lady Bradshaigh in the composition of Richardson's *Sir Charles Grandison*, as described, for example, in Jocelyn Harris's 'Introduction' and 'Note on the Text' in her edition of Richardson's novel (vii–xxiv and xxviii–xxxvii); or Eaves and Kimpel, 363–74, *passim*.

Female authorship of explicitly pornographic novels,[8] however, seems to have been almost unthinkable at the time; or at least the publication of such texts would have been increasingly unlikely[9] because of economic power structures in combination with changing gender expectations (due to the 'two-sex model'): it was men who dominated the printing business and they would hardly have approved of (or even been approached by) female authors of pornography.[10] But even if we should come across the odd pornographic text under a female author's name, Harvey warns us that

> [w]e have to be extremely cautious of ascribing female authorship to erotic [even more, I add, to pornographic] books when this can not be verified with other sources, as we know that publishers marketed many novels as being female-authored when they were not, because they sold more. (44)

A similar reason can also be suspected for the high number of female narrators of pornographic fiction. But here we already leave the level of production and enter that of the text.

Narration, Plot, and Characters

Sentimental and pornographic novels soon developed a number of specific conventions which corresponded and contributed to the gendering of the respective genre – be it in terms of narrative style and technique, structure and development

---

[8]   I do not consider amatory fiction to belong to that category, since (despite its daring openness in sexual matters) '[t]he explicit description or exhibition of sexual subjects or activity' (*SOED*; cf. note 2 above) is not prominent or even usual in this genre. Indeed, as Wagner writes, 'the amatory novel draws the curtain, so to speak, where explicit sexual scenes have their beginning' (1990, 216). A frequent constellation, for example in Eliza Haywood's *Love in Excess; or, The Fatal Inquiry* (1719/1720), seems to be the interruption of a sexual scene shortly before intercourse (cf., for example, 58–9, 117–18, 124–5, 225–6, and 258–9 in David Oakleaf's edition of Haywood's novel).

[9]   Peakman's examples of 'licentious material' (38) written by women all stem from the earlier part of the century, that is, from the period before the establishment of a genuinely English pornography. His suspicion that 'with the advent of pornographic fiction, women were ... asked by their publishers to provide for this market anonymously' (39), must therefore remain highly speculative.

[10]   Though Peakman states that in the earlier eighteenth century women 'were also involved in the seedier, less respectable end of the [literary] market' (see also MacDowell 1998, 294), and that '[b]y the mid-century, [they] had all but disappeared as major publishers and printers' (Peakman, 25), Harvey mentions only one erotic book being published by a woman in the eighteenth century, and that in continuation of her deceased husband's publishing business: Mary Cooper's *The Man-Plant* of 1752 (cf. Harvey, 42–3). Generally speaking, female booksellers were always the exception to the rule and, what is more, even in the days of Behn, Manley, and Haywood they 'were not usually involved in the production of women's fiction' (Turner, 89).

of plot, or presentation and constellation of characters. The following paragraphs will investigate some of these conventions and try to establish their function in the construction of gendered identities within the fictional world.

Despite the fact that the canonical examples of sentimental fiction are authored by male writers, the (dominant) narrative voices in these texts are frequently female.[11] In the genre's prototype, Richardson's *Pamela* (1740), an epistolary novel and thus (due to its association with the private sphere) regarded as feminine in itself, the female autodiegetic narrator fills more than 90 per cent of the novel's pages with her letters and diary entries. The story's point of view thereby clearly becomes a dominantly female one.[12] However, this does not automatically mean that the text serves female interests. Rather, the authorial construction of a female point of view tends to veil the masculinist gender bias of the values presented.

The plot structure of the typical sentimental novel is that of pursued innocence or 'Virtue in Distress' (see Brissenden, and Todd, 75). This pattern coincides with contemporary notions of delicate, naïve, but virtuous middle-class femininity (as criticized in Wollstonecraft's *Vindication*), which is opposed to male aristocratic worldliness, debauchery, and vice. Feminine virtue is frequently presented as a result of restricted contact with the world or public sphere. Connected to this principle of innocence is a certain (involuntarily) seductive quality, so that as soon as the protagonist lacks the protection of a patriarchal family, she threatens to become – in parody of the initiation pattern – prey to the ruthless 'men of the world'. Paradoxically, however, the corruption of female middle-class innocence (attempted or successful as it may be) also influences the male aristocratic villains, who either are reformed (*Pamela*) or repent and die (*Clarissa*). Thus, while the female heroine is characterized by a refined sensibility and moral sense,[13] the male antagonist, initially at least, lacks all moral standards and interprets sensibility in terms of sensuality and sexuality.[14]

---

[11] Even in those famous cases where, as in Mackenzie, the narrator is a *Man of Feeling* (1771), the writing would possibly be characterized by some as *écriture féminine*. The great exception here (as usual) is Laurence Sterne, whose narrators are – despite their claim to refined sensibility – decidedly masculinist.

[12] With *Clarissa*, the case is more complex, because the multiple narration of this text gives other voices, and particularly the male voice of Lovelace, considerable say – and in the latter half of the novel even makes him the dominant voice. This structural circumstance (together with Lovelace's wit) posed a serious problem for Richardson, who repeatedly revised the text in order not to make his masculinist rake-villain all too fascinating for the reader (cf., for example, Todd, 75–6).

[13] For the feminine 'gendering of sensibility' and morality in Richardson, see, for example, Todd, 78–81.

[14] There are, of course, also 'Men of Feeling', like Harley in Mackenzie's novel of that title (1771), Goldsmith's Primrose in *The Vicar of Wakefield* (1766), or even Richardson's protagonist in *Sir Charles Grandison* (1753). These cases are particularly interesting in terms of gender identity, because, as could be shown in the case of Harley, great pains have to be taken by the authors of these works in order to forestall the danger of their

Pornographic novels of the eighteenth century, like sentimental novels of the time, also frequently chose female first-person narrators (even if for slightly different reasons),[15] and they share the latter genre's preference for the epistolary form or autobiographical confession.[16] Cleland's *Fanny Hill*, as the first English example, also reflects these genre conventions, albeit in a rather parodistic vein: it is a parody of the female epistolary novel because each of its two volumes consists of only one long letter by the protagonist to an unspecified 'Madam'. Fanny (in a probably ironical hint at Pamela's obsessive writing habits) even ends the first one after over 100 pages with the words: 'surely, it is high time to put a period to this' (*FH*, 126). It is a parody of the autobiographical 'confession' (ibid., 129) because – similar to Defoe's *Moll Flanders* (1722) – Fanny's moralizing 'tail-piece' (ibid., 223) and praise of virtue at the end of the book sound anything but convincing.

Plot structures of pornographic novels also usually affirm the conventions of diaries, autobiographies, and confessions, and arrange sexual episodes in chronological order, following the principles of repetition, variation, and intensification. The story often follows a pattern of initiation and thus is akin to the sentimental plot of pursued innocence – the difference being that it is the initiation itself (the loss of innocence and virtue) that brings reward here, and not its prevention. Fanny Hill, like the protagonist of many a sentimental novel, leaves her rural home after the loss of her family, moves to London, and gets initiated into the world and into sexuality. After a long and varied series of (increasingly self-sought) sexual experiences she finally becomes heiress to the fortune of her latest keeper, regains her lost romantic love, and 'retire[s] to a virtuous middle-class existence of domesticity' (Wagner 2001a, 20). For Wagner,

> [t]here can be no doubt that the resemblance to the happy ending in *Pamela* is intentional; but Cleland explodes rather than apes Richardson's denouement: for Pamela there could be neither sex nor sexual pleasure before marriage, and she trades her "virtue" for the marriage licence; Fanny, however, tries to show that vice can also lead to virtue and that there is a difference between sexual and erotic love, her love for Charles being both *eros* and *agape*. (Ibid.)

---

being accused of effeminacy. Despite their lack of interest in sexual pursuits and sensual pleasure, their heterosexuality and masculinity has to be foregrounded by other means, like a hopeless romantic heterosexual infatuation (Harley), a number of children (Primrose), or an exaggerated sense of honour and duty (Grandison). Again, only Sterne's 'men of feeling' seem to be able to reconcile their refined sensibility and their (often problematic!) masculinity.

[15] For the functions of first-person narrative in pornographic novels see Goulemot, 120–30 and the latter part of my section on 'Reader Response' in this chapter.

[16] Peter Naumann (177–8) sees the converging point of moral and pornographic novels in the tradition of confessional literature. For the genre traditions of the whore biography and the whore letter, and for Defoe's *Moll Flanders* (1722) and *Roxana* (1724) as models, see Wagner 1990, 222–5, and Wagner 2001a.

In terms of eighteenth-century gender discourse Fanny thus becomes a highly problematic character. On the one hand, her interest in sexual gratification and her obvious lack of moral sense seem to confirm the sensualist 'notion of an essential female lasciviousness' (Peakman, 189); on the other, her sensibility is refined enough to be capable of differentiating between two subtly distinct kinds of pleasure like sexuality and love, even enhancing the one by the other (cf. Naumann, 190). By that she (con)fuses contradictory eighteenth-century expectations of femininity (the sinner and the saint) in a highly ironical, maybe even emancipatory vein.

In contrast, most of the male characters in *Fanny Hill* are astonishingly one-dimensional and limited in their sensibility. They are neither sublime villainous heroes nor sensitive men of feeling. The women either make them dupes of their narrow sensualism (*FH*, 164–75) or they turn them into sexual objects for the satisfaction of female interest and desire (ibid., 107–21, 196–202). Charles alone is presented as a male character of sympathy and respect – and he shows quite a number of feminine traits (Ibid., 81–2).[17] Interestingly enough, his masculinity, like that of many sentimental heroes, has to be repeatedly foregrounded in order to suppress the suspicion of effeminacy (ibid., 74, 82, and 216).

Reader Response

Having looked at authors and texts of both sentimental and pornographic fiction, it is now time to finally ask questions concerning the gender specificity of these genres with regard to their readers. But who are they? Reader response theory since the 1970s has produced a plethora of terms and concepts for the recipients of a (literary) text, among them the actual, empirical, historical, imagined, intended, informed, fictitious, implicit, and implied reader, who are not always easily distinguishable from one another. For my purposes here I shall concentrate on the three categories of empirical, fictitious, and – most important – the 'implied reader', whom Iser defines as a textually determined reading performance (Iser 1994a, 9).[18] This performative aspect, in my opinion, makes it legitimate to see the implied reader as gendered (although Iser's term is rather to be understood as a structural position than as a real or imagined person). After all, the 'act of reading' (Iser 1994b) involves, for example, the dynamics of identification with or the voyeuristic gaze at male or female characters. The gendering of the implied reader is, of course, strongly informed by that of the fictitious reader on the story level, and it should itself have an equally strong influence on the empirical readers and their empirical act of reading, which in turn was/is part of their performance of gender and thus the (re)construction of their gender identity.

If women in the eighteenth century, as Wollstonecraft regretted, were culturally constructed as feeling rather than thinking beings, it must have appeared natural to

---

[17]   Cf. Elizabeth Kubek, who calls him 'epicene' (188).

[18]   For a different typology of readers, see Harvey, 35–77.

find them reading a genre of literature which had emotional sensibility at its core; and the scarce material available seems to confirm the suspicion that a majority of empirical readers of sentimental fiction were female. Richardson started his *Pamela* as a 'letter writer' for young women; and although he declares in the preface that the intended audience of the finished novel is 'the YOUTH of *both sexes*' (*P*, 31), the original catering for a female readership can still strongly be felt in the published version (Watt, 148 and 151–4). Because of the female autodiegetic protagonist alone, the process of reader identification can be assumed to be much easier for a female than a male readership.[19] What is more, the private and therefore 'typically' feminine form of epistolary writing suggests a similarly private act of reading which safely remained within the hegemonic limits of feminine social decorum.

As for the fictitious readers: Pamela's letters are, of course, intended for both of her parents; but, maybe more importantly, most of them are actually read (and from a certain point undoubtedly also meant to be read) by Mr B. Only in the beginning do we encounter Pamela as a reader of her parents' letters, and only rarely of Mr B.'s epistles. The fictitious readers of the novel in terms of gender thus correspond only marginally (in Pamela's mother) with the empirical, probably mostly female readership of the novel.

But neither is the implied reader of *Pamela* identical with any of the fictitious readers of Pamela's writing, as this structural position results from the text's presentations of these letters, their fictional writer, and their imagined or represented reception by the reading characters. The gendering of this implied act of reading certainly involves identification with the feminine heroine and her ideals of female virtue. These ideals, however, differ somewhat from those of the fictional readers, of Pamela's father and mother (let alone of Mr B.). While her parents represent traditional norms of class and gender hierarchies and try to make their daughter unconditionally submit to them (*P*, 45–6), Pamela's sensibility tacitly undermines these conservative conventions and, through her preference for genuine feeling over conventional morality, subtly reverses the established gender and class hierarchy by making the aristocratic libertine finally succumb to middle-class virtue.

The text thus encourages its implied readers to mediate between their own different models of femininity: On the one hand, it affirms contemporary gender stereotypes like sensibility, virtue, and passivity. On the other hand, these qualities, which are supposed to be simultaneously performed by the reader in the act of reading itself, result in a potential subversion of conventional gender hierarchies and, through identification with the protagonist, enable the reader to experience

---

[19]   Nevertheless, one should beware of an all-too-simple model of reader identification. As Barbara M. Benedict has convincingly argued, sentimental novels almost always are characterized by a 'dialectic between formal control and emotional release' and '[r]eaders are hence directed not just to sympathize, but also to detach themselves from the action and the characters' (11; see also 18, *passim*).

a sort of female empowerment without having to subvert the hegemonic gender pattern. That this empowerment is ultimately contained in an overall attempt to stabilize patriarchal power structures becomes, of course, nowhere more obvious than in Pamela's long catechism of marital duties (as prescribed by Mr B.!) in the latter part of the novel (*P*, 467–71).

Statements about the empirical reader of eighteenth-century pornography are bound to be paradoxical, for although we know very little about historical reading habits, it is generally assumed that such books were hard to get, read privately, 'with one hand', and almost exclusively by male readers.[20] All of these assumptions meanwhile have to be qualified.[21] Nevertheless, I would still maintain, with Shoemaker, that '[m]ost obscene literature was written by and for men' (65).

It is only at first sight that this predominantly male empirical readership stands in contrast to the mostly female narrators and fictitious readers in pornographic texts. Far from excluding an actual male readership, such intimate feminine correspondence is a widespread convention in pornographic texts at least since the so-called 'whore dialogues' (Wagner 2001a, 25–6) and, as Goulemot has shown (59–60),[22] serves the creation of a voyeuristic distance in its male readers, quite opposed to the recipients' identification with the characters, which is typical for sentimental fiction. 'To put it in its crudest terms', Goulemot writes, 'the reader [of pornography] is not seized with a desire for *jouissance* because the author describes the desires of his characters, but rather because there are bodies and an embrace' (59). It is doubtlessly true, therefore, that eighteenth-century pornography in general – despite its female narrators and fictitious readers – is not really interested in a female perspective, but is dominated by the 'male gaze [, which] projects its fantasy onto the female figure' (Mulvey, 837).[23]

---

[20]   In his *Confessions*, Jean-Jacques Rousseau talks of 'those dangerous books that a fine lady finds inconvenient, because they can only be read with one hand' (quoted in Goulemot, 36). It is interesting to note, in our context, that Rousseau obviously did not share the last of my listed assumptions, that about the all-male readership of pornographic fiction.

[21]   As to availability. there is general agreement that after the lapsing of the Licensing Act in 1695 and the ensuing abolishment of pre-publication censorship, '[e]rotica circulated relatively unfettered' in England (Harvey, 38). Besides, the general assumption of the solitary reader of pornography has been questioned by showing that the perusal of pornographic fiction was also part of an upper-class culture of (mainly) homosocial bonding in clubs and coffee houses (ibid., 60–77). Finally, the implication of an all-male readership was challenged by Peakman, who insists that 'women read and enjoyed obscene literature' (37). Peakman's (careful enough) speculation about such a readership is, however, based on reader addresses in 'prefaces' (35) or the access of '[f]emale servants' (36) and '[m]istresses' (187) to their masters' and lovers' libraries.

[22]   Also Naumann, 220 and 319, *passim*.

[23]   I borrow this term from feminist film theory without, of course, paying tribute to the media-related aspects of this concept. Harvey, with reference to erotic material, mentions its 'imagined female reader' (54) but states that it was 'explicitly aimed at men' (55). Later, she talks of a 'clear disparity between the imagined female readers of erotic texts and the actual

Nevertheless, and despite Goulemot's argument for the reader's voyeuristic distance from the pornographic text, the structural devices of a female first-person narrator and a feminine point of view, as well as corresponding strategies of directing the implied reader's sympathy, will not remain without effect and, I would argue, cannot but create a certain amount of reader identification. If this can be conceded, however, an affirmation of conventionally masculine gender identity through the reading of pornographic fiction, in the case of *Fanny Hill* at least, faces considerable problems. Identification of the implied reader with the female narrator-protagonist (cf. Naumann, 317) clearly privileges feminine readings of the conventionally heterosexual scenes (and for a male heterosexual empirical reader might result in a 'queer' reading experience). But identification of the implied reader with any of the male characters in the text would counteract the construction of a masculine heterosexual gender identity as well, because the book's inherent image of masculinity is a rather unflattering one (with the possible exception of Charles, who, however, only rarely appears on the scene and ends up as economically dependent on his wife [*FH*, 222–3]). In order to establish a safe masculinist reading, therefore, the recipient has to counteract identification and try to position himself at a safe distance of voyeuristic observation from the story world. But even then, *Fanny Hill* in several aspects obviously contradicts the general assumption of the implied reader's undisputed masculinity in pornographic texts. Granted, the realistic description of Fanny's painful defloration (ibid., 76–8) can still be interpreted as catering to some male readers' 'latent sadism' (Naumann, 198); but her account of the unsatisfactory intercourse with Mr Norbert (*FH*, 164–77) or the mentioning of her miscarriage (ibid., 93) are not likely to represent male heterosexual fantasies. The same is true for the many elaborate descriptions of male bodies and organs (for example, ibid., 81–2, 108, 116, and 139), which seem to imply a female gaze rather than a male one – and even more so for the elaborate male homosexual scene toward the novel's end (ibid., 193–6).[24]

For a male heterosexual reader, therefore, whether at a voyeuristic distance or in identificatory closeness to the characters, the act of reading *Fanny Hill* is bound to lead to a potentially confusing gender performance, the outcome of which could eventually be a disturbance rather than an affirmation of hegemonic masculine identity.

---

male readers of external evidence. The latter leads us to regard the former not as proof of female readership, but as one of a range of techniques which characterized women (and men) in a particular way. […] Images of women as enthusiastic and receptive readers of erotica were not a source of pleasure for women, but a source of sustenance for erotica's male readers' (77).

[24] This scene, which was cancelled from most later editions (cf. *FH*, 230, n120), was repeatedly taken as evidence of Cleland's (latent) homosexuality (see, for example, Peter Sabor's introduction to his edition of *Pamela*, xiii), but cannot, in my opinion, suffice to make a male homosexual position for the implied (let alone the intended) reader of the novel plausible. Nevertheless, Lisa Moore, in *Dangerous Intimacies: Toward a Sapphic History of the British Novel*, argues that '[t]he unusual prominence and availability of male bodies in the novel both assumes and creates a male homosexual gaze and desire' (67).

Conclusion

My investigation of the English prototypes of eighteenth-century sentimental and pornographic fiction is based on the implication that these two seemingly contradictory genres share the common background of eighteenth-century culture. Nevertheless, or rather (following Laqueur): consequently, they appear as strictly antithetical with regard to their gender politics. The emerging two-sex model implied a gendering of sensibility and sex, and thus of sentimentalism as feminine and pornography as masculine. An increasingly close investigation on the levels of author, text, and reader, however, at the same time revealed some surprising contradictions within this binary constellation and quite a number of parallels and connections between at least the chosen English prototypes, if not the two newly established genres in general. Through the implied readers of what seemed to be clearly gendered genres, their internally aporetic structures imply a wide range of possible mediations of gender identities for the empirical readers at the time – and maybe even today.

Chapter 4
Paratexts and the Construction of Author Identities: The Preface as Threshold and Thresholds in the Preface

Katharina Rennhak

Paratexts as Thresholds

As a paratext the preface is 'what enables a text to become a book' (Genette, 1; Derrida 2004, 3–65). According to Genette, paratexts are characterized by their generative power: they generate the books they are an integral part of (Meißner, 2), and they set the parameters which are fundamental to any reading experience (cf. Genette, 2).[1] The preface, in particular, which is very often a site of theoretical self-reflections, is a medium that transmits a message which does not only refer to and discuss questions concerning (the medium of) literature or the literary, but defines and even generates it. The French title of Genette's study of paratexts is, of course, *Seuils*, and the metaphor of the threshold is central to the conceptualization of the paratext:

> More than a boundary or a sealed border, the paratext, is rather, a *threshold* [...] that offers the world at large the possibility of either stepping inside or turning back. It is an 'undefined zone'[2] between the inside and the outside, a zone without any hard and fast boundary on either the inward side (turned toward the text) or the outward side (turned toward the world's discourse about the text), an edge, or, as Philippe Lejeune put it, 'a fringe of the printed text which in reality controls one's whole reading of the text'. Indeed, this fringe, always the conveyor of a commentary that is authorial or more or less legitimated by the author, constitutes a zone between text and off-text, a zone not only of transition but also of *transaction*: a privileged place of a pragmatics and a strategy, of an influence on the public. (Genette, 2)

If the paratext in general and the preface in particular generate the book, they do so in the process of mediating between various different systems or entities: the

---

[1]   See Leujeune, *Le pacte autobiographique* (Paris, 1975), 45; quoted in Genette, 2.

[2]   Genette refers to Duchet and to Compagnon, who talks about 'an intermediary zone between the off-text and the text' (328, quoted in Genette, 2).

extratextual and the core text, the world beyond the book and the world within the book, as well as between the text and its reader, the author and the reader, and the author and the text.

Genette's concept of the preface as threshold triggers and enables my analyses of the construction of gendered author identities in the prefaces of eighteenth-century novels. Unlike Genette, but together with Kevin Dunn (who bases his claim on Foucault's reflections on the author function), I will assume that '[t]he "I" that speaks the preface [...] is always a rhetorical figure, [...] an attempt at self-authorization' (Dunn, xi, 11).[3] While I also agree with Dunn that prefaces often mediate between 'the public and private roles of the author' (Dunn, xi), I will not work within the parameters Dunn develops in his gender-*blind* study of Renaissance to late seventeenth-century prefaces,[4] but rather use Genette's structuralist tools, which have the advantage of being, at least, 'gender-*neutral*', and (in the last part of this chapter) expand on his spatial metaphor of the threshold by relocating it in its historical context.

Genette's first (of three) chapters on the preface, entitled 'The prefatorial situation of communication', describes the object of study via 'the characteristics of place, time, substance, or pragmatic regime' (12). Genette distinguishes three possible roles which the preface-writer can assume 'in relation to the text' (179): 'authorial' (as the author of the text), 'actorial' (as a character in the story), or 'allographic', a term Genette uses to designate a different third person (178–9). Genette's observations about the sender's position with regard to the relation of fact and fiction are also relevant here:

> A preface may be attributed to a real person or to a fictive person. If the attribution to a real person is confirmed by some other [...] paratextual sign, we will call the preface *authentic*. [...] [I]f the person to whom the preface is attributed is fictive, we will call the attribution, and therefore the preface, *fictive*. (179)[5]

Genette's tools are useful because they help to describe the processes at work in the construction of prefatorial identities. That the application of Genette's categories of the 'authorial' and the 'actorial', the 'authentic' and the 'fictive' will

---

[3] Genette is far from sharing this view concerning the concept of the author. He apodictically claims that the paratext 'is characterized by an authorial intention and assumption of responsibility' (3). According to Genette, paratexts provide their readers with a fairly direct access into the author's mind.

[4] I will also argue for a different conceptualization of the public and the private from that of Dunn, who defines them as 'the common and the particular' (8). Dunn's notion of the private, especially, with definitions such as 'one's person, the domestic self' (13) and the 'autobiographical' (23), remains vague throughout *Pretexts of Authority*; and, ultimately, it mirrors what I would describe as the analyzed male writers' attempts to postulate an *individual* self. They construct this individual self by claiming it to be so unique that it cannot be described and is utterly inaccessible or (in their terms and Dunn's) private.

[5] Genette's third category of the apocryphal need not interest us here.

also be shown to lead to his system's breakdown does not disable the tools it provides. On the contrary, in what follows it is their limited utility which will help to explain how prefaces of eighteenth-century novels written by women and written by men construct author identities.

Mediating Female and Male Author Identities in the Preface

In a stimulating article, Cheryl L. Nixon analyzes the prefaces of Jane Barker's *A Patch-Work Screen for the Ladies* (1723), Eliza Haywood's *Adventures of Eovaai, Princess of Ijaveo* (1736), and Sarah Fielding's *The Governess* (1745), and shows '[that p]refaces by early eighteenth-century women […] often blur the boundaries created by Genette's categories' (Nixon, 133). The preface to Sarah Fielding's *The Governess*, for example, begins as follows:

> *My young Readers,*
> Before you begin the following Sheets, I beg you will stop a Moment at this Preface, to consider with me, what is the true Use of Reading; […] One Thing quite necessary to make any Instructions that come either from your Governors, or your Books, of any Use to you, is to attend with a Desire of Learning, and not to be apt to fansy [sic] yourselves too wise to be taught. For this Spirit will keep you ignorant as long as you live, and you will be like the Birds in the following Fable. "The Mag-pye alone, of all the Birds, had the Art of building a Nest" […]. (vii–viii)

It could not be more obvious: the 'sender' of this preface clearly introduces herself as the author of the whole book by directly addressing her 'young Readers'. She is well aware of the various functions of the preface, as identified, for example, by Genette (196–236). At the same time, however, she shows 'character traits that duplicate those exhibited in the fictional text' (Nixon, 133). Like the fictive Mrs Teachum, the governess who features in the title of the book, the authorial sender of the preface uses the didactic potential of stories for her purposes. She explicates her salutary lesson concerning 'the true Use of Reading' by drawing on a story about the magpie and the birds that were too impatient or conceited to profit from the former's knowledge about the true 'Art of building a Nest': 'Fielding's author becomes a governess, mimicking the character types found in her novel' (Nixon, 133).

The 'sender' of the preface in Jane Barker's experimental *Patch-Work Screen for the Ladies* (1723), which mingles poetry with various stories from love to murder tales, first clearly identifies herself as the author of the book by pointing to her '*two former* NOVELS' (iii), by self-consciously reflecting on the function of different narrative structures, by comparing her strategy to that of Defoe (iv), and, finally, by prompting 'the Reader' to '*be sure to buy* these Patches *up quickly*, […] *thereby you'll greatly oblige* […] *the* Author. *Who is*, Your humble Servant, JANE BARKER' (viii; emphasis in original). Like Fielding's preface, however, Barker's also creates a realm where author and character meet. While Fielding's prefatorial sender identifies with the eponymous governess, Barker's meets the fictive protagonist (and first-person narrator) of her earlier novel, *Love Intrigues; or, The History of the Amours of Bosvil and Galesia* (1713), who also features prominently in this novel's narrative: '[In] *the open Field, I met with the poor* Galesia [...]. *With her I renew'd my Old Acquaintance; and so came to know all this Story of her Patch-Work*' (Jane Barker 1723, vii). Nixon comments: 'Author and character come together in a preface, forming a female community of two who initiate the creation of the universe of the novel' (137).

It is exactly this blurring of the categories of the 'authorial' and the 'actorial', and the intermingling of the authentic with the 'fictive', which distinguishes Barker's preface and those of many other women writers from Defoe's, Richardson's, and other male authors' prefaces. As is well known, Defoe and Richardson invest most of their prefatorial energy in emphasizing the authenticity of their stories. The prefatorial voice of Richardson's first novel claims that *Pamela* collects non-fictional documents: his heroine's 'Letters [...] have their foundation both in *Truth* and *Nature*' (Samuel Richardson 1980, 31). Likewise the sender of *Robinson Crusoe*'s preface famously declares the 'thing to be a just history of fact; neither is there any appearance of fiction in it' (Defoe 1994, 7). The 'authentic' authors of Sarah Fielding's and Jane Barker's prefaces meet and blend with their characters in the undefined region at the threshold between the extratextual and the textual, whereas the canonical eighteenth-century male novelists favour one of two alternative strategies to keep the two ontological spheres clearly apart:[6] Defoe's and Richardson's prefaces try to eradicate every hint at something 'fictional' altogether and use the prefatorial threshold in order to argue that their books will enable their readers to approach something real through a new medium rather than their immediate sense perception.[7] The Fielding of *The History of the Adventures of Joseph Andrews* (1742) proceeds differently in that he uses the prefatorial threshold to demarcate a strict borderline between the 'factual' and the 'fictional'. Just in case a reader of his preface misses the irony about his claim that 'every thing is copied from the Book of Nature, and scarce a Character or Action produced which I have not taken from my own Observations and Experience' (Henry Fielding 1980, 8), his authorial speaker ultimately emphasizes the artificiality and constructed nature of the protagonist of his story: 'I have *made* him a Clergyman', he stresses (ibid., 9; emphasis added). This strategy abandons the claim of authenticity in order to point to the authentic authorial sender's exceptional creative energies and his power over the fictional realms he fathers, but it also demarcates two ontologically different realms: beyond and within the text.

---

6   For exceptions, see, for example, the prefaces of William Godwin's *Caleb Williams* (1794) and *Fleetwood; or The Man of Feeling* (1805), which also blend the authentic and the fictive, if not the authorial and the actorial.

7   Their well-known practice of installing an allographic sender as the speaker of their prefaces also serves 1) to further support their authenticity claim, and 2) to distance the author as far as possible from the fictional world. The author whose name decorates the title page does not even enter the prefatorial site, but remains decidedly extra-textual and authentic.

The prefaces of Charlotte Smith's late eighteenth-century novels are notorious for their construction of the authoress as a heroically suffering mother figure. Smith's autobiographically informed authorial prefaces repeatedly depict the desolate life of the wife of an unfaithful and profligate husband and a mother of seven, who must earn a living by selling poems and novels in order to support her family. She also, again and again, vents her frustration about a never-ending lawsuit over her father-in-law's inheritance, unjustly kept from her.[8] Her preface to *Desmond* (1792) does not only, like those of Fielding and Barker, simultaneously claim and problematize the authenticity of its authorial speaker, but also hints at the authorial speaker's method of generating the fictive characters which people the main text of her book:

> *I* [...] may safely say, that it was in the *observance*, not in the *breach* of duty, *I* became an Author; and it has happened, that the circumstances which have compelled me to write, have introduced me to those scenes of life, and those varieties of character which I should otherwise never have seen: Tho' alas! it is from thence, that I am too well enabled to describe from *immediate* observation, "The proud man's contumely, th'oppressors wrong; / The laws delay, the insolence of office." [*Hamlet*, III, i] [...] in consequence of the affairs of my family being most unhappily in the power of men who *seem to exercise all these with impunity*, I am become an *Author by profession* [...]. (Smith 1997, 6; emphasis original)

Some characters of this novel's text, the prefatorial voice explains, emanate from the very same 'circumstances' which also produce '[the] *Author by profession*' who has written this book. In other words, the same circumstances which force the speaker of the preface into her role as author also provide her with the material which she needs to construct her novel's plot and characters. Surprisingly, however, Smith uses a quotation from *Hamlet* to enumerate some of the figures and plot elements typical of her novels. The prefatorial discourse of *Desmond* thus points to a peculiar reciprocal effect: the characters that enter the fictional story have been taken from real life; they are as 'authentic' as the 'authorial' voice.[9] At the same time, however, all these 'real' people have always already accrued their lifelike personalities, regardless of whether they find access to the fictional world or not, because they conform to character types or fulfil roles which have been provided by literary texts. The authorial speaker of the preface to Smith's *Marchmont* (1796) explains, for example:

> [...] I do not affect to deny that I have occasionally drawn from the life; and I have no hesitation in saying, that in the present work the character most odious [...] is drawn *ad vivum* – but as it represents a reptile whose most hideous features are too offensive to be painted in all their enormity, I have softened rather than

---

8   See, for example, Smith 1794, v–vi. For biographical information see Fletcher.

9   In what follows, I use the terminology Genette develops for his description of the sender of the preface for all the characters that walk across the prefatorial threshold, as it were.

overcharged the disgusting resemblance [to the prototype]. It has often been observed to me, that such an obscure wretch [...] is too contemptible for satire. As an individual he is; but as a specimen of a genus extremely poisonous and noxious he becomes an object to be held up to detestation; [...]. (xi–xii)

This paragraph concentrates on the first prefatorial '*transaction*' (Genette, 2), the transference from the extratextual to the textual, from the world beyond the book into the fictional text. This movement from the outside into the inside of a text is a rather conventional one, of course. Smith's handling of this transaction, however, differs from the famous authenticity claims in Defoe's or Richardson's allographic prefaces. By reflecting on her '*ad vivum*' characters, Smith's prefatorial sender does not emphasize her story's authenticity or probability, but rather explains the purpose of her reliance on real-life 'prototypes'. This purpose lies in holding them 'up to detestation' in a satire which is less interested in the authenticity of its objects than in the generic features of the type the 'prototype' stands for.

Another passage, which introduces a second authentic, actorial villain, further complicates the transference of an entity from one side of the prefatorial threshold to the other. Here the authorial speaker stresses her own creative intervention, which accompanies this 'real-life' character's transportation into the fictional world. In this passage the prefatorial sender also explains how the villain's identity can only be understood by having recourse to parabolic or figurative strategies:

> What will be thought of my peculiar ill fortune, when I assert that I have it in my power to produce a counterpart to this demon? The *Great Man* [...] put us, by way of *protection*, into the trust of a worthy cousin of his own. The worthy cousin, instead of driving away the evil spirit whom he found preying on the wreck, began to consider how he might appropriate a share of it to himself – He croaked, and, lo! [...] his agents, flocked around; and numberless vultures fed instead of one: – so that our *Great Director* was like the man in the parable, who being infested with a devil, goeth forth and taketh unto him seven devils [...]. (Smith 1796, xiv–xv)

The reciprocal effect which characterizes the relationship between 'fact' and 'fiction' and the reciprocal infection, as it were, of authentic persons with 'fiction' and of fictitious characters with the 'authentic' becomes even more obvious in the preface to Smith's *The Young Philosopher* (1798):

> But as no distresses can be created without such men, as in the present state of society stand in place of the giants, and necromancers, and ogers of ancient romance, men whose profession empowers them to perpetrate, and whose inclination generally prompts them to the perpetration of wickedness, I have made these drawings a little like people of that sort whom I have seen, certain that nothing I could imagine would be so correct [...]. (vii)

Smith can easily transfer 'real-life' people across the prefatorial threshold and integrate them into her fictional text, because in the world beyond her text those people already fulfil a typically literary plot function which constructs their (authentic as well as fictive) identities.

I will come back to these examples, but would like to briefly summarize what has been discussed so far. What I have shown (by drawing on the argument developed by Nixon) is that the prefaces in eighteenth-century novels by the female writers analyzed do not so much use the paratextual threshold to lead the participants of the prefatorial communication from one world into another, but rather swing wide open the door on the threshold between the extratextual and the textual, between Genette's 'factual' and 'fictional' and between authentic prefatorial figures on the one hand and fictive characters on the other. The prefaces analyzed could also be said to be sites where 'two rules of law [...] cancel each other' (Maclean, 273); their particular 'cancelling power' takes effect, however, beyond the prefatorial transition zone, which does not so much lead from one world into the other, but rather connects two realms which it shows to abide by similar, rather than different, rules. The intermingling within the preface of authorial and actorial characters, and the processing of fact into fiction and vice versa, demonstrates that the construction of identities, in particular, follows a similar set of rules in both realms. (With Paul Ricœur's concept of narrative identity and Judith Butler's performativity in mind I will label this set of rules 'narrative-performative'). Nixon describes the modes of operation which structure the construction of identity succinctly:

> A close examination of [these] preface[s] reveals how this marginal space encourages self-definition that blurs the distinction between author and character, fact and fiction, and text and pre-text. The formal strategies used to construct the character of the woman author within the preface are used to construct the female characters within the text and, it is implied, should be used by the reader to construct herself outside the text. (123; also see 133)

My own readings of the construction of prefatorial identities above have shown that I share Nixon's view that the preface plays a central role in demonstrating the general modes of operation of the 'narrative-performative' strategies which take effect beyond the paratextual site as they construct the identity of all the 'characters' involved in the literary communication: the identity of the author, the character, and the reader.

However, the passage just quoted also allows me to disengage my argument from Nixon's. While I am as interested in a gendered reading of prefatorial constructions of identity as she is, I differ from Nixon where it comes to evaluating the gender implications of our shared observations. Nixon argues 1) that '[the prefatorial] moment of authentic/fictive self-definition' provides insights into 'the process of [a specifically] *female* self-legitimization', which 2) as such allows Fielding, Barker, and Haywood to offer (in their prefaces, at least) 'empowering female self-definition[s]' (133 and 137; emphasis added). My analysis of Smith's prefaces, however, has demonstrated that the construction of (authentic and fictive) male characters operates according to the same laws as that of the female authorial characters in Barker's and Fielding's prefaces. I would argue, therefore, that the female novelists' prefaces analyzed describe the 'narrative-performative' strategies of the process which reigns over the construction of everybody's identity, be it male or female. If that is the case, 'the process of [...] self-legitimization' depicted is certainly not *per se* 'empowering' for the woman writer.

The Prefatorial Threshold Metaphor and the Ideology of the Separate Spheres

In order to locate gender-specific strategies in the preface, I will make use of another metaphor which builds on the notion of the threshold and is constitutive for eighteenth-century gender(ed) discourses: the ideology of separate spheres.[10] It is a basic assumption in eighteenth-century gender studies that one of the greatest challenges of every woman writer is to justify her 'going public', and it is in the preface where such justifications and other, often self-reflexive meditations on the spatial image of the separate spheres are discussed. While there is, of course, no agreement on how exactly 'the private' and 'the public' are to be conceptualized, gender-oriented scholars today certainly concur that any notion of an 'overly simplistic concept of separate sexual spheres' must be avoided (Mellor, 7). The rediscovery and intensive analysis of many eighteenth-century female-authored texts has made it quite obvious 'that women had an enormous [...] impact on the formation of public opinion in England between 1780 and 1830' (ibid., 11).[11] After all, as many historians have stated, around 1800 more books written by women writers were available than ever before.[12] Knowledge of the socio-historical context is, of course, relevant. The main reasons for me to draw on the language of the separate spheres, however, is that it allows me to focus my analyses on *gendered* and *the gendering of* prefatorial discourses more carefully than Nixon, whose analyses ultimately rest on one main criterion: the biological sex of the author.

In what follows, I will look at how some female novelists use the metaphor of separate spheres in their construction of gendered identities in general and their female authorial identities in particular. In the process it should become clear that the linkage I suggest between the spatial metaphor which has been used to understand prefatorial discourses and the spatial language of the ideology of separate spheres is more than just an associative-speculative relation triggered by the image of the threshold. Throughout my analysis of the way prefatorial

---

[10]   For a discussion about the advantages and disadvantages of using the concept of the separate spheres in twenty-first century literary and cultural studies, see Rennhak and Richter.

[11]   Also see Colley 1996, 262–3, and Eger, Grant, Gallchoir, and Warburton, 15: 'Despite the manner in which some feminists have cast the Enlightenment as a monolithic patriarchal movement, there is strong reason to suspect that what we have come to regard as the Enlightenment public sphere was in fact constituted and defined by women as well as men'.

[12]   See Bannet, 1. For statistical evidence see Garside, Raven, and Schöwerling (eds), vol. 1: 39–49; vol. 2: 72–6. See also Stanton, 247–54.

reflections about the public and the private are projected onto the realms that are delimited – or, rather, opened up onto each other – by the preface, I am well aware that notions of the extratextual and the textual realm beyond the preface do not correlate in any simple or natural way with gendered notions of the public and the private. A person's or character's movement within, along, or across the threshold which delimits the gendered spheres is categorically different from the transferences enacted within the preface. The main trajectory of the publishing activity makes this quite obvious: it is always the novel in its entirety of text and paratext which is transmitted into a public realm. Whether the realm from which it originates is conceived of as private or public or as yet another liminal space is less obvious, and a question which many a prefatorial reflection turns to. However this latter question is answered, what can always be said is that the novel, which travels into the public realm, takes its starting point from wherever the authorial I sees her- or himself situated. In this context, the precarious localization of paratextual authorial identities somewhere between (Genette's) 'authentic' and 'fictive' realms once again becomes pertinent. Some textual examples will help to illustrate my point.

An instance of *the* standard version of eighteenth-century conceptualizations of the notion of separate gendered spheres can be found in the preface to Frances Brooke's second edition of *The Excursion* (1785):

> To govern kingdoms, to command armies, to negotiate, to fight; to investigate the hidden powers of nature, to traverse the abstruser regions of philosophy and science, to bend the stubborn mind to the yoke of rational obedience, be the province of man. To sway the softer empire of private life, to cultivate the milder powers of the understanding, to impress the gentler, the social, duties, on the hearts of the rising generation [...]; to watch the opening infant mind, necessarily committed at that early season to our tender cares, [...] to expand (as well by writing as conversation) the bud of reason, "And teach the young idea how to shoot," Be the task, as it is a pursuit not unworthy the retired dignity, the feminine softness, of woman. (2)

Before the reader encounters this passage, however, Brooke has opened her preface with a rhetorical cliché which – as the authorial sender herself explains – 'was the celebrated form in which a citizen of ancient Rome refused his acquiescence in any sentence of which he felt the injustice', as follows: 'I appeal to the people' (1). Consciously and explicitly, she borrows from political rhetoric to formulate her 'appeal', which concerns exactly that problematic situation which she has just re-enacted through her performative utterance of appealing: the fact that a woman addresses 'the public'.

> On giving a new edition of The EXCURSION to the public, I find myself irresistibly impelled to use the same form of appeal from an illiberal spirit of prejudice, and perhaps of affectation, which has lately endeavoured not only to depreciate works of imagination in general, but to exclude from the road of literary fame, even by the flowery paths of romance, a sex which from quick sensibility, native

> delicacy of mind, facility of expression, and a style at once animated and natural, is perhaps, when possessed of real genius, most peculiarly qualified to excel in this species of moral painting. (Ibid.)

The authorial sender not only 'appeals to the people', she also claims that women can be 'possessed of real genius' and thus partake of what is – ever since Young depicted him in his influential *Conjectures on Original Composition* (1759) (see Schabert, 374–5) – an eminently masculine and utterly independent spirit, whose mind soars above both the private and the public, but who certainly writes in order 'to deliver [his truths] up to the public' (Young, 106–13).

The rhetoric of political appeal and the claim that women are well able to compete with their male colleagues seem to clash here with the acceptance and 'stylized repetition' (in the sense of Judith Butler)[13] of the ideology of separate spheres. The prefatorial discourse of Brooke's *The Excursion*, however, sets out to reconcile these seemingly irreconcilable performances. What has to be taken into account, according to the authorial sender, is, firstly, the fact that the textual world beyond the preface depicts an *imaginary* realm – even if this imaginary realm, as 'moral painting' (Brooke, 1), has implications beyond the other side of the prefatorial threshold for the extratextual world. A female author's imagination is better suited to fulfil the task of producing an imaginary textual realm than a man's, because women are used to 'sway the softer empire of private life' (ibid., 2). 'The province of man', the public sphere of action, is characterized by violence and cold rationality, and the male imagination is therefore less qualified to create and depict an imaginary *moral* world. Men are always in danger of making their novels 'the vehicle of depravity and licentiousness' (ibid., 1).

What the female authorial sender of this preface (like so many others) also stresses is that the mere fact that she is publishing a book does not mean that she herself enters the public realm. Her novel and her 'appeal *at the* unprejudiced *bar* of the Public' (ibid., 2; emphasis added) reach an audience without its authoress having to cross the bar and leave the private sphere that enables her to formulate her appeal with propriety. On the contrary, she is convinced that her 'retired dignity' is neither compromised nor lost just because she publishes a novel. The advantage of the print medium book, she argues, is that it enables a woman to communicate beyond the border of 'her' sphere and thus to influence public discourses without having to leave the private realm, which guarantees the construction of a stable female identity, which in turn guarantees that she write

---

[13]   'Gender ought not to be construed as a stable identity or locus of agency from which various acts follow; rather, gender is an identity tenuously constituted in time, [...]. If the ground of gender identity is the stylized repetition of acts through time and not a seemingly seamless identity, then the spatial metaphor of a "ground" will be displaced [...]. The abiding gendered self will then be shown to be structured by repeated acts that seek to approximate the ideal of a substantial ground of identity, but which, in their occasional *dis*continuity, reveal the temporal and contingent groundlessness of this "ground"' (Butler 1999, 179).

moral tales. Brooke's prefatorial discourse can thus be said to exhibit a number of (Butlerian) *dis*continuities in the dominant gender(ed) discourse of the separate spheres, and, as a consequence, to 'reveal [...] the groundlessness' of the notion of 'a substantial ground of identity' (Butler 1999, 179).[14] At the same time it must be noticed, however, that the 'stylized repetition' of the ideology of separate spheres in Brooke's preface is as '*con*tinuous' and affirmative as can be imagined.

Like Brooke's, Charlotte Smith's prefatorial authorial sender also repeatedly emphasizes that she has absolutely no difficulties reconciling her authorial role with the ideology of the separate spheres. In the preface to *Desmond* she counters the prejudice that '[k]nowledge [...] is [...] of so difficult attainment, that it cannot be acquired but by the sacrifice of domestic virtues, or the neglect of domestic duties' with the declaration, '*I* however, may safely say, that it was in the *observance*, not in the *breach* of duty, *I* became an Author' (6; emphasis in original). This reference to her being forced to make money as a professional author clearly hints at the inevitable permeability of the threshold between the public market and the private home, where more than half a dozen mouths want to be fed. It is therefore more daring than the rather abstract elaboration of the language of the spatial image in Brooke's preface. Ultimately, however, the line of argument in the prefaces of both authors is the same. The last sentence of the preface to the sixth edition of Smith's *Elegiac Sonnets*, for example, declares: 'I am well aware that for a woman – "The Post of Honour is a Private Station"' (6). The last words are taken from Addison's neo-classical *Cato* or rather from the eponymous hero's advice to his son to 'Content thyself to be obscurely good. / When vice prevails, and impious men bear sway, / The post of honour is a private station' (Addison, 140–42). Like Brooke's prefatorial sender, who refers critics who doubt her assertion of the peculiar qualities of the private sphere to Samuel Richardson, Smith's sender models herself on a male 'illustrious example' (Brooke, 1), who championed the moral virtues characteristic of the private realm. While both certainly hope to partake of Addison's and Richardson's indubitable moral authority, they also imply that even though their male colleagues *may* write moral tales (provided they succeed in suppressing their more 'worldly', public knowledge),[15] the female writer who is firmly anchored in the private sphere cannot but produce fictional worlds which offer their readers morally salutary advice. In short, the female author's movements, as they are depicted in her preface, repeatedly lead her toward the very borderline between the private and the public. Ultimately, however, the authorial identities constructed in female novelists' prefaces are characterized by the claim to be firmly situated in the private sphere, which confers moral authority. What 'goes public' is the book, not the author.

---

[14]   See the previous footnote. Also see my (and Nixon's) argument in the first part of this paper.

[15]   See Tosh, who stresses that it was always the privilege of 'men [to] operate [...] at will in *both* spheres' (230).

A fairly enigmatic passage in Jane Barker's preface to *A Patch-Work Screen for the Ladies* can also be understood along these lines. Barker, I argue, stages a rather radical displacement of an obsolete and unhelpful masculine author concept by a new feminine one. She, too, however, remains within 'the allotted boundaries and appointed province of Females' (Burney, iii). When the authorial voice reports how, during a 'Tea-Table *Entertainment*' among several ladies, their different political and religious opinions and 'Sentiments *are as differently mix'd as the* Patches *in their Work*', she is suddenly reminded of the assertion of '*some* Philosophers [...] *about the* Clashing *of* Atoms, *which at last* united *to compose this glorious Fabrick of the* UNIVERSE' (Jane Barker 1723, v–vi). But she apologizes immediately:

> *Forgive me, kind Reader, for carrying the Metaphor too high; by which means I am out of my Sphere, and so can say nothing of the* Male Patch-Workers; *for my high Flight in Favour of the Ladies, made a mere* Icarus *of me, melted my Wings, and tumbled me Headlong down, I know not where.* (Ibid., vi; emphasis in original)

A metaphorical '*high Flight*' catapults the prefatorial sender beyond and above the separate spheres and into the decidedly masculine sphere of the male author-as-prophet; her entry into this world high in the sky transforms her into an Icarus figure, somebody who attempts to fly, does fly, but is doomed to failure right from the beginning. In this airy sphere she is neither at home nor welcome.

The landing place, too, is a peculiar realm. It is characterized by its lack of a hierarchical structure and the equality of persons of '*all Ages, Sexes, and Conditions*' who admire a '*wonderful* Piece *of* Patch-Work', '*a* New Creation' (ibid., vi, emphasis in original). However, the 'Patch-Work' she encounters in this sphere is not identical with the patch-work the authorial speaker will offer in the main text of her book. So where has she landed? I would argue that she has dropped *down* (an interesting topological dimension) into the public sphere which the male writer, who is a much better aviator than the prefatorial female author, directs and manages from above. What is, certainly, in full swing at this landing place is the thorough reconstruction of social relations within a prelapsarian world. The prefatorial sender has *fallen* into a world temporarily located before the fall, as it were. '*I was greatly rejoyc'd at this my* Fall, *when I found my self amongst these happy Undertakers*', she comments, and goes on to report that she '*hop'd to unite* [her]*-self in their Confraternity*' (ibid., vi–vii). The experienced gender-oriented scholar rightly expects that the con*fraternity* will not admit the *female* author into their community. This is what happens, but Barker's preface offers an interesting variation on this topos. What is expelled is not so much the female authorial sender of the preface, but rather her masculine instantiation of an author, the female poet-prophet:

> [*B*]*ut they finding some Manuscript* Ballads *in my Pocket,* [the Confraternity] *rejected me* [...]; *so I was forc'd to get away, every one hunching and pushing me, with Scorn and Derision. However, as the Sequel prov'd, I had no small*

Reason to rejoice at being thus used; for soon after, their Patch-Work Scheme, *by carrying the Point too high, was blown up about their Ears, and vanish'd into Smoke and Confusion*; [...]. (ibid., vii, emphasis in original)

The whole masculine world of the '*Confraternity*' explodes – again because a '*Point*' was '*carr*[ied] [...] *too high*'. The prefatorial sender does not regret this destruction. Rather, the next paragraph relates her encounter with Galesia, her most important collaborator on the decidedly female 'Patch-Work' referred to in the title of the novel. Galesia is neither flying above nor falling into a chaotic and unrealistic Utopian and prelapsarian world. The authorial sender meets her while she is '*walking to stretch her Legs, having been long sitting at her Work*' (ibid.).

While Kathryn R. King (like Nixon), in her reading of Barker's preface, emphasizes the 'empowering possibilities' which 'the woman writer's entrance into the print world' offers (81), I find it important to take into consideration the fact that the analogy between pen and needle, patch-working and writing, and the ensuing 'extension of traditional forms of women's work' into the 'London literary market' – again – does not engender a greater mobility of the authoress (as constructed in this and the other prefaces analyzed). The patch-work metaphor, as King also notes, rather 'seem[s] to express [...] the need of their creators to ground an unfamiliar activity (writing) in a homely, familiar, and secure activity' (ibid., 81). Barker's authorial voice in the preface, as well as the actorial figure with whom she joins forces, are securely anchored in the private sphere; their work is conceived of as 'home-work'.

Conclusion

My contention that the prefaces analyzed invest a great deal of their argumentative energy in constructing an authorial identity that never enters the public realm does not imply that I would like to contradict scholars like Mellor or Colley, who have argued that '[n]ot only did women participate fully in the discursive public sphere, but their opinions had definable impact on the social movements, economic relationships, and state-regulated policies of the day' (Mellor, 3). Smith's *Desmond* is the first novel which unfolds its plot in revolutionary France, after all. And the 'Apology' to Frances Burney's 'Brief Reflections Relative to the Emigrant French Clergy' (1793) – another eminently political text which certainly participates in public discourse – is yet another paratext which demonstrates how women writers, even if they acknowledge 'the allotted boundaries and appointed province of Females', cleverly work with, extend, and adapt the metaphor of the separate spheres to their own purposes (Burney, iii).[16]

---

[16] Burney emphasizes that houses have windows, which invite the women inside to become 'spectatresses of the moral as well as of the political economy of human life' (iii), and doors, through which guests, news, and sometimes even people in need, like the emigrant French clergy, enter.

What I find striking, however, is that none of the authorial voices in the prefaces analyzed suggest any radical readjustment of the spatial metaphor that reigns the gendered discourses of their time. All of them, however radical their literary experiments or political arguments in the fiction beyond the prefatorial threshold, perform 'stylized repetitions' that consolidate the 'spherical structuring' of gender(ed) relations. I am well aware (and hope to have shown) that there are ways in which the language of separate spheres can be used strategically to justify a woman writer's intervention in what seem to be exclusively or predominantly male public discourses. However, given that the binaristic ideology of separate spheres must always inevitably serve to perpetuate traditional hierarchies, I would hesitate to enthuse – like Nixon, King, Mellor, and others tend to do – over allegedly 'empowering strategies'.

There are differences in the handling of the spatial metaphor which help to differentiate between constructions of authorial identity in women writers' prefaces. What makes a difference, I suggest, is the degree to which a prefatorial discourse demonstrates 1) that the notion of separate spheres is nothing but a metaphor, and 2) how this metaphor is affected by the same laws that take effect at the prefatorial threshold between the extratextual and the intratextual, the (allegedly) authentic and the (allegedly) fictive, which have been shown to constitute the construction of prefatorial identities. Of the texts analyzed, only the preface to Barker's *Patch-Work Screen for the Ladies* points to the constructedness of the gendered spheres. All the other prefatorial voices may point to the narrative-performative status of the authorial identities they construct, but the equally discursive status of the highly influential spatial metaphor of the separate spheres is never critically reflected. The female authorial speakers rather go on using it uncritically in their attempts to reconstruct authorial identities and to endow them with moral authority.

Chapter 5
Owning Identity:
The Eighteenth-Century Actress
and Theatrical Property

Felicity Nussbaum

I curse all Squibs, Crackers, Rockets, Air-Balloons, Mines, serpents & Catherine Wheels, & can think of nothing & Wish for nothing, but laugh, Jig, humour, fun, pun, conundrum carriwitchet & Catherine Clive!
—Letter from David Garrick to Clive (26 August 1774)

Catherine Clive (1711–1785), the finest comedienne and singer on the mid-eighteenth-century stage, was, according to actor-manager Tate Wilkinson,

> a mixture of combustibles – she was passionate, cross, vulgar, yet sensible, and a very generous woman, and as a comic actress, of genuine worth – *indeed, indeed*, she was a diamond of the first water. The valiant Boadicea never hurled her spear with more furor than Clive, that Amazonian Thalestris of Drury-Lane theatre, [who] pursued that great general, Garrick, whenever he offended her; indeed the whole green-room dreaded her frowns. (Wilkinson, 42)

Clive's virago-like temper may have been not just a personality quirk but also her recognition of the historic strategies that thespian women needed in order to possess cultural authority. The eighteenth-century London theatre has recently been defined as 'the crucible of celebrity' – a place of confluence of powerful political, economic, and social forces (Tillyard, 20–27).[1] Stella Tillyard convincingly claims that 'celebrity was born at the moment private life became a tradeable public commodity' (25). The emergence of celebrity may be linked not only to the marketing of privacy but also, I suggest, to the unprecedented appearance of women on stage after the Restoration. Celebrity, according to Tillyard, grants special attention to women: 'It had, and still has a more feminine face than fame, because private life, and the kind of virtue around which reputations could pivot, were both seen to reside in femininity and in women' (ibid.). The increased presence of women in the very public arena of the theatre meant that gossip about the private lives of a significant number of women, and especially sexual scandal, advanced with vigour. The most canny of celebrated actresses paradoxically

---

[1]   She argues that the cult of celebrity fades after the 1790s, and only arises in its modern form at the end of the nineteenth century.

generated agency from their historically unprecedented situation: they carved out a coherent public personhood while projecting an accessible, layered interiority that traversed the boundaries between public display and personal revelation, and between dramatic character and private self.

In her influential study on the theatre, Lisa Freeman has argued that in eighteenth-century plays, character is largely determined by generic conventions which were more clearly formulaic than those of realist novels, and that this difference in expectations meant that the stage excluded from its dramatis personae a 'public/private split', resulting in 'only public space and public displays' (Freeman, 27). The character's consciousness as imagined by the audience derived largely from drama's generic and formulaic conventions. In brief, Freeman believes that genre conventions provided characters with codes that at times simulated an interiority, and thus 'character' affords a more appropriate paradigm than 'subjectivity' when speaking of performative identity. But if we take the actual performative moment into account, I am suggesting, a talented actress could affect a persona that carried far beyond the surface codings typical of a particular genre. Actors – and especially actresses – created what I am calling an 'interiority effect'. This simulation of interior depth blends the star actress's putative personality with the character's emotions and thoughts, and it may be constructed and exposed alongside them. Each subsequent repetition of a familiar role allowed the actress to revise and perfect in an ongoing way the combination of personal and generic elements in a given character.

Talented star actresses affected to possess consistent personae in plays, and especially in epilogues, to produce characters that displayed an apparent interiority to which celebrity could attach itself and flourish. This came about to some significant degree because of the interaction between actresses and their parts, their self-referential allusions, and the reciprocal relationship of mutual give-and-take realized between audience and stage. As Robert Weimann has pointed out, the precipice between stage and audience provided 'a precariously built-up tension between both worlds, the one associated with the fiction of the text, the other associated with its *actual use in society*' (221). Rather than disrupting or competing with the public image of the actress, the character's consciousness often evolved in performance to meld together with it. In the eighteenth century's highly collaborative theatre, this interiority, imagined to be 'real', competed with the interiority of assumed fictional characters in a shifting, reiterative identity. Much of what was of interest to the audience was the interplay between the two as spectators tried to speculate about what portion of the inner consciousness of the actor was shared with the character.

Here I am going to describe some general concepts of identity before I turn to a specific discussion of one of the eighteenth century's most celebrated actresses, Kitty Clive. The 'interiority effect' that she and other celebrity actresses realized was not, then, a transparent interiority, but rather a fluid, multilayered, situational, and virtual one bolstered by the circulation of celebrity gossip. The dramatic characters they represented were indeed governed by genre within the theatre, as

Freeman has argued, but also by rumour at its borders. The interiority effect is thus less about probing an actual interior consciousness than about regularly engaging its improvisational nature.

The staged character also possessed a value assigned by the marketplace, and it earned credibility toward an approximation of a 'real' person whose worth fluctuated. The best actresses allowed themselves to seem to be accessible while continuing to enact flexible identities. They exploited the fact that the 'I' they were impersonating, even in self-referential epilogues, was different from the 'I' who was performing. James Boswell recognized this manoeuvre in 'On the Profession of a Player': 'A player is the character he represents only *in a certain degree*.' An actor maintains 'a kind of double feeling' (469) while remaining conscious of his own life. The most successful eighteenth-century actresses, I suggest, recognized the importance of creating this interiority effect, which allowed the drama to vie with other nascent forms – such as the epistolary novel, the periodical, and autobiographical writing – in fostering a sense of individuality and intimacy. These women on stage, I am arguing, combined unprecedented social leverage with a new kind of value to invent what I am calling 'performative property' in their public/private identities.

Introducing Kitty Clive

Among the actresses who participated mightily in celebrity's invention, Catherine Raftor Clive understood that cultivating fame meant not only acting assigned roles superbly but also keeping aspects of her personal life in public circulation. Born to an Irish father and an English mother in 1711, Clive debuted on the stage a scant two years before Anne Oldfield died, thus inaugurating a second generation of actresses who followed upon Elizabeth Barry and Anne Bracegirdle; she was sometimes made to seem the heir apparent to these extraordinarily talented actresses. Her generation of actresses differed from the earlier ones in that they could benefit from the mistakes of their talented predecessors, develop new strategies for becoming respected professionals, and serve as mentors for younger actresses.

During the eighteenth century, new forms of patronage dependent upon personality developed alongside the increasingly commercial theatre. The talented and spirited Kitty Clive took advantage of these changes to successfully rival male actor-manager playwrights: she clearly believed she was their talented equal. Clive's expert management of her career and her accumulation of theatrical properties meant that she cultivated a collaborative relationship with her audiences and interlocutors. Attempting to avoid being construed to be someone else's property, Clive served as her own agent; she was propelled by the belief that as a subject who possessed rights, she had the prerogative to appropriate her own labour and to possess her own 'self'. Unlike many earlier actresses, Clive constructed a consistent simulated personality that defined her character on stage and off, and that allowed audiences to feel they knew her intimately. Clive attempted to project an illusion of coherent identity that referred not to a precedent 'real' person, but to a fabrication of a coherent self. Her person, social standing, national affiliations, and costuming worked together to shape this 'public intimacy' into a recognizable and yet supple theatrical persona.[2]

For Clive and for other celebrity actresses, private identity had the potential in its public performance to metamorphose into a commercial property that merited the highest wages. While the reader of fiction might take a proprietary interest in the imaginary characters of the novel, thus claiming them as his or her 'own' to make them 'real', in the theatre Clive transformed performative property into a kind of currency. This extended to her proprietary right to 'own' certain roles, to invent idiosyncratic actor-character parts for herself in the afterpieces she wrote, and to promote her own person as Irish and English at once. These endeavours allowed her to generate a cultural value which, rather than being located in a mercenary sexual exchange, arose from her steady labour as a singer, playwright, and actress, and from her savvy cultivation of a personal relationship to the Town. Performative property was thus constituted through hard work and through stimulating social relationships.

Clive's savvy recognition of the way the forms of mobile property were changing – shifts which paralleled the historical development of authorial copyright law beginning with the 1710 Statute of Anne (when authors, rather than printers, were given the right to reproduce their work for profit) – allowed her to keep pace with changing times and to be responsive to an audience's changing modes of perception in an emergent modern market economy. This strategy also let the celebrated actress sustain her career over four decades and transform potential liabilities – including her Irish heritage, coarse humour, fiery temper, faulty education, fading beauty, and diminishing powers – into strengths that contributed to an ever-maturing formation of a recognizable, but still protean, identity.

Clive, unlike so many fellow actresses, largely managed to escape innuendo about her sexual life and avoided conventional assumptions about actresses as prostitutes. Though Clive married barrister George Clive of Hereford (second cousin to Robert, Lord Clive) in 1732 or 1733, they soon separated. They maintained amicable relations, but she was never to live with her husband again. If *The Life of Mr James Quin* is to be believed, Clive endured untoward advances from male admirers, but Quin's memoirist makes even a fellow actor's 'taking some liberties with her in the dressing room' (70–71) an occasion to buttress Clive's reputation for virtue.[3] Clive thus heightened her marketability by aligning virtue and commerce at the very time when the larger culture was struggling with the incongruity of these linkages. Clive's activities, including her writing, gave considerable evidence of proto-feminist sympathies, bolstered by her economic

---

[2]   Joseph Roach (2003 and 2007) employs the term 'public intimacy'.

[3]   When Quin accosted her with 'coarse and indelicate' talk, Clive complained to the manager.

independence in earning her own living. Beginning at a mere 20 shillings per week, Clive quickly gained a substantial reputation and a high salary through hard work. Known as 'the Clive' (the article being added frequently to the names of opera divas) and thus anticipating 'the Siddons', she had extraordinary longevity on the stage for 41 of her 74 years (for 22 years of which David Garrick served as her manager). Upon her husband's death, Clive scoffed,

> Poor Mr Clive is gon [sic], and I think made but a bad exit, he promis'd me all his goods and chattels and has given me none; but, thank God, I am quite happy and contented, and don't feel the least malice to his memory. I have fortune enough to purchas [sic] every thing I *cannot* do without. (Letter from Catherine Clive, in *The Harcourt Papers*, 8.171)

The difficulty, of course, was for an actress to appear sufficiently distant from commercial transactions to command a reputation for virtue and to incorporate decorous femininity into her public image.

Clive posed a triple threat to her manager and to fellow actors of both sexes as a consummate actress, accomplished singer, and innovative playwright. By her own account, Clive was stage-struck from age 12, when she 'used to tag after the celebrated Mr [Robert] Wilks whenever they saw him in the Streets, and gape at him as a Wonder'.[4] One unlikely, though much repeated, version of Clive's discovery recounts that she was a lodger to Miss Eleanor Knowles, happily scrubbing the porch steps, when her lilting singing voice attracted the attention of theatre patrons in the Beef Steak Club, which met opposite in the Bell Tavern. This story resonates with Clive's most popular roles as a singing chambermaid on stage (until 1747–1748) and testifies to the extraordinary sweetness of her voice. She was the most popular female comic singer of her time, making entr'acte songs her own. As *The Comedian* (1732) remarked with admiration, only Italian opera singers could rival her: 'Miss Raftor is without a *Superiority*, if we except the foremost Voices in the Italian Operas.'[5]

Clive successfully played the singing shepherdess Phillida in Cibber's *Love in a Riddle* (1729), but her greatest triumph came as the cobbler's wife, Nell, in Charles Coffey's *The Devil to Pay, or the Wives Metamorphosed*, a character she debuted in 1730, which established her reputation, doubled her salary, and guaranteed that the farce would become a fixture of the repertoire for the rest of her career – that is, for 35 seasons (*The Life of Mr James Quin*, 69; Joncus, 16–17).[6]

Part of what may have driven Clive's ambition and sense of entitlement was her father's obligatory forfeiture of an estate to which he had been heir

---

[4]   The anecdote is recounted by Chetwood, 127.

[5]   *The Comedian, or Philosophical Enquirer* (7 October 1732): 37–42, 39. I am grateful to Ilias Chrissochoidis for this reference.

[6]   Joncus beautifully describes aspects of Clive's manipulation of social codes through the masque form. She and I, largely relying on different sources, share similar conclusions regarding Clive's public persona.

Fig. 5.1   *Mrs Clive from the Picture at Strawberry Hill*, engraving by A.
                Van Haecken, after J. Van Haecken. Harvard Theatre Collection,
                Houghton Library, Harvard University, Cambridge, Massachusetts.

Fig. 5.2   *Mrs Clive in the Character of Phillida in Cibber's* Love in a Riddle, 1728–1729, engraving by Faber, after Schaklen. Harvard Theatre Collection, Houghton Library, Harvard University, Cambridge, Massachusetts.

(Richards, 24). She was the daughter of William Raftor, an Irish lawyer from Kilkenny, who, according to William Chetwood, had surrendered his land after he fought on the losing side with James II at the Battle of the Boyne (1690), though he was later pardoned by Queen Anne. Despite her origins, Clive's onstage performance of social class was remarkably labile. As a comic actress Clive was able to impersonate servants, women of quality, and the characters in between, and she offered a consistent thread that enlivened her roles. Best known in her early career for acting chambermaid characters, Clive often mimicked the airs of her onstage mistress while outwitting her. She was especially well known for her parts as would-be fine ladies who imitated – but could not fully inhabit – the genteel manners and dress that signalled their characters. Clive played on this doubleness by alternating between chambermaid and fine lady to thoroughly intermix them in the persona the audience came to identify as constituting the 'real' Clive. The social class codings for an actress, signalled in part by her ability to engage in conspicuous consumption of carriages, fashionable clothing, and jewels, often did not fit cultural expectations for properly decorous women.

Newfound celebrity was unsettling because it established, through star power, an intangible but negotiable property. 'Property was both an extension and a prerequisite of personality', J.G.A. Pocock declared in his classic formulation of eighteenth-century economic change. Property afforded a citizen the autonomy 'necessary for him [sic] to develop virtue or goodness as an actor within the political, social and natural realm of order' (Pocock 1985, 103). 'Actor' used in this way describes, of course, an agent of action rather than a thespian player, but the definition nevertheless points to the centrality of the theatre in grappling with these cultural issues. Women were classified as unable to possess property themselves, as Blackstone's *Commentaries on the Laws of England* (1765–1769) made clear, and upon marriage they were legally required to subsume themselves and their right to property within their husbands' identity. Thus actresses who possessed property in themselves functioned in a new realm of uncharted territory.

Just as 'real' property gave way to the ephemeral nature of credit in the eighteenth century, Clive's relationship to her own celebrity evolved as it gained greater worth. 'Once property was seen to have a symbolic value, expressed in coin or in credit', as Pocock argued in a much-cited passage, 'the foundations of personality themselves appeared imaginary or at best consensual: the individual could exist, even in his own sight, only at the fluctuating value imposed upon him by his fellows' (1975, 464). As Carole Pateman brilliantly explained in *The Sexual Contract*, Locke implicitly limited the possession of one's self to the male sex. Locke wrote, 'Every Man has a *Property* in his own *Person*' and a person can only claim an object as property insofar as he intermingles it with labour, and thereby 'fix a Property' within it (Locke 1988, 287–90). Coming into possession of her *self*, Clive, along with other celebrity actresses, adopted this definition as her own. Clive came to personify the individualism upon which modern feminism was founded (and has sometimes faltered), as it has met with critiques of its rejection of larger social connections; but, unlike that liberal self which is presumed to pre-exist its actions and seek only self-promotion, Clive shaped her subjectivity in conjunction with the dramatic characters she portrayed, and sometimes collectively on behalf of the other actors whose interests she shared. For Locke the self was determined not by its substance but by its identity with a consciousness that appropriates self to itself. When Clive created a persona with an identical name, performed by her self-same person – 'the self is one and the same, "the same to itself" because it "owns itself" or is its "own self"' (Balibar, 27) – Clive queried the relationship of self to person and property in her roles and writings, and jockeyed what might be termed 'the uneasy relationship of identity and difference' (Balibar, 33) as she both identified with what she had named (by appearing in her own person) and disowned it (by claiming not to be herself).

When Clive referred to the 'customs' of the theatre with respect to property relations in her pamphlet *The Case of Mrs Clive* (1744), she drew on the longstanding English reliance on common law. Having been a victim of salary price-fixing, she implicitly defined the status of an actress within its brief history since women had come to the stage in the Restoration, but the 6d. pamphlet also, importantly, attacked the legitimacy of patriarchal power and its sovereign authority. Common law derived, of course, from precedent rather than statute, and it began to assume a rather more permanent shape as local practices became more fully entrenched and widely accepted as authoritative. Common law frequently rested on verbal transmission; as such, it was contingent, informal, and arbitrary. What Clive sought throughout her career was fair and consistent application of the existing body of practices relating to acting. To firmly establish these practices was especially critical to the well-being of women players, who were vulnerable to exploitation – particularly in Clive's case, because, as a wife separated from her husband, her property was by law subsumed under his. The intricacies involved in property arrangements of contracts and wills, of personal property and land, were vital components of many popular Restoration and eighteenth-century dramatic plots. This reliance on common law is particularly evident in the treatise that forcefully asserted Clive's right to *own* her own labour and, by virtue of that labour, to own her 'self' as a subject with rights.[7] In Clive's case, women's property did not rest in its traditional location in the domestic setting, and *The Case of Mrs Clive* argues the case informally but passionately in the court of public opinion. Susan Staves has described women's legal status regarding property during the Restoration and eighteenth century as having moved through several stages. The lengthy first stage involved considerable experimentation in the courts in terms of establishing any rights. In the second stage (1778–1800), 'separate maintenance' developed as a viable alternative for women, and they sought to enter into contracts on their own.[8]

---

[7]   I am very grateful to Lisa Freeman for the stimulating correspondence that helped me formulate these ideas, though she is not responsible, of course, for my interpretation of our exchange.

[8]   Susan Staves, entering the controversy as to whether married women's situation *vis-à-vis* property improved, on the side of an early nineteenth-century retreat from earlier advances, posits the three stages described here.

Thus the 1770s contributed to a revolution for women (followed by a decline in women's legal status in the early nineteenth century), as part of which several celebrated actresses attempted to erode married men's right to possess their wives' income and property. Clive anticipated this move in daring to assert the right of a *feme sole*, a single woman independently able to make contracts in her own name, for all actresses, regardless of their marital status.

In short, Kitty Clive claimed that an eighteenth-century actress, though dispossessed of ordinary property because she was a woman, was able to command, in addition to a substantial earned salary and gratuities, a new kind of property located in her identity, which I am calling 'performative property', and which we might locate somewhere between real property and paper credit. Though this practice of respecting an actor's right to a role was generally followed, in fact there were celebrated infringements of this tradition, and actresses were more vulnerable to its abuse than actors and less likely to convince managers of their right to a dramatic property. The potential for difficulty was greatest when an actress returned to the stage after a leave of absence, such as for pregnancy or illness, or when her aging face and body spurred another actress in the company to appropriate her roles. Unlike their situation in marriage, in which their legal existence was suspended or sublimated, women were unquestionably placed at a disadvantage regarding both wages and inheritance: 'No amount of equal inheritance could counteract the law of covertures and its legal "fiction" that a husband and wife were one person – the husband – and therefore their property was his' (Erickson, 19).[9] Performative property, differing from real or mobile property, is embodied within one's person; it cannot be transferred without permission, and it avoids the self-alienation intrinsic to contractual prostitution.[10] In sum, Clive maintained that inherent within the actress was her right to act a given role in perpetuity and to claim that role as hers for lucrative benefit performances.

One might argue, then, that performative property was the first significant property that a woman could possess in her own name, which depended upon her identity rather than that of her husband or her family. A woman deriving from the least privileged classes could thus rival the elevated standing which the aristocracy possessed because of their claim to land, and she could even exceed the economic and social mobility that accruing moveable property had made newly accessible to the trade and merchant classes. Performative property was located in possessing a role of one's own, and yet also becoming representative of a property which was abstracted from the real in that its actuation was realized in a unique performance that could never be exactly replicated. I would like to turn now to a specific instance of Clive's ingenuity in manipulating onstage and offstage aspects of her identity.

---

[9]   Nicola Phillips, however, finds that married women could defend their property in court, and that the law was not consistently applied.

[10]   See Laura Rosenthal for a recent discussion of actresses and prostitution.

The 'Irish-English' Clive

Clive fought throughout her career for her right to 'own' parts and epilogues, and to establish a celebrated identity. Like other celebrated eighteenth-century actresses, Clive frequently 'kept a distinguishing role in epilogues, creating a character quite as definite as those which she represented in the play itself, and authors wrote their epilogues to suit the speaker' (Knapp, 68).[11] Many of the epilogues allude to her writing talent and seem to prod her toward producing her own original theatre pieces. In the epilogue following Frances Sheridan's *The Dupe* (1763), speaking openly of herself as a 'Sister Scribbler' ('Not Mrs *Friendly* now, I'm Mrs *Clive* / No Character from Fiction will I borrow'), she shares the female playwright's lament that she cannot convince a man to write the epilogue. Consequently the playwright begs Clive as actress and playwright to produce one on the spot: 'What's to be done, she cry'd? can't *you* endeavour / To say some pretty thing? – I know you're clever.'[12] Similarly, Garrick's epilogue written for the 19 March 1751 performance of Clive's *The Rehearsal; or, Bays in Petticoats* (1753) is a rousing call to action on behalf of women writers:

> But pray, Sirs, why must we not write, nor think?
> Have we not Heads and hands, and Pen and Ink?
> Can you boast more, that are so wondrous wise?
> Have Women then no weapons but their Eyes?
> Were we, like you, to let our Genius loose
> We'd top your wit, and Match you for abuse.[13]

The richness of the epilogue in performance, spoken by Clive as Mrs Hazard, would have arisen from its enfolded layers of reference to actress, playwright, role, and private person, thus extending the joke of the play through meta-dramatic references. Though one might interpret the feminism of the epilogue as contained by its misogyny, the force of Garrick's epilogue is at least as much a grudging recognition that Clive's comic talent truly rivalled his; her delivery of the lines, along with appropriate gestures, may have reinforced the way her arguments for women's equality constituted part of her ongoing epilogue persona. Garrick's avoidance of a 'struggle for victory' with Clive, according to Thomas Davies, could be 'attributed to his dread of her getting the better of him' (Davies, 200), especially since her salary and benefits often rivalled his.

Clive's development of performative property also involved her mediation in the eighteenth-century playhouse's critical function in the invention of a theatricalized British identity.[14] Especially during the 1760s, London audiences

---

[11]   Clive was 'the most amusing as well as the most consistent' of such women.

[12]   The popular epilogue is reprinted in *The Theatrical Bouquet*, 132.

[13]   The epilogue in the Folger Library collection is printed in Kinservik, 322–3.

[14]   Michael Ragussis argues that toward the end of the century a double move occurred: legitimizing the native voice was accompanied by a trope of failing to pass as an authentic

welcomed plays by Irish playwrights, including Isaac Bickerstaff, Arthur Murphy, Hugh Kelly, Richard Cumberland, and Oliver Goldsmith.[15] Clive brazenly capitalized on the English audiences' appetite for Irish fare, which had been demonstrated in their taste for Thomas Sheridan's afterpiece *The Brave Irishman; or, Captain O'Blunder* (1743), as well as Charles Macklin's comedies *Love à la Mode* (1759) and *The True-Born Irishman* (1760), revised as *The Irish Fine Lady* (1767). The relationship between Irish and English theatre in the eighteenth century was arguably an asymmetric one negotiated by actors, performances, and theatres on both sides of the Irish Sea, though recent critics suggest a more dynamic and reciprocal relationship than a colonial model might allow.[16] That transnational relationship subverts more traditional paradigms that emanate from nations: an alternative model emphasizes more productively, I think, the traffic between them (Hall 2005, 543–60).

A long-reigning assumption has been that the eighteenth-century Irish theatres in Smock Alley and Aungier Street were largely colonial institutions that merely fostered English loyalties. Helen Burke (2003) has vigorously contested this view, and she convincingly traces a native Irish counter-theatre to reveal that the seemingly extraneous matter surrounding the main piece, especially prologues and epilogues, often resisted the status quo. In discussing Clive's afterpieces here, I am suggesting that her farces, staged first in London, also served this contestatory function, and that even the London stage was sometimes the site of ferment stirred by Irish actors and playwrights.[17]

In the characters Clive created for Irish *women* on stage and on the page, she counters common expectations that Ireland was merely 'a rural backwater', a landscape populated by harmless comic Gaelic peasants, 'where the English visitor could experience a welcome release from the pressures of modernity'.[18] While the typical Irish working-class man was frequently portrayed as a blustering, ignorant buffoon and the Irish maid as a lusty local, these popular conventional images were expanded and complicated in Clive's renderings. In her dramatic pieces, Ireland becomes less a murky bog swarming with primitive people and ideas than a rich cultural resource for women to draw upon. At some level Clive also recognized that she was playing on English fears of what intermarriage between individuals – and,

---

English person. While both these tendencies may certainly be traced, Ragussis does not consider the third possibility of happy hybridity that Clive proposes.

[15] See Morash, 51. He speaks of this trend toward Irish comedies at the turn into the eighteenth century.

[16] See, for example, Susan Cannon Harris, who builds on Mary Louise Pratt's concept of the 'contact zone'.

[17] Helen Burke remarks that British theatre was most often exported to Ireland, but Irish theatre was also occasionally imported into England, exerting more influence than she suggests (2007, 219–32). Greene and Clark show that from 1720 to 1745 only 26 of 175 original plays on the Dublin stage did not premier first in London (72).

[18] Helen Burke describes stereotypes of the Irish with these words (2005, 88).

metaphorically, a union between the two countries – might bring; and she masks any potentially serious political and social satire with self-deprecating humour.

After her success with *The Rehearsal*, Clive further developed performative property in herself and her dramatic pieces and ultimately carried them to Ireland. Kitty Clive, though reputed to have displayed a rough, vulgar Irish temper, actually spent very little time in Ireland, acting in Dublin only in 1741 and again in the early 1760s. An anonymous author attacked her as stereotypically Irish in Hugh Kelley's *Thespis* (1766): she was 'Formed for those coarse and vulgar scenes of life, / Where low-bred rudeness always breathes in strife' (Kelley, 22 and 33). She had, however, also been long identified with more attractive Irish associations, such as singing 'Ellen a Roon' in *The Miser* at her benefit on 19 August 1741.[19] Clive's Irish patriotism may have sufficiently revived during her trip to Ireland in 1762 to prompt her to transform her role as the English Mrs Jenkings in *Sketch of a fine Lady's Return from a Rout* (1763) into the central Irish character Mrs Oconner in the final afterpiece.[20] That farce is among the few Irish plays on Irish subjects written during this period, and among a very few composed by a woman of Irish heritage.[21]

The one-act farce, *Sketch of a fine Lady's Return from a Rout*, like her two-act revision, *Every Woman in her Humour*, comically resists mid-eighteenth-century norms of appropriate feminine behaviour. It repeats a familiar theme of conflict between a woman's real desires, whether serious or trivial, and her social and domestic obligations.[22] Produced for Clive's benefit night at Drury Lane, 12 March 1763, *Sketch* focuses on Lady Jenkings, a newly minted lady of quality who insists on being addressed as 'your Ladyship' rather than 'Madam', and who shares Clive's passion for card playing. She is representative of a new English aristocracy uneasy about its identity, which may have been familiar to Clive because of her acquaintance with the Anglo-Irish ascendant elite.[23] Because the character Lady Jenkings's husband, the docile Sir Jeremy Jenkings, had recently been knighted, Clive/Jenkings is deeply self-conscious about her newly acquired status. Lady Jenkings represents a delinquent Ireland whose debt is forgiven as a consequence of its promise of reform.

---

[19] Benefit of Mrs Clive in *The Miser*, DNL 4–8.8 in the Dublin music calendar, see Greene and Clark. 'Ellen a Roon' first appeared in Charles Coffey's ballad opera, *The Beggar's Wedding* (London, 1729).

[20] See Frushell 1968, to whom I am indebted throughout. According to Susan Cannon Harris, 207–30, Dublin theatres were beginning to compete with the London stage in the 1730s and 1740s.

[21] Greene and Clark remark, 'Few distinctly Irish plays were staged in our period' (89). In addition, *The London 'Prentice* (1754) and a translation, *The Island of Slaves* (1761), have been attributed to Clive, but these plays are much less certainly her creations.

[22] The manuscript afterpieces in the Huntington Library Larpent collection, *Sketch of a fine Lady's Return from a Rout* (LA220), *Every Woman in Her Humour* (LA174), and *The Faithful Irish Woman* (LA247), are unpaginated.

[23] Morash finds a trend toward mocking the uncertain identity of the Anglo-Irish aristocracy in Irish comedies in the early decades of the eighteenth century (41).

The Sketch was also performed at least once in Dublin, on 27 June 1763, during the time that Clive visited the city. When Clive revised it into the afterpiece, *The Faithful Irish Woman*, she stressed her Irish ethnicity and seemed to identify with a growing Irish patriotism. The spirited farce, submitted to the Lord Chamberlain and signed by James Lacy (March 1765), inserts an Irish plot into the earlier *Sketch* along with would-be English aristocrats. The play admits of Irish vulgarity but relegates such characters to a specific class location. In large part it good-humouredly defends Irish traditions and language.

Having acted Lady Jenkings in *The Sketch*, Clive switched roles and nationalities in *The Faithful Irish Woman* to play the Irish Mrs Oconner, the good-natured cousin of the gambling, would-be fine lady Jenkins (the 'g' is dropped in the later farce). The play resembles Thomas Sheridan's *The Brave Irishman* in that the central character displays manners that, in spite of her being Irish, mark her as possessing more humane instincts than her English cousin. Showing considerable feistiness and not a few peculiarities, the uncouth Irish woman defiantly takes snuff in the first scene. She tentatively accompanies Lady Jenkins to her late-night gambling rambles, only to mock her pretensions and irresponsibility. Mrs Oconner displays enviable money management skills and values, and she urges her reprobate English cousin to renounce her addictions and affectations.

Mrs Oconner ironically instructs the English in improving their speech, and most significantly she defends 'the Irish-English Language' – rather than 'Anglo-Irish' – as the proper language of the upper classes in both countries. Clive and her character, Oconner, intimately recognize that a person's social standing could be significantly transformed through reforming her enunciation or regional dialect. Clive's newly aristocratic Irish woman was extraordinary in attempting to fix an *Irish-English* identity that brought together elements of both, making her superior to a purely English one. Clive/Mrs Oconner boldly insinuates that 'Irish' takes precedence over 'English,' and that the English have much to learn from their neighbours. For example, Mrs Oconner scoffs at English superstitions that Ireland teems with poisonous snakes and other animals, and that the Irish are toad-eaters: ''Tis an unaccountable thing what they get into their heads about Ireland.' The Irish woman twice tells her English cousin, Lady Jenkins, that sending her spoiled stepdaughter, Miss Nancy, to Ireland would 'make her good for something' by virtue of marriage to an Irish man. Social status also trumps the country of origin in the play. The genteel Irish, Mrs Oconner protests, speak without a brogue, though vulgar people in both countries garble the language into nonsensical jargon: 'But I'll tell you, if I was not worth a shilling in the World, I would Bett you 500£ that we speak truer English in the Castle of Dublin, than you do.'

There are significant textual indicators that Clive's views in *The Faithful Irish Woman* were not without controversy. Among the changes, the claim that the occupants of Dublin Castle speak finer English than 'is spoken in the circle at St James's' is emended, as is Mrs Oconner's remark that the Lord Lieutenant had indicated that 'English was spoken in the purest Manner in Dublin'

(Frushell 1970, 51–8).[24] At the same time, Mrs Oconner displays a bold lack of deference to the English: 'We are civil to the English when they deserve it, and when they don't deserve it, why —.' Still, Mrs Oconner is describing a chronic problem in England at mid-century, when emigrants with various dialects flocked to the metropole, all seeking a uniform pronunciation, a 'language properly so-called', that would afford them social mobility at a time when language academies were being founded in Britain (Barrell 1983b, 110–75).[25] The London stage became a cosmopolitan venue to hear these dialects spoken, satirized, regularized, and legislated.

The Faithful Irish Woman suggests that Clive herself, though an Irish patriot, had erased any sign of an Irish inflection, unlike some of her fellow Irish actors. Clive as Mrs Oconner speaks as actress and playwright rather than in character when she says,

> Well now I'll tell you a Story and it is very true ['in Dublin' is crossed out] some years ago we invited an English Actress ['Actor' is crossed out] to come over to Us; [...] So one day she was Dining at a person of Quality's house, & there was no less a Person than my Lord Chancellor, & so he was complimenting her, & said he had never heard any Lady upon the Stage, speak the English so well; Well then, a gentleman in Company reply'd, Faith & my Lord, there is no great Wonder at that that she shou'd speak English well, for her Grandfather was a Irishman.

If the 'English Actress' is meant to be Clive, then the joke clearly turns Irishness into an asset and champions Clive the actress and character as perfectly blending the two countries. Writing and acting her own performative property allowed audiences to imagine her interiority as diplomatically encompassing sympathy with both countries.

Clive's Irish woman takes pride in Irish values and in the hybrid language the Irish helped to shape. Rather than debating the respective merits of being Irish and living as a Briton, a potentially combustible mixture, Clive resolved cultural difference through the romance of an Irish woman and an Englishman instead of the usual reverse pattern; in short, she stands on its head the conventional plot of an Irish man marrying an English woman. Alluding to plots such as Thomas Sheridan's afterpiece *The Brave Irishman* (1743) and Charles Macklin's play *The True-Born Irishman* (1760), Clive/Mrs Oconner remarks, 'The English Ladies have sometimes done us the honour to shew a partiality for our Countrymen, & I am glad I have it in my power to return the Obligation by giving my fortune to an Englishman, who has behav'd nobly to his Kind & country'. Like Clive,

---

[24] Frushell carefully collates the two plays to argue that Clive probably approved the changes to *Irish Woman* in rehearsal, but my own examination alternatively suggests that the emendations in manuscript might indicate the censor's wishes.

[25] Barrell discusses a uniform language as a unifying force in mid-century Britain.

Mrs Oconner ascends to become part of the Anglo-Irish – or Irish-English – elite, though she mocks those who attempt to hobnob with people of rank.

In the second act of the play, Mrs Oconner receives word that her fiancé, Truman, an English sea captain, abruptly lost his fortune when his ship sank. Mrs Oconner generously shares her substantial fortune with him, and he seems not at all emasculated by the financial arrangement. Clive concludes the afterpiece with a satirical air from Gay's *Beggar's Opera*, playing on the popularity of her singing role as Polly and again reminding the audience of the bridge between theatrical representation and her person: 'And now I can sing to you with pretty Polly […] thus safe on Shore, I ask no more; / My All is in my Possession, Possession &c.' Serving as a metaphor for her native land, she embodies a loyal Irish woman who is willing to support both husband and self with money from selling property inherited from an Irish uncle. As I indicated earlier, Clive had given her estranged English husband, George Clive, a steady allowance from her earnings, yet upon his death he left her nothing. In addition, I suggest, Clive signals through her characters, onstage and off, that she willingly contributed her acting talent to England, and she also hints at England's trade inequalities vis-à-vis Ireland, its prejudices and misapprehensions about Ireland, and its extraction of Ireland's cultural and economic resources. Thus Ireland is personified as a wealthy, propertied independent woman – a woman closely resembling Clive – who generously assumes the debts of a suddenly destitute Englishman to share his identity in wedded bliss.

If Irish women were frequently depicted in eighteenth-century plays as domestic and maternal, Clive's interpretation of the Irish woman in her afterpieces, written and produced in London, is all the more radical in its divergence from this formulaic representation. Clive is highly original in her resistance to portraying the Irish, and particularly Irish women, as victims, suffering mothers, or even as fortune-hunters. Clive's comic female heroines, like the actress herself, are the antithesis of distressed femininity or anguished maternity. Instead they are savvy, moneyed, high-spirited women with hearts of gold who speak 'Irish-English' with true wit, eschew domestic duties, and generally defend Ireland and its 'civilized' culture – the very type of the celebrated actresses I have been discussing.

In short, Clive contributes to the formation of a peculiarly Irish female identity that is distinct from the stereotypic native Irish servant or the blustering, drunken Teague figure. Rather than an Irish adventurer voraciously seeking a wealthy English wife, Clive's Englishman hopes to endow an Irish woman who ironically ends up supporting him. Traumatized by hailing from a country with a history of being dispossessed of one's land, Mrs Oconner's 'Irish-English' identity is bolstered by becoming a landowner. She says, 'I have Secret to tell you, I have got 2000£ in good firm Land that the Sea can't wash away.' Just as Clive claimed a different sort of theatrical property in the parts she established as her own, her character reclaims the real property from which many Irish had been dispossessed. In promoting this identity, Clive made available a social space and a theatrical space which she could inhabit as a dislocated Irish woman who was not anyone's possession, but who instead took possession of theatrical properties in her dramatic roles. The afterpieces Clive acted and penned highlight the difficulty of negotiating a tenable relationship between participants who are unequal because of national, religious, class, and gender affiliations. In her invention of a novel version of the Irish woman character, both Irish and English identities were transformed in her formulation of the equation.[26]

When Garrick asked Clive 'how much she was worth' she reportedly replied, 'as much as yourself' (Davies, 195). Her long career, like the extended dispute waged over the actors' rebellion, was symptomatic of the growing conflict between a collective model of the theatre as a patent company versus one that relied for its success on celebrated individual personalities. Clive's achievements rivalled those of any actress and many actors to this point in theatre history. She competed with Garrick in performance, as a businesswoman, as a playwright, and most of all, as a celebrity who claimed her right to performative properties, among which were a would-be fine lady, chambermaid, Irish-English woman, and spokesperson for women's rights. She remained loyal to a craft that she believed deserved to command rights, privileges, and respect. In sum, Kitty Clive skilfully mediated identities – her own as well as diverse national, class, and gendered identities – to contest reigning assumptions regarding virtue, property, and commerce.

---

[26] David Lloyd describes popular and non-élite history as giving evidence of deliberate and 'persistent inassimilability to the state' (77–88).

Chapter 6

Constructing Identity in Eighteenth-Century Comedy: Schools of Scandal, Observation and Performance

Anette Pankratz

New Selves and the Theatre

According to – amongst others – Taylor, Seigel and Wahrman, the concept of personal identity as 'one that presupposes an essential core of selfhood characterized by psychological depth, or interiority, which is the bedrock of unique, expressive individual identity' (Wahrman, xi) emerges in the course of the eighteenth century. This correlates with a shift from the holistic cosmology of the body politic and status-based feudal hierarchies to a model of functional differentiation (Luhmann 1997, 731; Scholz, 1–2). Instead of the family one was born into, capitalist market forces and specialized social subsystems such as politics, religion, law, the economy or literature provide multiple frameworks for identity formation. In this changing culture, people are expected to conform to social norms, but at the same time they have to differentiate themselves from others (Elias 1993–1994; Luhmann 1998).

These processes can be related to the emergence of the mass media (Luhmann 2004, 11–12; Luhmann 1997, 291–302). Novels, magazines and newspapers circulate information for an anonymous mass market relying on an informed public of readers and writers (Luhmann 2004, 187–8). In this emergent subsystem, disembodied words replace face-to-face communications, physical presence and status-based representation. Moreover, printed texts need and produce privacy and interiority. They are usually perused in private (Seigel, 160–66; Koschorke, 169–84), and especially the new genre of the novel offers the soul/psyche as a sign of inner depth of both characters and readers (Koschorke, 157). At the same time, printed texts further processes of individuation. The corpus of more and more standardized information serves as a yardstick for one's belonging to a common culture and enables people to formulate new opinions and interpretations by means of which they can distinguish themselves (Luhmann 1997, 297). This leads to an acceleration and multiplication of information, which is potentially accessible to everyone. More and faster information, in turn, enhances contingency and potential dissension (Downie 2005, 74).

Theatre, with its emphasis on face-to-face communication and the co-presence of audience and actors, rather seems to be the odd medium out, attached to the status-based forms of representative publicness and lacking the means to adequately represent complex inner lives (Freeman, 6 and 16). And yet, as this article attempts to show, eighteenth-century comedies participate in the processes and debates about the shifting concepts of identity.[1] They do this by setting the theatre apart from the new mass media[2] and by highlighting the qualities and pitfalls of identities which are only discernible from the outside.

Prologues and epilogues allude to the cultural function of the theatre. They promote the neo-classical topos of theatre as reflection or mirror of reality with a clearly didactic intent (O'Brien, 186–9). As the prologue of George Lillo's *The London Merchant* (1731) puts it:

> If thoughtless youth to warn, and shame the age
> From vice destructive, well becomes the stage
> If this example innocence secure,
> Prevent our guilt, or by reflection cure;
> If Millwood's dreadful guilt and sad despair
> Commend the virtue of the good and fair,
> Though art be wanting, and our numbers fail,
> Indulge th'attempt, in justice to the tale. (265)

Plays theoretically provide either negative or positive examples for self-reflection and, more important, self-correction. These claims often pay mere lip service to critics and are sometimes undermined in the plays themselves.[3] Moreover, dramas do more than just passively reflect; they order and select, providing a model of the world which is recognizably related to the everyday lives of the audience, 'but a sufficient remove from it to enable critical reflection' (O'Brien, 190). The spectators observe a version of reality, which they have to relate to their own lives and by means of which they are able to establish a relationship to their own selves (Fischer-Lichte 1990, 4; Luhmann 2004, 115).

Theatre's exteriority and its generically given focus on 'interpretable surfaces' highlight the faultlines of individuation and interiority (Freeman, 27). Psychological depth, true emotions or a 'benevolent heart' are, per se, inaccessible (in both 'real' life and on stage); they have to be mediated by words, gestures or deeds (Sheridan 1979, 29). Hence, in the plays 'nothing remains but the outside' (Henry Fielding, 'An Essay on the Knowledge of the Characters of Men', quoted in Freeman, 26), an outside produced by a character's performances, which has to be

---

[1] For identity formation, especially in eighteenth-century domestic tragedy, see Weidle.

[2] Although printed plays, theatre reviews and critical reflections on the stage have to be considered as definite parts of the public sphere, see Fischer-Lichte 1990, 257–8; Weidle, 35.

[3] One example is Richard Brinsley Sheridan's *The Critic*, which will be discussed in this chapter.

observed and interpreted by others: 'the stage offers us a medium in which public exteriors were taken not merely as symptomatic of an interior, but rather as the only basis upon which judgments about character could be formed' (Freeman, 27). Eighteenth-century plays hence concentrate on the tensions between a character's unknowable, but assumed interiority, his or her representation of it and the reactions of the spectators, both on stage and in the auditorium. This interplay between performing and observing identities negotiates the discourses produced and distributed by the mass media, the dual publics created on stage as well as the performative tensions between role, character, actor and audience.

Theatre as Meta-Medium

Plays often self-reflexively position the theatre as a cultural institution in its own right offering a 'dynamic, though clearly biased, view of the battlegrounds in the cultural wars that dominated so much of eighteenth-century representation' (Freeman, 50; cf. O'Brien, 199). They point out the unreliability and manipulations of the new mass media and thus present the theatre as meta-medium, which appears to offer its audience a privileged position outside – or above – politics, religion or the economy, from which it is able to evaluate cultural processes and form its own judgment.

Sheridan's *The Critic* (1779) starts with the Dangles '*at breakfast, and reading newspapers*' (7). Mr Dangle's indignant recitation of headlines points toward the inundation of the public with information: '"Brutus to Lord North" – "Letter the second, on the State of the Army" – Pshaw! "To the first L dash D of the A dash Y" – "Genuine Extract of a Letter from St Kitts" – "Coxheath Intelligence" – "It is now confidently asserted that Sir Charles Hardy." Pshaw! Nothing but about the fleet, and the nation!' (ibid.).

The highly topical news alludes to the invasion scare in the summer of 1779 during the American War of Independence.[4] Characters being flooded by a welter of printed information, however, were nothing new. This had already figured large in Henry Fielding's *The Coffee-House Politician* (1730), which ridiculed Politick's undiscerning consumption of newspapers – 'you must read all that come out: about forty every Day, and some Days fifty: and of a *Saturday* about fourscore' (Fielding 2004, 433). *The Critic* takes up the topos of unreliable and confusing newspapers and explicitly juxtaposes it with the stage. In contrast to his wife, who follows the reports avidly and chides him for his lack of interest, Dangle prefers the theatre to politics: 'I hate all politics but theatre politics' (Sheridan 1989, 7). But he cannot escape the political discourse as the play-within-the-play, Puff's patriotic 'tragedy', *The Spanish Armada*, transposes the present threat of invasion into the secure Elizabethan past (ibid., 8).

---

[4]   For the historical and theatrical context, see Feldmann, 87, and the article by Robert W. Jones.

The Critic's play-within-the-play, however, makes fun of dramas which try to evoke a 'British Armada spirit' and by means of this imbue the theatre with a direct political function (Feldmann, 87). This critical attitude ties in with Dangle and Sneer's discussion of a new play called *The Reformed Housebreaker*, whose author intends to turn the theatre into a 'school of morality' (Sheridan 1989, 13). The ironical praise by Sneer highlights the futility of using a play to teach juridical norms:

> The Reformed Housebreaker; where, by the mere force of humour, Housebreaking is put into so ridiculous a light, that if the piece has its proper run, I have no doubt but that bolts and bars will be entirely useless by the end of the season. [...] it is written by a friend of mine, who has discovered that the follies and foibles of society are subjects unworthy to the notice of the Comic Muse, who should be taught to stoop only at the greater vices and blacker crimes of humanity – gibetting capital offences, in five acts, and pillorying petty larcenies in two. – In short, his idea is to dramatise the penal laws, and make the Stage a court of ease to the Old Bailey. (Ibid., 14–15; cf. Wiesenthal, 326)

In a similar vein, *The Spanish Armada* attempts to evoke patriotic feelings. But it turns out a badly written, absurdly plotted piece of bombast with some bits of Shakespeare thrown in for good measure.[5] Its alleged author, Puff, is introduced as a versatile hack writer who makes a living as 'Professor of the Art of Puffing' (Sheridan 1989, 31), which – just like the *Reformed Housebreaker* – supposedly serves important functions in all realms of society, 'yielding a tablature of benevolence and public spirit; befriending equally trade, gallantry, criticism, and politics' (ibid., 40). Puffing fuses a didactic impetus with the emergent capitalist marketplace and its 'new spirit of professionalism and free enterprise' (Feldmann, 91). Puff has to make his living by influencing public opinion. He has developed a variety of techniques from the 'puff direct' (Sheridan 1989, 35), the slightly manipulative advertisement, to the more subtle 'Puff Oblique', which 'delights to draw forth concealed merit, with a most disinterested assiduity; and sometimes wears a countenance of smiling censure and tender reproach' (ibid., 39). *The Critic* here refers to a broad variety of journalistic genres which had already figured large at the beginning of the play – 'the various forms of Letter to the Editor – Occasional Anecdote – Impartial Critique – Observation from Correspondent, – or Advertisement from the Party' – and relates it to one person (Puff) and one purpose (to earn money) (ibid., 35).

Sheridan's play implies that financial considerations, and not the disinterested reasoning among equals in the bourgeois public sphere, underlie the diversity of opinions.[6] Many eighteenth-century comedies allude to the fact that the multiplication of attitudes within the public sphere is shaped first and foremost by economic aims. In order to earn more money, Puff learns how to diversify

---

[5]   And as link to the original main piece of the evening, Shakespeare's *Hamlet*; cf. Miller, 99.

[6]   As Jürgen Habermas assumed in *Strukturwandel der Öffentlichkeit*, 105–7.

his talents and produce texts fit for as many factions as possible. Likewise, in Fielding's *The Author's Farce* (1730), the greedy publisher Bookweight makes his writers churn out article after article, not for the enhancement of public ratiocination but for the benefit of his purse:

> Fie upon it, gentlemen! What, not at your pens? Do you consider, Mr Quibble, that it is above a fortnight since your Letter from a Friend in the Country was published? Is it not high time for an Answer to come out? At this rate, before your Answer is printed your Letter will be forgot. I love to keep a controversy up warm. I have had authors who have writ a pamphlet in the morning, and answered it in the afternoon, and compromised the matter at night. (Henry Fielding 2004, 29)

The transmission of information by the mass media, the replacement of observable facts by printed words and untrustworthy discourses, are shown to control public opinion. In contrast to newspapers and pamphlets, drama appears visible and graspable in the immediacy of the performance. It is the privileged perspective of the stage which allows the audience to recognize the journalist's manipulations (Freeman, 65).

The theatre finds means not only to call Puff's bluff, but also to appropriate his writing for its own advantage. In the rehearsal of *The Spanish Armada* the (fictitious) performers, scene designers, prompters and technicians conspire against Puff and his pseudo-didactic, commercialized aims. All the lengthy descriptions of gallantry and heroism are cut by them 'in a most shocking manner' (Sheridan 1989, 68), as the frustrated author complains. Patriotic tragedy is thus turned into a snappy afterpiece (Miller, 99). It ends with a celebration of the English victory over the Spanish in 1588, including allegories of the Thames and a potpourri of emotionally fraught music, from Purcell's 'Britons, Strike Home' to 'Rule, Britannia' (Sheridan 1989, 84). In the first production, this mixture seems to have pressed all the right buttons and created a mood of 'common enthusiasm' (Crane 1989, xvii). The play succeeds by theatrical, not journalistic, means. It replaces words with music and technical effects (Miller, 103).

The Critic satirizes the manipulations of public opinion. At the same time it admits to being part of these manipulations. But in contrast to the newspapers and pamphlets, it draws the audience's attention to its apparatus for evoking emotions – from the dramaturgically apt Under Prompter, who constantly intrudes during the rehearsal, to de Loutherbourg's scenery, to the 'STAGE EFFECT, by which the greatest applause may be obtained, without the assistance of language, sentiment or character' (Sheridan 1989, 75; see also Wiesenthal, 324; Freeman, 57 and O'Toole, 151).

The 'here-and-now' of the stage thus attains more importance than the commercial or political aims of a play. This is highlighted in a passage about theatrical puffing. Puff explains about the proper advertisement for a play. On the literal level, this uncovers yet another facet of journalistic writing. Without having seen the performance, a professional writer is able to describe its success by recourse to superlatives and clichés:

the day before it is to be performed, I write an account of the manner in which it was received – I have the plot from the author, – and only add – Characters strongly drawn – highly coloured – hand of a master […]! Then for the performance – Mr Dodd was astonishingly great in the character of Sir Harry. That universal and judicious actor Mr Palmer, perhaps never appeared to more advantage than in the Colonel; – but it is not in the power of language to do justice to Mr King! – Indeed he more than merited those repeated bursts of applause which he drew from a most brilliant and judicious audience! (Sheridan 1989, 36)

On the level of *The Critic*'s first performance at Drury Lane, the actor of Puff, Thomas King, here praises himself in the presence of his colleagues Dodd and Palmer (as Dangle and Sneer), anticipating and probably cherishing the enthusiastic reaction of the 'judicious audience' (cf. Crane 1995, 91–2; O'Toole, 150). The 'puff', the distortion of reality, becomes a description of the truth – but only if one acknowledges the reality of the performance, that is, the physical presence of actors as actors and their interaction with the audience. This collaboration of performers and audience, and not Puff's text, also brings about the surge of patriotism at the end of *The Spanish Armada*. Moreover, the nod at the audience in Puff's/King's virtuoso piece ties in with the play's acknowledgment of the power of the 'public' (Sheridan 1989, 11). Puff points out that 'the number of those who go through the fatigue of judging for themselves is very small indeed!' (ibid., 37). By offering a privileged point of view, the spectators of *The Critic* are given the role of a discerning audience whose members judge for themselves and, by means of observation, become active participants in the theatrical performance.

Dual Publics

Even if plays do not explicitly juxtapose the liveness of the theatre with the discourses of the mass media, they operate with a framework of dual publics, the one established by the characters on stage plus a general, very often anonymous and depersonalized public offstage representing society at large. Similar to the characters manipulated by newspaper reports in *The Coffee House Politician* or *The Critic*, the general public is depicted as uninformed and gullible, taking the characters' self-fashionings at face value. The informed public again self-reflexively points towards the privileged positions provided by theatrical representations and indirectly includes the audience. The interplay between general and informed public is usually associated with the evaluation of a pair of socially similar, but ethically different characters, quite often a pair of brothers.[7] More than the contrast between the theatre and the mass media, these doublings highlight the need for close observation both in the world of the play and in the audience.

---

[7] Frequently using the classical pretext of Terence's *Andria*. Probably the best-known example of this juxtaposition is Thomas Shadwell's *The Squire of Alsatia* (1688).

In Sheridan's *The School for Scandal* (1777) Joseph Surface poses as 'Man of Sentiment' (13; cf. O'Toole, 123), exuding authenticity of feelings and moral depth. He at first seems to represent the norm and is 'universally well spoken of' (Sheridan 1979, 11 and 50–51); his brother Charles is damned as 'that libertine, that extravagant, that bankrupt in fortune and reputation' (ibid., 13). In the end, the reputations of the brothers are reversed and it transpires that they are not that different from each other after all (Worth, 152). The audience is not only confronted with the discrepancy between general opinion and the more discerning in-group, they also see the manipulation of public opinion by the eponymous 'school of scandal' presided over by Lady Sneerwell.

Just like the new mass media – to which they are implicitly related – the vicious circle's slander covers a broad range of techniques and topics and provides people with a host of contradictory pieces of information. Lady Sneerwell, Crabtree, Mrs Candour and Sir Benjamin Backbite manipulate public opinion, 'kill characters or run down reputations' (Sheridan 1979, 44). Sir Peter Teazle thinks gossip so dangerous that he wants to forbid it by act of Parliament (ibid.). But this is not the point of the comedy. Just as Surface is the family name of hypocrite, reforming rake and good-natured uncle alike and points towards the universal ramifications of identity construction and perception, the group of gossip-mongers undercuts any easy assumptions about truth and lies, surfaces and substances. Lady Sneerwell and her friends deftly mix invention, malicious lies, misunderstandings and, last but not least, truths. The arch-liar Lady Sneerwell herself explodes Joseph Surface's façade of sentimentality right in the exposition, while the upright Sir Peter Teazle goes on believing in Joseph's good character. Other essential information provided by the group is Joseph and Charles' rivalry for Teazle's ward Maria and the arrival of the uncle *ex machina*, Sir Oliver.[8] Moreover, the 'scandal group' serves as a central 'framing device' for the perception of protagonist Charles Surface (Wiesenthal, 321). Until his rather late appearance in III, iii, the audience has to rely on the judgements of others, mainly on the general public represented by Sir Peter Teazle and Lady Sneerwell's cronies. Probably well-versed in generic norms and comic plotting, the viewers might not trust the condemnation of Charles. The final proof, however, can only be got by the direct observation of the character on stage. In the merging of truth and lies and by undercutting too facile assumptions about other characters, *The School for Scandal* foregrounds the importance of discernment for the correct identification of others and, in turn, for the construction of personal and social identities. The 'school for scandal' thus serves as the audience's school for observation.

Dual publics and the need for close observation are put into relief in the screen scene (IV, iii) (cf. Wiesenthal, 324). When the secret rendezvous between Joseph Surface and Lady Teazle is disturbed by the arrival of Sir Peter, Lady Teazle hides behind a screen in order to maintain her and Joseph's reputations. Later on, Sir Peter

---

[8]   'Mr Surface, pray is it true that your uncle Sir Oliver is coming home? [...] He has been in the East Indies a long time. You can scarcely remember him, I believe?' (Sheridan 1979, 24).

hides in the closet to eavesdrop on Charles, whom he suspects of having an affair with his wife. In both cases the audience, and partly also the hidden characters, witness the difference between authentic and inauthentic performances. Not aware of his wife as secret listener, Sir Peter admits to his marital problems and elaborates on his act of generosity towards Lady Teazle, which is later to bring about the reconciliation of the couple. Afterwards, Charles denies any amorous involvement with Lady Teazle and asserts Joseph that he is only interested in Maria, which convinces Sir Peter of his innocence.

In contrast to these truthful, albeit unwitting, communications of interiority, Joseph is trapped between his public and private lives. Due to his surprising visitors and the subsequent games of hide-and-seek, he is made to act for different audiences. He tries to maintain his façade of sentimental morality for Sir Peter and Charles. At the same time, he wants to uphold his image as rakish suitor for Lady Teazle. The situation at first results in a spate of dramatic ironies that emphasize Joseph's hypocrisy. When, for instance, Sir Peter voices his suspicions about an affair between Charles and Lady Teazle, Joseph points out that a man 'who can break the laws of hospitality and attempt the wife of his friend, deserves to be branded as the pest of society' (Sheridan 1979, 97). His schizophrenic self-presentation becomes more frantic when Teazle mentions Joseph's involvement with Maria – something that Lady Teazle is not supposed to hear – and when Charles teases him about his flirting with Lady Teazle, which Sir Peter is not meant to find out. At the end of the scene, the screen falls discovering a repentant Lady Teazle and, more important, exposing Joseph to the credulous Sir Peter as 'smooth-tongued hypocrite' and 'villain' (ibid., 108–9).

The scene highlights the interplay between social identities and their performance in different publics. In the comically condensed succession of observers, who represent the multiple publics of the play, Joseph's double role collapses. The audience – which has been aware of his 'true' character from the very beginning – will hardly be surprised by the denouément of the scene, but is made to focus on the dynamics between the positions of the observers, the different levels of information and Joseph's more and more anxious attempts at coherent self-fashioning.

At the end of the play, it is not the emulation of Joseph as 'model for the young man of the age' (ibid., 29), as Sir Peter mistakenly advised at the beginning of the play, or the distrusting of appearances, as Lady Sneerwell cynically recommends (ibid., 116), but the importance of close observation and the awareness of the several publics which are celebrated. Significantly enough, the happy ending in *The School for Scandal* comes about through looks: Maria has 'looked *yes*' (ibid., 136; emphasis in original) and will assume the role as Charles's 'monitor' (ibid., 137), thereby guaranteeing his moral reform. The last look belongs to the audience, the final monitor: '*You* can, indeed, each anxious fear remove, / For even scandal dies, if you approve!' (ibid.; emphasis in original).

Performing Social Identities

The approval of the audience indirectly also involves the acknowledgement of common social values and class identities (Fischer-Lichte 1990, 215). The dominance of upper-class characters in eighteenth-century drama implicitly and tautologically results from their being born into the upper class, but their social identities have to be corroborated by appropriate performances in public through clothes, manners and words. It is these iterations of an assumed authentic original which, in the world of the play, 'produce the effect of an internal core of substance [...] manufactured and sustained through corporeal signs and other discursive means' (Butler 1999, 173). Performances in the theatre are always already framed as manufactured, which adds another layer of performativity, the tension between the liveness of the theatrical event and the characters being represented. Thus, the identity of Puff in the first performances of *The Critic* oscillates between the figure of a stereotypical hack author and star actor Thomas King. This, in turn, also points towards the constructedness of social identities. Manners and the signs of intellectual brilliance can be learned and reproduced. Talented actors are able to transcend the supposedly natural barriers of class – a fact which the comedies emphasize by role-plays within the role. In *The School for Scandal* Sir Oliver, for example, visits his nephews in the guises of the impoverished merchant Mr Stanley and the broker Mr Premium. All of these performances also involve the audience as constituent co-producers (and co-performers) of the precarious theatrical reality (Fischer-Lichte 2004, 26 and 46–7). The plays acknowledge this by addresses in asides, prologues and epilogues, in playful meta-theatrical framings as in *The Critic*, or in the collective and ritualized celebrations of happy endings.

The importance of social performances in the world of the plays is usually emphasized in scenes in which either assumed identities are exploded, as in *The School for Scandal*'s screen scene (discussed above), or a person's 'internal core' becomes discernible to the general public. Here Charles Surface's selling of the family portraits emblematically condenses the performativity of social identities in all its ambivalence. The paintings of the 'family of the Surfaces, up to the Conquest', featuring war heroes, judges, Members of Parliament, mayors – in short, the elite of the country – have to be turned into cash in order to secure his position (Sheridan 1979, 79–83). The aristocratic ethos of heredity, the long family tree and ancestors in eminent positions no longer suffice; only leading an ostentatious lifestyle – demonstrated by manners, fashion and discerning consumerism – maintains an advanced position in the general public.

Conspicuous consumption turns out to be a mixed blessing, though. On the one hand, it signals inclusiveness. Everyone can be part of the in-group as long as he or, less often, she has the necessary means and the appropriate manners. Characters often explicitly perpetuate the myth of an open elite, in which property, and not heredity, serves as the criterion for membership (Schröder, 32; Downie 2005, 62–6). Quite a few eighteenth-century plays allude to a mixing of landed and monied wealth, of aristocracy and the upper-middle class. In Richard Steele's

The Conscious Lovers (1722), the merchant Sealand claims that: 'we Merchants are a Species of Gentry, that have grown into the World this last Century, and are as honourable, and almost as useful as you landed Folks, that have always thought your selves so much above us' (75). Thorowgood, in Lillo's *The London Merchant*, likewise insists that 'As the name of the merchant never degrades the gentleman, so by no means does it exclude him' (11). In *The School for Scandal* no one comments unfavourably on Lady Sneerwell's background as 'the widow of a City knight with a good jointure', and the colonial merchant Sir Oliver Surface even represents the evaluative norms of the play (12). It is only characters like George Wealthy in Samuel Foote's *The Minor* (1760), like Charles Surface a young man on probation, who insist on an essentialized exclusivity between classes: 'I have been too well instructed in the value of nobility, to think of intermixing it with the offspring of a Bourgeois' (Foote 1974, 47).

As the examples of George Wealthy and Charles Surface demonstrate, however, leading the right lifestyle can be quite short-lived. Both young men assume the role of the gentleman by spending money amongst their friends and hangers-on. But ostentatious consumption has to be backed up by the approval of the public at large, symbolized by the legitimate inheritance of property, triggered by successful performances of interiority and the adaptation to social norms. In the case of George Farquhar's *The Beaux' Stratagem* (1707), the impoverished younger brother, Aimwell, poses as his older brother and tries to marry the rich heiress, Dorinda. In the end, the brother dies, and Aimwell does indeed become the wealthy Lord Aimwell and also marries Dorinda. This extremely happy ending not only establishes the 'comic ethos that appearance and reality can be brought into a relation not only of equivalence, but more importantly, of identity' (Freeman, 172), it also points out the necessity of correct performances. Aimwell has to admit to his earlier act of impersonation and give a demonstration of personal honesty and honour before he can reap his rewards. George Wealthy and Charles Surface, likewise, have to earn the financial support of father and uncle, respectively. In spite of his gambling and corresponding with procuresses and potential mistresses, George Wealthy convinces his father that he is indeed his worthy heir, when he takes pity on a young woman who was sent to him as a prostitute and promises by his 'honour' to protect her (Foote, 59).[9] In *The School for Scandal* Sir Oliver promises that 'if Charles has done nothing false or mean, I shall compound for his extravagance' (Sheridan 1979, 49). In contrast to *The Minor*, the final test has little to do with morals. Charles wins Sir Oliver's approval by not selling the portrait of his uncle, because the 'old fellow has been very good to me' (ibid., 83). The gesture merges the ethos of heredity with the spirit of (authentic) sentiment and meritocracy. Charles cannot completely do away with the aristocratic family model, but he justifies his decision as individual choice based on his uncle's financial support.

---

[9]   Later on, she is discovered as the 'Bourgeois' he refused to marry. It almost goes without saying that the happy ending celebrates their engagement.

This compromise encapsulates the paradoxes of eighteenth-century identity formation. Charles's rakish behaviour serves as a necessary stage of male individuation. As Sir Oliver explains: 'Egad, my brother and I were neither of us very prudent youths; and yet, I believe, you have not seen many better men than your old master was' (ibid., 49).[10] His wild life indicates that in contrast to his brother Joseph, who hypocritically imitates the literary models of sentimentality, Charles is a 'real' person. The gesture of repentance demonstrates that he is about to become a better man himself, to enter civilized society, finally 'acting up' to his social roles (ibid., 123).

Conclusion

The aspect of 'acting up' to one's role was part and parcel of an evening at the playhouse, which transposes the aspect of performativity to the auditorium and beyond. Going to the (legitimate) theatre indicated cultivation and distinction. Furthermore, in the seventeenth and eighteenth centuries, spectators did not only silently consume; they directly participated. Stage and auditorium were lit, thus spectators were constantly on display. Protests, loud conversations or – in extreme cases – direct action served as possible – albeit not welcome – performances in their own right (Freeman, 3–5; O'Toole, 113–18). In the eighteenth century, the audience gradually underwent a process of civilization. Spectators were banned from sitting on stage, the distance between auditorium and stage became larger and the potential for direct participation more restricted. This enhanced the already very prominent function of theatre as school of observation, channelling the social energy in the controlled performative autopoietic feedback.

The performative selves on stage were shown as under pressure from dual publics and a world shaped by the emergent mass media. These performances offered a variety of subject positions with which to experiment, to agree or disagree. The exteriority, superficiality and seemingly simple liveness turned the theatre into a 'site of resistance to the rise of the subject and to the ideological conformity enforced through that identity formation' (Freeman, 2). Yet, the new subject relied on self-observation and the observation of others, a technique which the theatre as meta-medium and society's 'other' taught as well (Luhmann 1998, 152; Seigel, 141–3). In other words, what at first sight might appear as marginalized cultural institution turns out as complement, teaching to look for interiority in exteriors and to make the necessary fine distinctions.

---

[10]   This is confirmed by the old and loyal servant Rowley: 'Their worthy father, once my honoured master, was, at his years, nearly as wild a spark; yet, when he died, he did not leave a more benevolent heart to lament his loss' (Sheridan 1979, 28–9).

Chapter 7
Material Sites of Discourse and the Discursive Hybridity of Identities

Uwe Böker[1]

In his *Complete English Tradesman* (1727) Daniel Defoe tells this anecdote:

> I heard once of a shop-keeper that behav'd himself thus to such an extreme, that
> when he was provok'd by the impertinence of the customers, beyond what his
> temper could bear, he would go up stairs and beat his wife, kick his children
> about like dogs, and be as furious for two or three minutes, as a man chain'd
> down in *Bedlam*; and when the heat was over, would sit down and cry faster than
> the children he had abused; and after the fit was over he would go down into his
> shop again, and be as humble, as courteous, and as calm as any man whatever; so
> absolute a government of his passions had he in the shop, and so little out of it; in
> the shop a soulless animal that can resent nothing, and in the family a madman;
> in the shop meek like a lamb, but in the family outrageous like a *Lybian* lion.
> (Defoe 1970, 94–5)

This anecdote highlights the question of personal identity, bourgeois self-control
and its historical socio-genesis. It suggests, above all, that identity is somehow
shaped or determined by sites of discourse. The patterns of discourse represented
in Defoe's anecdote are shaped by the specific sites of assembly: the shop and the
family. In discourse analysis, every site is a social place. Sites as different as the
shop, the alehouse, the coffee-house, or churches, law courts, libraries or drawing-
rooms of country houses do not only belong to heterogeneous socio-economic,
cultural or political fields but call for different modes of communication, different
manners and morals. All social places function as discursive spaces that define
and redefine identity through the interplay between the self and the other. In their
Politics and Poetics of Transgression Peter Stallybrass and Allon White remarked:

> Each "site of assembly" constitutes a nucleus of material and cultural conditions
> which regulate what may and may not be said, who may speak, how people may
> communicate and what importance must be given to what is said. An utterance
> is legitimated or disregarded according to its place of production and so, in large
> part, the history of political struggle has been the history of the attempts made to
> control significant sites of assembly and spaces of discourse. (88)

[1]   I would like to thank Isabel Karremann for her careful editing of my text and her
helpful suggestions when I happened not to be able to do this myself.

Although Defoe's shop appears to be a relatively insignificant site, the anecdote reveals that the tradesman is in fact master of the upper regions of his house, whereas the material and cultural conditions of the shop are determined by the economic interests of his customers. The tradesman, his body and his tongue have to speak at least two different languages.

Thus Defoe's anecdote suggests that personal identity is not a stable and permanent entity but is constantly changing under discursive conditions that lie beyond the control of the individual. According to Michel Pêcheux, each member of society is permanently 'existing in a field of different discourses, different message systems, [...] situated between those different systems' (Pêcheux quoted in Morley, 77), and thus continuously experiences a multiplicity of discourses that may be competing with one another at the same time, in the back of one's mind or more openly in all kinds of texts. The spaces in which the individual exists are continuously 'crossed by a number of different discourses, some of which support each other, are in alignment with each other, some of which contradict each other, some of which we relate to positively, some negatively [...] in the process of decoding and interpreting the messages [...], other messages, other discourses are always involved, whether or not we are explicitly conscious of it' (ibid.). Therefore we have to understand, he remarks, how one message relates to the other sets of representations, images and stereotypes that the audience is familiar with.

There is no reason not to apply Pêcheux's ideas to the period under discussion. In Defoe's case there are at least two different discourses, intersecting with and contradicting one another, both of which shape the tradesman's behaviour. On the one hand he participates in a private discourse within the family whose lord and master he is; and on the other hand there is an economic discourse dominating the shop that determines the welfare of his family and is obviously in the back of his mind at all times. But because of the necessity of self-control, the private discourse is suppressed the moment the tradesman is confronted with customers whose desires he has to fulfil, in his own commercial interest. Thus he is torn between professional countenance in the shop and frustration and violence bordering on Bedlam-like madness towards the members of his family who, from a psychological point of view, function as scapegoats.

It is true that the increasingly commercial, competitive and acquisitive British society needed a kind of aim-oriented rationality, resulting in 'reflexive monitoring'. Thus the anecdote demonstrates also, as Brean Hammond put it, 'the split between the public and the private self that emerges in the bourgeois sphere as a result of commercial ascendancy' (229). As economic forms of exchange proliferated through the entire society, the discontinuity of public and private, or public and private man, confronted contemporary observers with 'profoundly unsettling questions about the "authenticity, accountability, and intentionality"' (ibid.) of human subjects, that is, with unsettling questions as to the status, continuity and coherence of their identities.

The Discontinuity of Identity, or: Patchwork Identity

Eighteenth-century observers not only thought about the ongoing differentiation of society and social roles, they were also well aware of a split within their own selves. 'The personal Identity of Sameness', a concept defined by *The Spectator*, increasingly became a problem. The new empirical model of the mind showed that the ego, the self or identity, seemed to be discontinuous, subject to contradictory modes and not the indivisible substance held by traditional moral psychology (Dussinger, 31). The authors of the *Memoirs of Martinus Scriblerus* questioned 'how a man is conscious to himself that he is the same Individual he was twenty years ago, notwithstanding the flux state of the Particles of matter that compose his body' (*Memoirs of the Extraordinary Life*, 140), and the Earl of Shaftesbury asked 'whether the I of this instant be the same with that of any instant preceding or to come?' And again: 'That there is something undoubtedly which thinks, our very doubt itself and scrupulous thought evinces. But in what subject that thought resides, and how that subject is continued one and the same [...] this is not a matter so easily or hastily decided by those who are nice self-examiners or searchers after truth and certainty' (Shaftesbury, 275). Bishop Joseph Butler, too, questioned the new and disturbing idea 'that personality is not a permanent, but a transient thing: that it lives and dies, begins and ends continually: that no one can remain the same person two moments together, that two successive moments can be one and the same moment' (quoted in Fox, 6). Nevertheless, according to Butler, the self is able to survive through memory and history:

> Though the successive consciousnesses, which we have of our own existence, are not the same, yet are they consciousness of one and the same thing or object; of the same person, self, or living agent. The person, of whose existence the consciousness is felt now, and was felt an hour or a year ago, is discerned to be, not two persons, but one and the same person; and therefore is one and the same. (ibid.; cf. Dussinger, 35)

Whereas Butler and others presuppose an essentialist notion of identity, Defoe's narrative of the ideal tradesman puts forward a different idea. I would like to use for this the term 'patchwork identity', coined by present-day social scientists, although in a sense slightly different from their emphasis on the post-modern loss of coherence and the necessity of creative self-determination (see Keupp 1993 and 2002). In fact, the socio-genesis of self-control was a phenomenon relating to the emergence of the modern state, where physical violence as a primary means of regulating social conflicts shifted to the institutionalization of 'a social apparatus [...] in which the constraints between people [were] lastingly transformed into self-constraints' (Faller, 33–4, referring to Elias and Foucault). Self-constraint produces a sense of the self, however contested it may be.

If I am right in seeing something like patchwork identity, or at least traces of it, at work in eighteenth-century social life, then this must have consequences for our understanding of the mediation of identity as well. We should therefore look for points of fracture, for discursive incompatibilities or contradictions, for a writer's conscious or unconscious shifting from one discursive site to the next as well as for the shift among discourses in one site. In what follows, I will explore such shifts as well as civil society's attempts at regulating the discourses and the identities they produce. My first example is provided by the 1670 Quaker Trials and the Quakers' practice of 'bold speaking' as a means of appropriating the discursive site of the courtroom for the articulation of an oppositional political discourse. Then I will turn to the streets of eighteenth-century London as another material site of discourse and the Societies for the Reformation of Manners as civil agents of policing aberrant behaviour. While aiming at, in modern parlance, an internalization of surveillance as a private conscience, this inner self could also be perceived as a space of withdrawal from the very attempts at policing. In both cases, my focus will be on how these sites and their discourses were regulated, and how successful these attempts at regulation were – and could hope to be, given the inherent patchwork quality of identities.

'Bold Speaking': The 1670 Quaker Trials and the Emergence of Political Identities

As we know from contemporary courtroom dramas on TV, the participants in legal actions have to stick to certain rules and institutionalized procedures that are reiterated time and again and are thus made stable and permanent. During the period under discussion, these institutionalized rules did not only serve legal procedure but also political aims. Thus religious and political opposing groups such as the Quakers tried to subvert them by practicing what they used to call 'bold speaking' (cf. Böker 2002b). Through bold speaking they challenged not only ministers in their own pulpits[2] but also judges during examinations and trials, displaying a considerable amount of legal expertise. The Quakers thus sought to subvert the dominant rules of discourse and transform the old place of the courtroom into a new site of the public sphere (cf. Horle, 50–51; Greaves, 129 ff.; and Green, 202).

One of the bold-speaking Quakers was John Crook, whose trial account *The Cry of the Innocent for Justice* was first published in 1692. As mentioned before, the history of political struggle has been the history of the attempts made to control significant sites of assembly and spaces of discourse. This is why the Judge told him, 'Your tongue is not your own, and you must not have liberty to speak what you list' and 'we are to tell you what is law, and not you us' (Crook 1791, 153). Nevertheless, Crook succeeded in speaking boldly by invoking 'the laws of England' and referring the Judge to the Magna Carta and the Petition of Rights, King Alfred's laws, *The Mirror of Justices* and Coke's *Institutes*, so that at one

---

[2] They could be tried, however, for disrupting the routine of ministers and congregations; see Horle, 48.

point in the trial the common hangman was called in to enforce the rules of the court by means of gagging the accused.

Another example is the trial of William Penn and William Mead in 1670. After having addressed a crowd of some 100 people on Gracechurch Street, Penn and Mead were sent to Newgate for 'preaching seditiously and causing a great tumult of people [...] to be gathered together riotously and routously' (quoted in Green, 222).[3] They refused to obtain release through a payment of fines, but demanded jury trial. Right from the beginning, they refused to conform to the rules and the practices of the legal discourse. Penn argued that he was unable to remember the 26 lines of the 'Indictment *verbatim*; and therefore we desire a Copy of it, as is customary in the like occasions' (Penn 1670, 307). He began to challenge the Judge upon legal matters, asking 'upon what Law you ground my Indictment'. When the Recorder reminded him that the Law is *Lex non scripta*, the defendant, well educated in the law, explained that 'If the Common Law be so hard to be understood, it's far from being very Common: But if the Lord [Edward] *Cook*, in his Institutes, be of any consideration, he tells, That Common Law is Common Right, and that Common Right is the great Charter-Privileges'.[4] And again: 'The question is not, Whether I am guilty of this Indictment, but whether this Indictment be legal' (Penn 1670, 311). In addition, Penn repeatedly referred both the Bench and the audience to 'the Rights and Privileges of every Englishman', to the 'Ancient Fundamental Laws, which relate to Liberty and Property', and to the 'Rights and Privileges of English-men' (ibid., 314).

The Bench retorted with 'menacing Language', calling him a 'sawcy [...], an impertinent [...], a troublesome Fellow', and saying, 'You deserve to have your Tongue cut out' and 'Pull that Fellow down, pull him down' (ibid., 313–15),[5] and sending Penn and Mead to the bale dock.[6] When, in the end, the jurymen returned a verdict that Penn was guilty of nothing but 'speaking in *Gracious-street*', the Bench began to threaten the 12 jurymen, calling their foreman, Bushell, 'an impudent canting Fellow' (ibid., 316). Penn, in turn, instantly reminded the jury: '*You are* Englishmen, *mind your Priviledge, give not away your Right*' (ibid., 317). They were told 'not to be dismiss'd till we have a Verdict that the Court

---

3   Unauthorized religious meetings could be prosecuted as riots; three or more persons gathered, involved in violence or intending to commit a violent act, were said to constitute a riot; see ibid., 47.

4   Penn 1670, 311. Starling's own comment: 'Now the Common Law is Common Right, or *Lex Rationis*, imprinted in every man's understanding' (quoted in Green, 223, n. 101).

5   See Sir Samuel Starling's version of the trial account, and the Mayor ordering the gaoler to 'Stop his mouth; [...] bring Fetters, and stake him to the Ground' (Starling, 28). See also his comment: 'Upon this Mr. *Penn* was very silent and quiet, although nothing was done to him' (ibid., 29). In his answer to Starling, Penn speaks of the judges' 'Billingsgate Rhetorick' (ibid., 8).

6   '*Penn* made such an uncivil noise, that the Court could not give the *Jury* the Charge; he was therefore put into the *Bail-Dock*, which stands even with the Bar, and the Prisoners might hear the Charge as well as a Prisoner might hear at the Bar' (ibid., 21).

will accept; and you shall be lockt up, without Meat, Drink, Fire, and Tobacco; […] we will have a Verdict, by the help of God, or you shall starve for it'. And, as the Observer remarks, the 'Court swore several Persons to keep the Jury all night without Meat, Drink, Fire, or any other Accomodation: They had not so much as a Chamber-pot, tho' desired' and to 'bring in another Verdict, or you shall starve; and I will have you carted about the City, as in *Edward* III's time' (ibid., 315–19).[7] The jury foreman, Edward Bushell, refused to pay his fine and was jailed, but after two months the Court of Common Pleas issued a writ of *habeas corpus* to set him and the others free. A few months later, Lord Chief Justice Vaughan 'finally laid the problem' of fining the jurors to rest (Green, 237), ruling that a judge was not allowed to punish or threaten a jury that arrived at a different conclusion than the Bench, thereby establishing the principle of non-coercion. In this case we can witness the interdependence of legal discourse, the sites of discourse and the emergence or consolidation of a non-hegemonic identity in public.

Crook's and Penn's trial accounts were reprinted during the 1790s at a time of a growing repression of the radical supporters of a democratic change in society. The government was alarmed at the proliferation of the public debate over parliamentary reform. After the 1792 proclamation for preventing seditious meetings and writings and the suspension of the *habeas corpus* in May 1794, the radical leaders Thomas Hardy, J. Horne Tooke and John Thelwall were arrested and put on trial. As Christoph Houswitschka (2004) has shown at length, Hardy, Tooke and Thelwall likewise used the courtroom as a site of the public sphere for debating legal and political matters. As there was a widespread interest in the history of opposition, Crook's *The Cry of the Innocent for Justice* was reprinted in 1791[8] and *The People's Ancient and Just Liberties Asserted* was reissued under Penn's name by the Sheffield Constitutional Society[9] with a motto from James Thomson's poem *Liberty* (1735) on the title page. Taking their oppositional strategy from the Quakers over a hundred years earlier but shifting the medium, the radicals used print as a site of discourse to articulate their subversive ideas and politically oppositional identities.

---

[7]   The members of the jury were fined 40 marks. In a later trial, a case of two Nottinghamshire Appeals in 1676, the jury was unable to find a unanimous verdict. As one of the four jurymen, disagreeing with the rest, was taken ill and was in need of some refreshment, Justice Whaley told them: 'If they did not agree, they should be kept there till they died, and as one of them died, the Court would choose another, till they were all dead' (quoted in Braithwaite 1962/1964, 226).

[8]   McCalman, 309–33. In the 1791 edition of *The Design of Christianity, with other Books, Epistles, and Manuscripts*, 'The Cry of the Innocent' has a separate title page dated '1790'.

[9]   Penn 1794. The Society for Constitutional Information did not have local branches, but other Constitutional Societies corresponded with London; see Edward P. Thompson, 115, n. 3.

The Policing of Public Behaviour and the Emergence of a Private Conscience: The Society for the Reformation of Manners

At the beginning of the eighteenth century and with the increasing commercialization of leisure,[10] the 'great wen' of London, containing at least one-tenth of the national population, seemed to be, according to Defoe, a 'monstrous' city; some years later Henry Fielding called the metropolis 'a vast wood or forest, in which a thief may harbour with as great security, as wild beasts do in the deserts of Africa or Arabia' (McLynn, 2–3). Indeed, London, just like the rest of the country, lacked a central police and law enforcement was at best rudimentary. In 1718 the City Marshall pointed out the

> general complaint of the taverns, the coffee-houses, the shop-keepers and others, that their customers are afraid when it is dark to come to their houses and shops for fear that their hats and wigs should be snatched from their heads or their swords taken from their sides, or that they may be blinded, knocked down, cut or stabbed; nay, the coaches cannot secure them, but they are likewise cut and robbed in the public streets &c. by which means the traffic of the City is much interrupted. (Quoted in Tobias, 26; cf. McLynn, 17)

When, 30 years later, Fielding complained about criminal gangs – 'they are armed with every Method of evading the Law' (Henry Fielding 1988, 170) – the undermining of orthodox certainties during the struggle over the true faith in Europe and the revival of skepticism had led to a general legitimization crisis. Its centre was the rejection of all teleological, dispositional accounts of assent as the foundation of moral knowledge and the assumption of innate dispositions. The theory of a natural conscience was replaced, as James Tully remarked, 'by an account of the conscience as a completely non-dispositional power of judgement, and of the mind as a blank tablet, indifferent to true and false, good and evil' (16). According to John Locke, ideas and dispositions were a product of custom and education that had to be grounded in the formation of mental and physical habits or in training by continuous repetition as a means of habit formation (ibid., 56). Nevertheless, crime, sin and moral transgression could still be considered interrelated manifestations of the same innate and intentional 'aberration', 'mingled into one and same notion of an offence against the peace of the king, his crown and his dignity, that is against God' (Lamoine, 13).[11] Criminals' accounts of their motivation or, indeed, their awareness of agency and responsibility could vary greatly. Thus a prisoner at the bar of the Old Bailey would occasionally tell the court that 'he never was addicted to Drunkenness, Profane Swearing, Whoring,

---

[10] See Plumb, and Hoppit on the pursuit of pleasure that 'had emerged as a particularly distinctive feature of English society after the restoration to become a powerful motor of change around 1700'; see also Neumann.

[11] See Herrup, 102–23, for the overlapping of the categories of sin and crime. Cf. also Burtt, 45.

Gaming, and such-like Debaucheries, and could not tell how he came to take up this wicked Trade of Thieving' (*Old Bailey Proceedings Online*, Ordinary's Account, 21 April 1714.). But a second one knew that his love of 'jovial Company, Drinking, and profane Talk' and his being 'engag'd in Debaucheries or Idleness' had been stepping stones to all kinds of crime (ibid., 25 May 1723); and to a third one, to be 'a grievous Sinner, a great Swearer and Drinker, an Adulterer, a Prophane and Lewd Wretch' also meant to be 'a sworn Enemy to those who were employ'd in the Reformation of Manners' (ibid., 11 August 1703). If misconduct and crime were the results of education and habit rather than an innate disposition toward evil, they could be counteracted by close self-monitoring. This was the rationale of the reformation of manners.

In the past, the ecclesiastical courts (the 'bawdy courts') had exercised jurisdiction over all sorts of religious and moral misbehaviour, supervising the morals of the community, instigating cases on defamation, slander, unseemly behaviour in church, working or rowdy drinking on a Sunday, simony, heresy, witchcraft, usury, adultery, homosexuality, brothel-keeping, fornication, incest and bearing a bastard (see Outhwaite). When at the end of the seventeenth century the decline of the ecclesiastical courts became more rapid, moral regulation was being transferred to Quarter sessions and local courts. The control of vice, however, was since the 1690s taken over by the Societies for the Reformation of Manners,[12] which supervised the material sites of discourse and gave 'a Check to the *Open Lewdneß* that was acted in many of our Streets' (Woodward, 7). The idea was to go 'about into Streets, Markets, and other Public Places' (ibid., 21) and purge these spaces of transgressive social behaviour, and to change individual behaviour as well as collective identities.

The first society formed during the 1690s in the Tower hamlets drew up a formal agreement 'upon the best methods for putting the law in execution against houses of lewdness and debauchery and also against drunkenness, swearing, cursing and profanation of the Lord's day' (Curtis and Speck, 46). Acting as a kind of 'social police' (Linebaugh, 58), they resolved 'to inform the magistrates of swearers, drunkards, profaners of the Lord's day, and of lewd houses' (Curtis and Speck, 46). They were told to roam the material sites of discourse, that is, 'to go out into the Streets and Markets, and public places on purpose, and to observe the people's behaviour there' (quoted in Burtt, 43). The strategies of the reform societies ranged from surveillance of special meeting places to informing the authorities, from attempts at having temptations like theatres, alehouses, fairs, animal sports or bawdy and molly houses suppressed to providing good examples and private admonition. They also made use of the printing press, issuing propaganda pamphlets as well as printed booklets of arrest warrants. Since every English subject had the right to prosecute criminal offenders, these print products

---

[12]   See Curtis and Speck, and Isaacs. For the wider cultural contexts see Burtt, and Barker-Benfield.

enabled the upright citizen to identify and report prostitutes, drunkards, gamblers, blasphemers and other offenders. As Josiah Woodward remarked,

> in the little Book, call'd, *A Help to Reformation*, [...] Magistrates have *Forms of Warrants*, [...] Inferior Officers have Instructions laid before them [...] And Private Persons have *Prudential Rules* for the Giving of Informations [...]. I have likewise, *Sir*, sent you some *Blank Warrants* for Particular Offences, which those that give Informations are to keep by them, and to fill them up when they have any Informations to give against any prophane and vicious Persons, with the Offenders Names, Offences, Places of Abode, &. and to carry them thus filled up to the Magistrates. (19–20)

Details about the arrests and prosecutions are included in the 'Black Lists' and later on from annual accounts appended to the sermons by members of the Society. The appendix of Edward Lord's *A Sermon Preached to the Societies for Reformation of Manners* (1724), that is, 'The Thirtieth Account of the Progress made in the Cities of London and Westminster, and Places adjacent, By the Societies for Promoting a Reformation of Manners; By Furthering the Execution of Laws against Prophaneness and Immorality, and other Christian Methods', tells the reader that the societies have 'in Pursuance of their Design, from the First of December 1723, to the first of December 1724, prosecuted divers sorts of Offenders', including 'Lewed and Disorderly Practices' (1,951), 'Keeping of Bawdy and Disorderly Houses' (29), 'Exercising their Trades or Ordinary Callings on the Lord's Day' (600), 'Prophane Swearing and Cursing' (108), 'Drunkenness' (12), 'Common Gamesters and their Associates' (21) and 'Keeping Common Gaming Houses' (2). 'The Total Numbers of Persons Prosecuted by the Societies, in and near London only, for Debauchery and Prophaneness, for 33 Years last past, are calculated at Eighty Nine Thousand Three Hundred Ninty Three 89,393' (ibid.).

Daniel Defoe, among others, was well aware of the public sphere as a meeting point of conflicting discourses. In his *Reformation of Manners. A Satyr, Vae Vobis Hypcocrite* (1702), he points to 'The mercenary Scouts in every Street', informers representing the hegemonic ideas of a masculine elite setting out to reform the public behaviour of ordinary people. The upper and the propertied urban classes are left more or less unmolested: '[...] if you lash a Strumpet of the Town, / She only smarts for want of Half a Crown: / Your annual lists of criminals appear, / But no Sir Harry or Sir Charles is here' (quoted in Curtis and Speck, 63).

It has been suggested by historians that the campaign for the reformation of manners aimed at a more 'tight control over the unruly forces of the market' (Barker-Benfield, 57) in a concern for a severe and effective labour discipline and the regulation of all sorts of diversions (Malcolmson, 89ff). The consequences for the individual self and identity are obvious. Thus, to give an example, vice and lewdness, and especially profanation of the Lord's day, were considered an 'offence against God and religion'; according to William Blackstone, 'the keeping one day in seven holy [...] is of admirable service to the state [...]. It humanizes by the help of conversation and society the manners of the lower classes [...]; it enables the industrious workman to pursue his occupation in the ensuing week with health and cheerfuless' (Blackstone, IV, 63). Keeping the Lord's day emerges here not only as a spiritual and moral obligation but also as economic prudence. Apart from 'humanizing' the lower classes, observing the religious command against gambling, drinking and whoring will save not only one's soul but also one's assets, for 'what the expensive Vices draw after them, is the Reason that Taxes seem to be so great a Burthen, that Trade [...] languishes, your Markets want Money [...] and your Prisons are crowded with Debtors' (John Disney quoted in Burtt, 51). The aim is thus to control not only individual behaviour but also the forces of the marketplace.

'Humanizing' the lower classes through information given to the magistrates by the exclusively male members of the Societies for Reformation of Manners was considered to be an effective means to change a person's moral dispositions and inner sense of self. Thus, Blackstone remarked, referring to an older statute: 'Drunkenness is [...] punished by [...] sitting six hours in the stocks, by which time the statute presumes the offender will have regained his senses' (Blackstone, IV, 64). Punishment in the form of public display is supposed to shame the offender into regaining his sense of proper public behaviour along with his senses. Yet there is also the possibility that in his inmost being he might still be of the opinion that he is the victim of social and economic discrimination. The public stocks thus can be seen as the meeting point of conflicting discourses which define and redefine identity through an interplay between the self and the other. This interplay is said to be healing the offender's moral 'sense', but could also be productive of a private, resistant sense of selfhood.

In another case, a political one, a Joseph Carter was sentenced 'to walk round the four Courts in Westminster-Hall, with a Paper on his Forehead, denoting his Offence, and to suffer one Month's Imprisonment' (cf. McDowell 1998, 69, n. 7). In a scene of public shaming that recalls Eleanor Cobham's punishment in Shakespeare's *Henry VI, Part 2*, the offense is here doubly inscribed, on a piece of paper and on the criminal's forehead. The choice of the forehead as a physical site of exposure is telling: what might be considered the original seat of identity is here covered with the magistrate's written verdict, an official document that suppresses and overwrites the offender's own 'text' or version of his story. Taken together, both texts could stand for the competing or contradictory discourses of the emerging bourgeois public sphere.

We know that reform societies remained an important factor in British civil society until the end of the nineteenth century (see Innes), although they never really succeeded in achieving their stated aims. I would argue that this, too, points to the simultaneity and persistence of altogether different and competing discourses of gender, domesticity, plebeian culture, nation and so on, which could not be streamlined into a unified, regulated collective identity. Rather, we would do well to acknowledge the discursive hybridity of selves at the intersection of different material and medial sites of discourse, in the eighteenth century as in our own time.

Chapter 8
Constructions of Political Identity:
The Example of Impeachments

Anna-Christina Giovanopoulos

Traditional media such as sermons, oral communication, rumours and visual displays have always influenced political views (see Tim Harris, 135), but during the later part of the seventeenth century printed media came to play a vital role in shaping political consciousness. This article investigates processes of identity constructions at the interface between politics, law and journalism, focusing on the period between 1678 (Exclusion Crisis) and 1714/1715 (accession of the Hanoverians). In the first section, the concept of the public sphere will be related to the role of print in shaping politics. Subsequently, the emergence of the Whigs and Tories will be addressed in order to contextualize constructive modes of collective identity formation in both the legal and the journalistic public spheres. It will be argued that these processes were characterized by conflicting negotiations that involved the need to invalidate negative ideological ascriptions. In contrast to continental conditions, however, negotiations of identity in England were not restricted to those in the seats of power. In other words, they were not conducted exclusively in Parliament, but also outside Parliament, in public. A representative sample of publications written in the wake of three impeachments will be included, and my arguments will be based on the cases against Danby, beginning in 1678, against Somers in 1701 and finally against Harley (Earl of Oxford) in 1715.

The theory of the public sphere as developed by Habermas has met with considerable criticism.[1] However, as Mark Knights points out, some elements of the model can prove useful, especially when concentrating on what Habermas 'might enable us to do in terms of reconciling historical and literary publics' (Knights, 13). Therefore, Knights suggests treating the public as a fiction that is both constructed and continually re-negotiated through print and other media. By pursuing the top-down approach, I am not negating the importance of other media such as sermons and processions in the formation of political identities, nor the role of the people in shaping the political agenda,[2] but for the purposes of this paper I am focusing on parliamentary proceedings as represented in the publications of

---

[1]   See Isabel Karremann's 'Introduction' to this volume for an overview of this criticism.

[2]   See Tim Harris for an investigation of popular politics.

trial reports and pamphlets and on their role in transferring political discussions to an audience outside Parliament.

Politicians of all political persuasions used the public sphere by means of printed material (Müllenbrock, 26). Thus, the public sphere became a 'representative arena for interaction, where the '"political nation" was able to promote its own image' and where individuals attempted to construct and negotiate both their private and public or collective identities (ibid., 27). The circulation processes worked in two ways, and public debate influenced the political decision makers. As Tim Harris postulates, the key themes of Restoration politics were on the agenda not because the elites thought they were important but 'because they were issues of real concern in Restoration society' in general (151).[3] Away from the confines of Parliament with its rules of discourse, parties could even use the public sphere 'as a lever against their respective opponents' and test the popularity of their views, so that more people could participate in political discussions (Müllenbrock, 27).

Thus, one aspect that Habermas does correctly acknowledge is the importance of the new media and, regardless of when pre-publication censorship was abolished, it remains a feasible thesis that the emergence of a public sphere was vitally linked to the print media that made arguments available to a wider audience. However, in contrast to Habermas's contention (based on an analysis especially of journals and moral weeklies) that enlightened individuals entered into a rational discourse, empirical data such as pamphlets show that political propaganda did not appeal to its audience in an objective manner; these publications were argumentative and polemical, designed to appeal to their readers' emotions and shape their collective identities, with the aim of creating an increasingly stable group identity.[4] These findings are corroborated by research which proves that English (legal) culture was 'dominated by dissent', even though the appeal to common concerns, such as the ancient constitution or the rule of law, might lead to a consensual reading.[5] From a formal point of view, as might be expected, political and legal arguments are shaped by the normative rules of discourse, especially in the space of the courtroom. However, the form obfuscates the underlying real opposition between the emerging groups of the Whigs and Tories, whose political attitudes will be outlined in the following section.

The Succession to the English Throne, 1678–1701, and the Emergence of the Whigs and the Tories

Research has shown the importance of language in the process of identity formation: the identities of the parties were 'shaped and disseminated throughout the country'

---

[3]   The issues were 'the threat of political insurrection at home, the tensions over religious dissent, concerns about the abuse of law, fears about the standing army, concerns about the regulation of economy' (Tim Harris, 151–2).

[4]   On the role of partisanship in shaping identities, see Knights.

[5]   See Böker 2002a, 207–8, and Böker 2002b, 35.

(Knights, 7) through (polemical) discourse, thereby also reaching those who were removed from the centre in both regional and social terms.[6] A proliferation of publications, some of which will be investigated below, transcended the boundaries of time and place and helped to define the concepts of the Whigs and the Tories. These emerged in the period 1678–1683, during the Exclusion Crisis, amidst power struggles between king and Parliament over the succession of James II. The acrimonious battles fought in Parliament and in the law courts, marked by the impeachment of Danby (1678/1679) and the Rye House Plot of 1683, however, also resulted in the deaths of some of the political leaders,[7] thus proving the problems of claiming an assertive political identity that challenged the authority of the king.

A new phase in the development of the political identities of Whigs and Tories began in 1688/1689, during the Glorious Revolution, once more over debates on the succession to the throne. William of Orange received an invitation from leading politicians, purportedly to help strengthen England's law, liberty and religion (Nenner, 153), the three favourite concepts of the time, which, however, were interpreted differently by the Whigs and the Tories.[8] Perhaps the most important difference between the collective identities was the stance towards stability. The Tories defined the concept in hereditary terms, favouring the Stuarts, whereas the Whigs put their emphasis on Parliament, the Protestant faith and legal liberty (Owen, 111). However, constitutional continuity was proclaimed by both parties, even though the key questions were not settled (Martyn Thompson, 23–6). As Howard Nenner puts it, the effects of 1688/1689 did not become immediately apparent owing to the 'determination with which Whigs and Tories chose to avoid rather than confront these issues' (253), which proves that on the surface, consent, or at least an effort to avoid a repetition of the turmoil of civil war, was a shared concept (see also Weil, 6).

In 1701 the issue of succession re-emerged. While in 1688 there had been little hope of dealing with the problem in Parliament, by 1700 this forum was considered the place where such topics could be decided (Nenner, 228). The new Act of Settlement, which strengthened the role of Parliament, conferred the English crown on the House of Hanover, while the king had to agree for some of his advisors (amongst them Somers) to be impeached in 1701 (ibid., 256). These impeachments led to the emergence of fairly stable parties for the first time. As the Whigs saw themselves under massive attacks, they rallied around their leaders and had to define their identity under pressure while defending themselves in court against the Tories.[9] Electoral results and practical exigencies led to a climate during Queen Anne's reign (1701–1714) that was more congenial to the Tories (who won the 1710 elections), while the accession of the Hanoverians led to the

---

[6]   For electioneering, see Speck 1970; see also Knights, 5.

[7]   These were William Lord Russell, Algernon Sidney and the Duke of Essex; the Earl of Shaftesbury was exiled (see Nenner, 147).

[8]   Another aspect was the interpretation of contracts (see Martyn P. Thompson).

[9]   See Speck 1994, 15; Steffen, 51 and 71; Holmes, 342.

rise of Whig power, which they used to attack their opponents: in 1714, the Tory leaders Harley and Bolingbroke were impeached.

Assuming that impeachment trials are the focal point where political identities were defined in a competitive environment, the following section will be devoted to analyzing the arguments concerning private and public selves, as voiced in texts relating to the trials against Danby, Somers and Harley. I will first summarize the three cases, then I will discuss identity constructions, and in a final section I will arrive at a thesis to account for the historical developments of political identity formation.

The Impeachments: Danby, Somers and Harley

Impeachments are located at the interface between law and politics. Generally, they were directed against prominent advisors of the monarch. Therefore, politicians were accused not necessarily as specific individuals but in their function as politicians. Impeachments were used sparingly after the fifteenth century until the mid-seventeenth century, when they re-emerged, thus proving their pivotal role in the power games between Parliament and king and, in the early eighteenth century, between the parties.

As long as the king did not need Parliament, he could protect his favourites against accusations, as can be seen in the case against Thomas Osborne, Earl of Danby, initiated in 1678. Here, Charles II used his right of prorogation several times, and after 1681 there were no elections until his death. On 21 December 1678, Articles of Impeachment against Danby were read in Parliament. He was accused of having assumed royal power by negotiating in 'matters of Peace and War with Forreign [sic] Princes and Embassadors [sic]', by-passing Parliament (Leeds and Tewksbury, 1). Secondly, he had allegedly tried 'to subvert the Antient [sic] Form of Government, and to introduce an Arbitrary and Tyrannical way of Government' (*England and Wales*, 6). Furthermore, Danby's religious identity was invoked, as he was accused of having supported Roman Catholicism, implying support of a foreign authority and autocratic government (Leeds and Tewksbury, 3). The relationship between the House of Commons and the king worsened, and the Commons decided to criticize the king as much as they dared by thematizing the 'Irregularity and Illegality of the Pardon, and the dangerous Consequences of granting Pardons to Persons impeached' (*England and Wales*, 10).

This case became notorious and was re-evaluated in 1695 by an anonymous editor when the Licensing Act lapsed (cf. *England and Wales*). The re-publication is proof of interest in royal conduct and in impeachments in particular, at a time when King William III saw himself increasingly under attack:

> The Right of Impeachments by the House of Commons, being a Matter wherein the People of England are so highly concerned, it is hoped it may not be thought unseasonable to publish the ensuing Collections relating thereunto, out of several scattered Papers formerly published, and not at present to be recovered without

difficulty; and the rather, because in this Case were discussed several Points of no small Moment; As the King's Power of pardoning the Person impeached; the sequestring him from Parliament, and imprisoning his Person, and also the Right of the Bishops to sit and vote in Capital Cases. (*England and Wales*, 3)

What also becomes evident is that in 1695 the editor could condemn King Charles II by characterizing his continued prorogations as 'according to the Practice of that Time' (ibid., 29), thereby implying that such behaviour was not tolerated at the end of the century. Thus, political identities had changed and self-assurance had grown, as is also proven by the next case.

Parliament explicitly asked King William not to grant any pardons to the accused members of the Whig Junto in 1701. The impeachment began officially on 1 April; the 14 articles against the Whig Junto, or specifically against Somers, can be subsumed under the following four categories: foreign policy, constitutional law, economy and (financial) corruption (Hargrave, 345–55). The last article, which succinctly summarized the opposing ideologies of the Whigs and the Tories, exemplifies how leading concepts were used to create a negative identity of the opponent. Referring to the Magna Carta and to 'divers good Statutes of this Realm' (ibid., 335), Somers was accused of having abused his power by giving 'divers Arbitrary and Illegal Orders, in Subversion of the Laws and Statutes of this Realm', and usurping an 'Arbitrary and Illegal Power' (ibid.). The article also mentioned actions that were 'highly dangerous to the legal Constitution of this Kingdom, and absolutely destructive to the Property of the Subject' (ibid., 355). These are leading concepts that were shared by Whigs and Tories, but they were interpreted in different ways: the Whigs assumed that the best way to protect English interests was to end the war, thus diminishing the financial burden, while the Tories believed that English interest lay in supporting the allies and fending off French expansionist policies (cf. Hargrave, Art. 5, 349). Somers reacted by denying all charges, without offering a counter-image; as the accusers from the House of Commons declined to attend the trial, Somers was found not guilty.

The articles of impeachment against Harley in 1715[10] can be grouped in the same way as the articles against Somers. Articles 1–7 were concerned with peace negotiations and included the particularly problematic secrecy agenda: Harley was accused of having acted without consulting the allies (Articles 1–3), and Article 6 could be interpreted as if Harley had assumed royal power (*The Whole Proceedings*, 55). In contrast, answering Article 11, Harley claimed that he had 'always acted by the immediate Directions and Commands of the late Queen, and never offended against any known Law', implying that he was not guilty of high treason (ibid., 60–61). Articles 12 and 13 were concerned with trade; Article 14 dealt with foreign policies once more, ceding Sicily to the duke of Savoy, disadvantaging the allied Austrian monarchy (ibid., 64). A similar accusation

---

[10]   *The Whole Proceedings against Robert Earl of Oxford and Earl of Mortimer* (London, 1715).

had been levelled against the Whig Junto, which proves that this was one of the standard offences incorporated into articles of impeachment.

Spaces, Mediatization and Identity Constructions

As Stallybrass and White point out, '[d]iscursive space is never completely independent of social place and the formation of new kinds of speech can be traced through the emergence of new public sites of discourse and the transformation of old ones' (80). Each '"site of assembly" constitutes a nucleus of material and cultural conditions which regulate what may and may not be said, who may speak, how people may communicate and what importance must be given to what is said' (ibid.). Two spaces will be considered, the legal space of Parliament and the journalistic space.

First, the legal spaces of Parliament and of the courtroom determined the rules of discourse. The publication of texts relating to impeachments show that the House of Commons and the House of Lords, as well as the individuals against whom impeachment proceedings were instituted, jealously guarded their perceived rights; 'tradition', and thus stability and continuity, were key concepts that determined ideal political identities. Two main findings emerge from the analysis of impeachments when they are considered as part of the internal legal culture.[11] Firstly, specific formulas were used in the prosecution and the defence arguments (with the latter often being mere replies in the negative), and secondly, only particular types of transgressions in connection to political conduct were mentioned. Reactions and counter-reactions created irreconcilable narratives, as the accused had to invalidate negative ascriptions of being the transgressive 'other' by using an alternative construct. Thematically, priority was given to the conduct of foreign policies, especially in relation to warfare and treaties, as well as to internal matters, that is, rewards and remunerations. Parliament increasingly criticized the institution of placemen and pensioners who were (at times wrongly assumed) to ensure that the legislature voted according to court policies (Holmes, 223).

As far as identity constructions are concerned, it becomes apparent, especially from the 1701 impeachment, that identity attributions were based on exclusion rather than inclusion, which subsequently led to the dissolution of consensual relations. While common ideals can be established on the surface, the underlying values that formed a politician's identity were very different. That language could be manipulated was criticized by contemporaries, who even provided their readers with polemical glossaries to interpret contentious terms according to their political leanings and to teach 'the true Intent of these few *significant* Words' (Hoadly, 2; original emphasis).[12]

---

[11]   The concept of internal and external legal culture is discussed, for example, in Friedman 1975.

[12]   Among the words explained are 'Hereditary Right' and '*Men of Republican Principles*', through which the '*Revolution,* and *Protestant Succession*' could be allegedly attacked without fear of repercussions (Hoadly, 2; original emphasis).

The antagonistic model can also be applied to the formation of collective identities: the procedures in Parliament were characterized by the extremely obstructive behaviour of the Lords and Commons, who, despite their projected self-image as rational protectors of rights, were reluctant to deviate from their positions.[13] In the example of Somers, the House of Lords decided on the date of the trial but took a vote in the absence of the accusers from the Commons and exonerated the accused (Hargrave, 377–8). It has to be noted that the impartial mode of discourse may have been the ideal propagated in weeklies and that such competitive practices were criticized. The very nature of politics demanded an antagonistic exchange, but rather than invalidating the thesis of an antagonistic relationship, contemporary critique can be interpreted as upholding an ideal, namely the eighteenth-century vision of the disinterested, polite gentleman in contrast to the actual political mode. Both the Commons and the Lords subscribed to a positive model of politicians on the surface, but in actual practice their value systems, which were intimately linked to power claims, did not lead to harmonious relations between the Houses. In electioneering, the strategies by their very nature are antagonistic, and a common technique was to invert one's own, positively connoted political identity. As Jonathan Swift wrote, a '*Whig* forms an Image of a *Tory*, just after the things he most abhors, and that Image serves to represent the whole Body' (*The Examiner* 1.34, 15–22 March 1710–1711: 1).

Political actions are therefore considered as manifestations of particular identity constructions that are to be seen relationally and as antagonistically evolving from discursive identity offers. Such identity offers were mediated through increasingly complex narrations, which remained open to negotiations and to subscriptions by representatives of different political convictions, especially when the second space, which was not subject to the narrow rules of Parliament, was involved. This was the journalistic space, which was created through mediatized versions of impeachments, either in the form of reports from Parliament and trial reports or, often, as polemical pamphlets and books.[14] Apart from the ministers' legally relevant conduct, which represented political convictions and values, their private conduct was also left open to discussion in pamphlets. Consequently, the impeachment proceedings were deliberately retold in the journalistic public sphere to rectify identity constructs and to find a forum to revise rulings from the parliamentary sphere of influence. Such publications pre-supposed that their readership possessed a certain degree of knowledge, and the progress of printing

---

[13]　Just before the trial of Somers, the Commons sent an indignant message to the Lords, stating amongst other things that they were not prepared to participate in the proceedings until Lord Haversham made '*Reparation for the great Indignity offer'd to them at the free Conference*' (Hargrave, 375–6, original emphasis). The Lords claimed not to understand what the Commons mean by 'that Resentment they speak of in their Message' (ibid., 376), and the matter was not resolved.

[14]　See the pro-Danby *An Impartial State* (1679) and its anti-Danby answer, *An Examination of the Impartial State* (1680).

led to the emergence of a dialogic culture where one could use print to answer publications from the previous day.

These discussions, however, proved to be controversial, as various attempts to manage the print media show. Roger L'Estrange, Surveyor of the Press since 1662, strongly believed in the power of written words in inciting the rebellious potential of the readers (Raymond, 324). But even after the Restoration, control was not completely re-established, and with the temporary lapse of the Licencing Act in 1679 during the Exclusion Crisis, printed publications increased in quantity and were circulated not only among the literate but also among the illiterate (Pincus, 807–34; Love, 203–7). As censorship proved to be difficult to maintain, the seemingly dangerous potential of the press was countered by the government through the active use of the medium. The licensor of the press, Roger L'Estrange, wrote in the *Observator* 1 (13 April 1681): 'the press had "made 'um [the people] Mad" and "the Press must set 'um Right again"' (quoted in Tim Harris, 134).

The effect of this co-option was a consolidation of the press (cf. Raymond, 323), and, as Kathleen Wilson points out, the political impact of the press 'lay in its ability to organize knowledge, shape expectations, mobilize identities and proffer ideals, perspectives and attitudes through which politics could be interpreted' (53–4). In this journalistic public sphere, new rules of discourse emerged. Apart from political interests, the private conduct of both the accused individual and his family was scrutinized, thus extending identity constructions beyond the collective political to the private sphere. In connection with the campaign against the Whigs in 1681, deliberate exclusion practices were used relating to Stephen College (cf. Weber, 172–208). Another such strategy was to link the Whigs with licentious behaviour, an example being the trial against Ford Lord Grey of Werk (1682),[15] and these practices added to negative identity constructions of the Whigs. Clearly, in this context, constructions of identity also occurred in an antagonistic mode, with the ultimate aim of gaining the support of an arbiter. One of the most successful propaganda pieces was Charles II's *Declaration To All His Loving Subjects, Touching the Causes and Reasons that Moved Him to Dissolve the Two Last Parliaments* in April 1681, which was instrumental in swaying the masses to become loyal to the king once more (Tim Harris, 134 and 147–8).

There was the tendency towards a more emotional discourse, which employed persuasive strategies mixing allegedly factual accounts with polemics to denounce the opponent and to seek, as in courtroom practice, the approval of readers as judge and jury. 'Each side represented the other through a set of imagined characteristics but also through different representational prisms that created very different, often

---

[15]   'The Trial of Ford Lord Grey of Werk, Robert Charnock, Anne Charnock, David Jones, Frances Jones, and Rebecca Jones […]', in *A complete collection of state-trials, and proceedings for high treason, and other crimes and misdemeanours; from the reign of King Richard II to the end of the reign of King George I* (London, 1720), 15–514. This trial was fictionalized by Aphra Behn in her *Love-Letters Between a Nobleman and his Sister* (1684–1687).

conflicting, claims about what was "fact" and "true"' (Knights, 8). Partisanship led to different interpretations of language, a development which Jonathan Swift, but also Daniel Defoe, saw negatively because they both supported the ideal of a shared language, according to the consensual model (ibid., 9). In contrast, partisanship meant the struggle over defining concepts. Each side claimed to provide the best version of the common good, even to the extent that party loyalty influenced everything. Without problematizing the question of 'truth' and 'reality', but believing in their existence, Henry St John, the later Viscount Bolingbroke, wrote in 1709: 'no man looks on things as they really are, but sees them through that glass which party holds up to him'.[16]

What emerges further on, especially during and after the first decade of the eighteenth century, is that identities were constructed independently outside the courtroom and that journalistic media demanded sanctions well in advance, as seen in the case against Harley in 1715. In anticipation of future developments, punishments exceeding legal provisions were demanded. One cause lies in the growth of the press, which was linked to an increased politicization of the public. It is due to this that the conduct of the Tories was more widely and critically scrutinized by the public than the actions of the Whig Junto had been over a decade before. Both cases dealt with similar accusations, yet led to different public reactions. For instance, the peace negotiations with France during the War of the Spanish Succession found much more interest than the negotiations to end the Nine Years' War at the end of the seventeenth century. In this respect, Arthur Mainwaring's 1711 poem 'An Excellent New Song, Called Mat's Peace, Or, The Downfall of Trade', set to the melody of 'Greensleeves', is a typical example. Comparing the impeachment of Somers and the stance towards Harley, the poem contains the line: 'If that Treaty then did Impeachment require / Sure this calls at least for the Rope or the Fire' (Mainwaring, 512, ll. 59–60), and Parliament was asked to act accordingly (ibid., 513, ll. 75–6 and 78–9).

Historical Development of Collective Identity Constructions: Phases

The focus of this paper was identity constructions at the interface of law, politics and journalism, and it was argued that identity is considered to be a discursive, fluid construct based on circulation processes. To start with, identity constructions were questioned, defined and re-defined in the legal discourse, and trial publications served as the medium to negotiate between the internal and external legal structures in an attempt to achieve political and social stability, but also, especially when the censorship system was temporarily out of order, to persuade the readers to follow alternative interpretations.

One result of the impeachments during the Exclusion Crisis was the stabilization of royal power and the failure of the Whigs to define their identities. The collective

---

[16]   *Camden* Miscellany, 26 (H.T. Dickinson [ed.]), 'Letters of Henry St John', Cam. Soc., 4th series, vol. 14 (Cambridge 1975), 147, quoted in Knights, 8.

concept of contractual relationships that overrode the doctrines of divine right and passive obedience continued to be of importance, but its supporters became marginalized. The supporters of Exclusion Crisis ideals re-emerged during the Glorious Revolution and defined themselves, by now in more consensual terms that could find assent among a wider political public, turning away from radical Whig positions. Political identities, however, remained fluid and did not determine votes and actions along party lines.

It is therefore interesting to note the influence of foreign politics on domestic identity constructions, because it was over secret negotiations and partition treaties or peace treaties that Whigs and Tories clashed. It took the hostile environment of Tory attacks on the Whigs from the late seventeenth century onward, in particular the impeachment trials of 1701, to create a climate conducive to the formation of relatively stable political identities. In contrast to the Exclusion Crisis, there might not have been as many deaths and convictions, but the parliamentary and journalistic arenas were used to negotiate identity offers and to display a firm stance in a process of differentiation. As far as political power and influence are concerned, the Whigs lost, but they came back with a vengeance in 1714 and turned their attention to the peace treaty of Utrecht[17] to indict the Tory leaders. When comparing the two periods, it becomes obvious that the idea of political strife and factions contravened the ideal of dispassionate debate, but that, once issues were at stake, the standardized discourse only narrowly hid dislike and very real oppositions. As David Zaret has shown, these ideal identity constructions were often propagated by eighteenth-century philosophers whose 'idealized descriptions of critical uses of public reason' (Zaret, 16–17) served a self-promoting function. Guy Miège's assessment (in connection with the impeachments of 1701) that '[...] the Differences which have happened between the two Houses of Parliament in the Course of Impeachments, have proceeded more from the Temper of some leading Men on each Side than the Nature of the Impeachments themselves' (Miège, 66–7) is true insofar as the impeachments were an instrument, reflecting power relations, which were used to attack members of the other party (that is, their collective identities); the nature of these attacks, however, was determined by the opposing political identities of society at large. There were shared ideals, but these referred to principles of conduct and not to principles of ideology.

---

[17]   See Müllenbrock for an analysis of the pamphlet war.

Chapter 9
The Public Sphere, Mass Media, Fashion and the Identity of the Individual

Christian Huck

The public sphere is now a well-established notion in eighteenth-century studies,[1] especially when it comes to analyzing periodicals like *The Tatler* and *The Spectator* (Newman, 21–4). Most of these studies refer – rather uncritically, as J.A. Downie has recently shown (2005, 58–79) – to Jürgen Habermas's classic political study *The Structural Transformation of the Public Sphere*, which was written 45 years ago. In this chapter, I would like to re-examine Habermas's concept in detail and take a specific look at the role Habermas ascribes to the mass media in the emergence of a public sphere – an aspect largely misconstrued by Habermas, as I will argue. The topic I have chosen to question the workings of the public sphere and mass media directly opposes Habermas's grave, apparently rational, male realm of politics: it is the ephemeral, apparently irrational *mundus muliebris* of fashion. As we will see, such a shift in focus might lead to a different understanding of the public (sphere) than that of Habermas. This new understanding will also make it possible to reconsider the role of the public (sphere) in the construction of individuals' identities. Schematically, my argument will revolve around the following oppositions:

.	Old: Habermasian Public	New: Popular Public
Typical Topic	Politics	Fashion
Aim	Consensus	Distinction
Mode	Rational-Critical Conversation	Affective Compact Impression
Medium	Interaction	Mass Media
Form	Letter	Advertisement
Place	Coffee-House	'Sphere' of Expectations
Identity	Prerequisite	Consequence

It should have become clear by now that the following discussion will be theoretical in perspective. Historical studies, like any other form of science, cannot

[1] I am not only indebted to all members of the research network 'Mediating Identities: Medialisierung und Vermittlung von Identitäten im England des 18. Jahrhunderts' for invaluable discussions of earlier incarnations of the thoughts presented here, but also, and especially, to Anna Christina Giovanopoulos and Annette Pankratz for discussing 'Öffentlichkeit' (public sphere).

be conducted without a theoretical framework. Sometimes, we are unaware of the distinctions we draw before we search for material, select and interpret it; some even think that we should just let the sources speak for themselves. Nevertheless, no material can speak for itself: it can only answer to questions we ask. And these questions we ask are dependent on our present preconceptions of bygone societies and their historical development; as every hermeneutic endeavour, historical studies begin with a *Vorurteil* (prejudice). Many studies of the eighteenth-century public sphere have started out from those conceptions outlined by Habermas; as mentioned above, most of these studies found fault in Habermas's description of the eighteenth century and revealed his preconception as a prejudice. However, by exposing Habermas's approach as ideological, it seemed easy to claim a common-sense, bias-free position for oneself. I do not think such a position is possible: the hermeneutic *Vorurteil* can never be overcome entirely; it can only be adequately reflected and adjusted. Rather than claiming to work without all preconceptions, one should, I think, try to explicate one's theoretical framework as precisely as possible. If there really are too many findings that cannot be integrated into Habermas's model, one should look for a new model that might be better suited to give meaning to new historical evidence. It is such a new theoretical framework that I want to propose here. In order to do so, a meticulously detailed examination of Habermas's framework is necessary to find out which theoretical decisions led to the shortcomings of his approach. Following this re-examination, I will try to construct a new framework that avoids Habermas's shortcomings. Of course, this new theoretical framework will only be as good as the extent to which it is able to integrate historical evidence and extricate meaningful answers from these sources. Unfortunately, however, there is not enough space here to put the new framework to the test – that will have to be done elsewhere.[2]

The 'Public Sphere' and Its Media

First published in German in 1962, it took until 1989 for Habermas's *Strukturwandel der Öffentlichkeit* to be published in English as *The Structural Transformation of the Public Sphere*. However, despite it having taken so long for the complete work to appear in English, a summarized version of Habermas's concept had been published 15 years earlier by the *New German Critique* under the title of 'The Public Sphere: An Encyclopedia Article', which was a translation of a 1964 entry to the *Fischer-Lexikon Staat und Politik*.

This quick glance at the publishing history reveals at least two points that are worth highlighting. First of all, Habermas's account of the public sphere is written from a perspective of loss. The liberal bourgeois public sphere that Habermas believes to have emerged in the eighteenth century has long been transformed, or corrupted; the historical image of this public sphere functions mainly as an ideal

---

[2]   For a more materially saturated engagement with this new framework, see Huck 2010.

for the current state of post-World War II crisis in Habermas's political critique of the present. Habermas, after all, is not a historian but a political theorist. Secondly, as the journey from *Staat und Politik* to *New German Critique* indicates, Habermas's theory of the political public sphere has been turned – not necessarily by Habermas himself, but by editors and adepts – into the foundation for studies of cultural phenomena. Although Habermas refers to central works of cultural publicity such as *The Tatler* and *The Spectator* (the 'literary public sphere', as he calls it), these are nothing more than preliminary steps towards his definition of a 'political public sphere'. The simple question that arises from this is whether Habermas's (idealistic) concept of the political public sphere is an adequate tool to analyze the (cultural) effects of *The Tatler*, *The Spectator* and similar papers.[3]

In his encyclopaedia article Habermas states that 'by "the public sphere" we mean first of all a realm of our social life in which something approaching public opinion can be formed' (Habermas 1974, 49). According to Habermas, 'public opinion', 'arising from the *consensus* of private *individuals* engaged in public *discussions*' (ibid., 54; my emphasis), is the designation, and the fate, of the public sphere. The function of this public opinion is defined precisely: 'The expression "public opinion" refers to the task of criticism and control which a public body of citizens informally [...] practices *vis-à-vis* the ruling structure organized in the form of a state' (ibid.). The public sphere, then, is something that allows or enables those that are not part of the official state to form an (unofficial) opposition, in that 'a portion of the public sphere comes into being in every conversation in which private individuals assemble to form a public body' (ibid., 49). These 'private individuals' are precisely those 'who were excluded from public authority because they held no office' (ibid., 51), but nonetheless, as 'private individuals' had a legitimate interest in the 'publicly relevant sphere of labor and commodity exchange' (ibid., 52). Does this extend to all individuals? It appears so, since 'access [to the public sphere] is guaranteed to all citizens' (ibid., 49). In this sense, the public opinion of the public sphere is merely an 'informal' equivalent, or supplement, of formal 'periodical elections' (ibid.); the public sphere as a whole is 'a sphere which *mediates* between society and state' (ibid., 50; my emphasis): via public opinion the public body is enabled to supervise public authority (cf. ibid., 49). Here, the public sphere is itself a medium and, as we will see, does not need another medium: it comes into being when private individuals come together.

How is the 'public opinion' formed in the 'public sphere' by the 'public body'? 'Citizens behave as a public body when they confer in an unrestricted fashion – that is, with the guarantee of freedom of assembly and association and the freedom to express and publish their opinions – about matters of general interest' (ibid.). It is of central importance that Habermas's 'public sphere' consists of personal

---

[3]   This is not to say that the cultural cannot be political, or that there is no 'political culture'; nonetheless, analytically, both realms work according to different sets of rules, and in order to analyze their interplay and their overlapping it might be best to first note these differences.

gatherings (in coffee-houses, clubs or salons), because it is only here that we can find the civilizing, or rather rationalizing, effects at work, as these are a product of (free) social interaction. Such a 'reasoning public' (ibid., 50) can thus overcome personal (idiosyncratic) opinions and prejudices in free interactional discourse. On the basis of publicly accessible information – a necessary prerequisite – in publicly accessible assemblies, the public body is enabled to control political affairs: 'the process of making proceedings public (*Publizität*) was intended to subject persons or affairs to public reason, and to make political decisions subject to appeal before the court of public opinion' (ibid., 55). Throughout the eighteenth century the 'public' was thought of in interactional terms, in terms of co-presence: the public was a place where individuals came together in person to discuss public matters. And it is important to emphasize that in Habermas's view, 'private individuals' exist as private individuals with private opinions before they come together. Everything else is grounded upon the preceding existence of such individuals and their personal interests in labour and commodity exchange.

There is one element of Habermas's theory that I have neglected so far: the role of (mass) media. In the genealogy of the public sphere that Habermas provides, he elaborates upon the 'important role' (ibid., 53) newspapers play in the formation of public opinion. Taking the developments in Britain as a model example in his more extensive monograph, he highlights precisely those publications that have long been an integral part of English studies, and particularly eighteenth-century studies: 'the *Tatler*, the *Spectator*, and the *Guardian*' (Habermas 1989, 43). However, while the importance of these publications is emphasized historically – and quite rightly so – their place in the systematic account is less prominent. In his encyclopaedic approach, the reference to media is brief: 'In a large public body this kind of communication [at 'free' assemblies] requires specific means for transmitting information and influencing those who receive it. Today newspapers and magazines, radio and television are the media of the public sphere' (Habermas 1974, 49). Similarly, in the longer historical exposition, the emergence of newspaper is cast as a *reaction* to the growth of the public sphere, not as its instigator: 'When Addison and Steele published the first issue of the *Tatler* in 1709, the coffee-houses were already so numerous and the circles of their frequenters already so wide, that contact among these thousandfold circles could only be maintained through a journal' (Habermas 1989, 42).

If there had been big enough coffee-houses, it appears, full of well-informed citizens, newspapers would have been unnecessary for the formation of a public opinion in the public sphere by the public body on the basis of public information. However, simply because of the sheer numbers of 'private individuals' in eighteenth-century London, newspapers became necessary for ensuring that all members of the public were given access to information. For Habermas, the moral weeklies were a platform for negotiations between individuals who were looking for the same 'agreement and enlightenment' (ibid., 43) as it was pursued and practised in the coffee-houses; newspapers were nothing more than an extension of interaction in co-presence: 'One and the same discussion transported into a different medium was continued in order to re-enter, via reading, the original conversational medium' (ibid., 42).

Mass Media

As I tried to explicate, Habermas's preference for interactional situations grants no more than a supplementary role to the mass media: conversation is 'original', newspapers are a 'continuation'.[4] 'The press', Habermas elaborates, 'remained an institution of the public itself, effective in the manner of a mediator and intensifier of public discussion, no longer a mere organ for the spreading of news but not yet the medium of a consumer culture' (Habermas 1974, 53). In its heyday, according to Habermas, the press worked as a kind of catalyst. Newspaper makers provided the necessary information for private individuals, who would then discuss it in the coffee-houses; these discussions, then, could be reflected in the papers. As a catalyst the newspapers added nothing to the information they secured and remained neutral, without an agenda of their own: they were merely, noiselessly, mediating.

As the antagonist of this neutral function, Habermas identifies 'consumer culture' as such: 'rational-critical debate had a tendency to be replaced by consumption, and the web of public communication unravelled into acts of individuated reception, however uniform in mode' (Habermas 1989, 161). This mode of consumption, which Habermas identifies as typical of mass culture, apparently 'leaves no lasting trace; it affords a kind of experience which is not cumulative but regressive [sic]' (ibid., 166).[5] The medium can no longer fulfil its function when it is consumed in 'individuated' (albeit 'uniform') form. Information received in this mode, according to Habermas, cannot (re-)enter the interactional, rational discussion of the coffee-house – it is lost in consumption. Habermas even gives a date for when the mediating function of 'the press' was transformed into a commercial one: 'In England, France, and the United States the transformation from a journalism of conviction to one of commerce began in the 1830s at approximately the same time.' From then on, 'private interests' began to rule the mass media. Before, 'the publishers insured [sic] the newspapers a commercial basis, yet without commercializing them as such' (Habermas 1974, 53). What had instigated the emergence of a public sphere – capitalism in the form of 'commodity exchange' – now came to swallow it.

It is not exactly clear what Habermas means by a 'commercial basis' that is not 'commercializing', but presumably he means that commerce was merely a

---

[4]   Habermas refers to readers' letters as proof for his thesis, and indeed these played an important role in early stages of the newspaper genre. However, they are an attempt to familiarize a new medium rather than an adequate reflection of the medium's structural status – many wrote letters, but most did not; they merely consumed.

[5]   Cf. Calhoun, 23–4.

means to the editorial end, the material basis for the newspaper to function as a neutral medium. Whether such a situation ever existed is an important question but difficult to answer. According to recent historical studies, politically motivated parties subsidized most periodicals of the early eighteenth century (Downie 1993). The publishers of these newspapers were dependent on financial backing, and their papers were surely engaged in providing not simply the factual basis for rational discussions, but biased rhetorical opinions that eventually led to mud-slinging and a two-party dissensus rather than a consensual public opinion. This can hardly be Habermas's ideal of a free press. Neither, presumably, does he mean those commercially successful publications with pornographic, voyeuristic and spectacular content, which he (deliberately?) ignores in his account of eighteenth-century media. However, the papers Habermas refers to as positive examples – *The Tatler*, *The Spectator*, *The Guardian* – seem to have been the only ones that were able to work autonomously, independently of direct subsidies. Here, indeed, 'the *publishers* ensured the newspapers a commercial basis'.

But how were they able to do so? According to Daniel Defoe, the commercial basis of independent newspapers could be ensured neither by sales nor subscription. In an answer to a reader's letter complaining about the increase of advertisements in his paper, he declares: 'The Author lets him know, that first of all 'tis apparent the Principal Support of all the Publick Papers now on Foot, depends upon the Advertisements.'[6] In order to be public, that is, open to all, newspapers needed someone else to pay the bill for the delivery of information: advertisers. Newspapers were and are more than just printed conversation, or fodder for sparking and continuing rational debates. To communicate via printed material produces financial costs that do not occur when talking to those present only – paper and ink have to be bought, machines have to be purchased and maintained and so on. If readers were asked to pay the full price for these costs, the audience would be (even more) severely restricted and the papers no longer 'publick'. As a consequence, communication is no longer a matter between just two parties: alter and ego, author and reader. Nor is it a mere transportation of interactional discussions into another medium. A third factor has now entered the equation with its own motivations: The medium, from now on, adds a message of its own. Communication, from now on, is triangulated, and it becomes impossible to keep an eye on every party involved: front and back, as we will see, start following different agendas.

There is, of course, a lot to be said about the ways in which information is selected for mass media and how it is published, and much can also be said about the categorical difference between spoken and printed discourse that Habermas seems to ignore. For example, newspapers constantly have to produce (spectacular) news items, and therefore they have a tendency to report in quantities and numbers and prefer topics that have pros and cons, or perhaps entail a conflict (cf. Luhmann

---

6   *Little Review*, No. 10 (1705), 37. Michael Harris supports Defoe's assessment from a twentieth-century perspective (19–24).

1990, 170–82). Instead of simply revealing what had hitherto been unknown to the public, newspapers, as we know today, create a specific version of reality. However, it is not my topic here to investigate the distorting effects of newspapers competing for attention in an embattled market.

Rather, I am interested in finding out what kind of public (sphere) is created by advertising, especially by fashion advertisements, since fashion is the prototypical topic of (popular) mass-mediated communication and a distinguishing feature of newspapers. More than any other paper, *The Spectator* relied not only on general advertising, but also, and especially, on advertisements for fashionable goods, cosmetics and clothes in particular.[7] In contrast to Habermas's interpretation, the mass consumption of consumer goods is not a consequence of the rise in production caused by the industrial revolution. The lust for consumption and demand for goods did not have to be artificially created after large corporations increased production – consumption, retailing and production have a much more intricate and entangled history. The public sphere is part of this history, and not something that has been consumed by it. As is well known, *The Spectator*, *The Tatler* and other papers excessively reported on questions of fashion,[8] sometimes even more than about literature, art or even politics. In economic terms, clothes were the second largest expenditure in private eighteenth-century households. The fashions (for example *Spectator*, No. 478, 1712) and cosmetics (for example *Tatler*, August 20, 1709) criticized and regulated again and again in the essays on the front page of the broadsheets were regularly promoted on a back page that was often completely filled with advertisements. Advertisements, as I want to argue here, encapsulate perfectly the essence of (popular) newspapers and mass media in general: they speak to you, and to you specifically and especially, but they expect no (direct) answer – they explicitly do not want to start a debate, rational or otherwise. Even more importantly, the popular talks to many 'yous' at the same time. It is personal and common at once.[9]

Advertising and Fashion

As seen above, Habermas situated the political public sphere as a mediator between the interests of 'private individuals' on the one hand and 'the state' on the other. But what oppositional forces are there in cultural matters? Does such a clear-cut opposition exist, as appears to be the case in the political sphere? If there

---

[7] For details of the quantity and quality of advertisements for fashion in *The Spectator* and *The Tatler*, see Huck 2007.

[8] For *The Spectator*'s stance towards fashion, as it is to be found in the essays, see Mackie.

[9] My notion of the popular goes beyond eighteenth-century definitions that situate the popular among so-called common or plebeian people only. Rather, what we can witness in the eighteenth century is an emancipation of popular forms from a well-defined demographic section of society: the popular becomes a semantic open to all forms of discourse.

are no elections, what is the 'informal' equivalent that reveals the public opinions concerning fashion? What secret knowledge, hitherto kept secret by interested parties, is to be revealed by the media? Is there a private opinion on fashion that individuals can bring to the public body? Is fashion open to discussion?

In the realm of culture there is no direct counterpart that the public body could challenge with its consensual opinion. Instead, the public provides its own opposition; there are no sumptuary laws passed by the state, for example, which the public opinion could supervise.[10] Taste is something that is discussed among the public itself. Fashion is unofficial, social and inherently public. There are no private fashions and no official ones; a fashion that nobody knows of is not a fashion, nor can fashion be dictated. There are, of course, the institutions Habermas mentions, such as the coffee-houses, literary salons and so on, that facilitate the (rational?) discussion of works of art, books and fashions on the basis of the information provided by the newspapers, and these institutions surely play a role in attempting to create a public opinion about fashion, art, and so on. But are the judgements about 'Culture', resulting from interactional discussions inspired by *The Spectator* and similar papers, really the central effect and function of those discourses?

For Habermas, at least, everything else would signal decline:

> Where works of literature, for example, had previously been appropriated not just through individual reading but through group discussion and the critical discourse of literary publications, the modern media and the modern style of appropriation "removed the ground for a communication about what has been appropriated" […]. (Calhoun, 23)[11]

This judgement is doubtful in both directions: it is neither sensible to suggest that 'individuated reception' has not been a central mode of reading in the eighteenth century nor reasonable to propose that today's books and films are not eagerly discussed – in fanzines, on fan-sites, in reviews, at parties and so on. However, neither modern-day nor eighteenth-century discussions of works of literature are mere continuations in speech of preceding printed discourses. There are no arguments to be taken up, no single propositions to be extricated. Instead, as I will explain in the following paragraphs, the 'compact impression', as I will call it, of a mass-mediated work forms the basis for further communications.

In any case, it cannot be said that the result of discussions about culture is consensual. More than anything else, fashion is a matter of distinctions, or different judgements and opinions about certain modes of dress. Is there, indeed, any need to produce a consensus about fashion? Who would benefit if there was just one public opinion about fashion and everyone wore the same clothes?

---

[10]   Only a few, very specific sumptuary laws, concerning the wearing of highland dress, printed calicoes, or swords, for example, were renewed or even introduced after Jacobean times; general fashions, that is, the cut, colour, and wear of apparel, were not regulated.

[11]   Calhoun quotes Habermas 1989, 163.

Aside from some authors of social utopias, no one has ever argued for a uniform dress for every citizen of a state. There were times, of course, when the state attempted to regulate differences in dress. However, at least since the eighteenth century, 'personal appearance is no longer determined by social consensus' – quite the opposite, as the sociologist Gilles Lipovetsky emphasizes:

> [Fashion] affronts habits and prejudices; it is violently condemned by church leaders; it is judged ridiculous, inappropriate, and hideous by contemporary chroniclers. The latest vogue is viewed as sublime by the elegant set, as scandalous by the moralists, and as ridiculous by the ordinary honest person; fashion and discordant opinion henceforth go hand in hand. (28)

This disagreement is by no means an involuntary or unintentional effect; the moralists try just as hard as the elegant to distinguish themselves through different (opinions on) fashions. Since the field of cultural capital is a contested realm, a consensus concerning matters of fashion can never be attained. Here, 'Culture' becomes culture – the transparent and transitory cement that binds and regulates society, at least momentarily. Fashion, deemed by many as the medium of compliance, is indeed the perfect example of how the sameness of objects and the divergence of opinions go hand in hand. A consensus about what exists does not imply a consensus about how it is – and this how, the way we see and do things, is what defines culture.

According to Niklas Luhmann, who was Habermas's great antagonist in German post-war sociology and is still largely unknown to English-speaking non-sociologists, the function of the mass media is precisely to produce objects that can be taken for granted in (further) communications, irrespective of individuals' perspectives regarding them:

> It seems that interest in [the various] programmes [of the mass media] lies in being presented with a credible reality, but one which does not have to be subject to consensus. Despite living in the same world (there is no other), viewers are not expected to join in any consensus of opinion. They are at liberty to agree or disagree. (Luhmann 2000, 60)

One can talk about this 'credible reality' (defined as consisting of things, but also schemata, scripts, types and so on) without relying on or getting involved with other people's idiosyncratic views.

Without necessarily having to be believed, mass-mediated impressions of reality inform the reader of what others have also been exposed to, providing common ground for future (inter-)action. People do not start discussing whether hoop petticoats actually exist, even if few have ever actually seen one in real life, but they probably all have different opinions on the matter. Mass-mediated impressions of reality can produce a credible reality simply because we expect others to know about them as well: 'Attention is paid to what is emitted just because it has been emitted and may be worthy of consideration; the emission makes it part of a background reality, frames of normality and a horizon of expectations' (Helmstetter, 54; my translation). This, as Elena Esposito has pointed out, seems especially true when it comes to fashion. Mass media 'provide the individual with fashion styles in the form of general semantic tendencies […], which the individual can follow or oppose' (Esposito, 168; my translation). Therefore, the possibilities of deviance only come into existence as a flipside of conformity. Mass media present/establish a certain behaviour, or appearance, as is realistically to be expected (to be accepted), yet there is always the possibility that readers use the knowledge specifically to differentiate themselves from such expectations.

This (popular) public sphere, then, is not a place were people come together to engage in rational-critical discourse; this public sphere is a sphere in the more elusive, almost celestial sense. It is the shared 'background reality' (Luhmann 2000, 65), the 'latent everyday culture' (ibid., 66) that remains un-uttered and un-contested, the knowledge that one expects others to expect oneself to have. Such a sphere is open to everyone who can be expected to have access to mass media, regardless of whether they choose to take advantage of it. The idea that what is published in the mass media is out in the open, potentially accessible to everyone, becomes more important than the question of who actually – empirically – accesses it. The 'reality of the mass media' is therefore real because it has real consequences, because it informs people's actions, not because it (mis-)represents a real reality (Luhmann 1997, 1102; cf. Müller 2006, 192).

In this sense, Habermas is perfectly right, willingly or not, in claiming that 'the public held up a mirror to itself' (Habermas 1989, 43) with the help of newspapers. Indeed, the public cannot see reality in this mirror, but an assembly of observers looking for reality – the mirror enables the observation of observers (Luhmann 1990, 181). Therefore, it matters little how real the image of reality they see is; it is enough to know, or even to believe, that others see the same image. And, as Habermas's metaphor of the mirror also reveals, the newspapers are stared at rather than being active agents in critical-rational discourse. The glance into the mirror of the mass media provides the spectator with popular 'compact impressions' (Luhmann 1997, 579; cf. Zorn). In other words, they are presented with condensed, easily accessible, highly charged and alluring impressions of reality that are imagined to be shared with others.

But although the public sphere is potentially open to everyone who has access to mass media, the background reality is not the same for every reader, as it is determined by their choice of reading material, their needs and interests, their economic means and hermeneutic skills, other forms of knowledge and so on. Only the most popular, or fashionable, utterances become part of everyone's reality, and not everything that is made public becomes that popular. As a consequence, the public sphere cannot be analyzed by examining interactional institutions, nor can it simply be analyzed by examining sales figures and the size of readerships. Instead, one has to enter the much more elusive realm of suppositions of suppositions and expectations of expectations, and as these remain unattainable to (historical) analysts, they can only try to determine the popularity of mediated utterance.

What is in fashion, what can be expected to be expected, is not hitherto secret information that simply has to be publicized. It only exists once it is public, and it becomes effective once it is popular. Which forms and topics become popular at a certain time and place is as difficult to determine for the cultural analyst as it is to produce them.

However, to make things popular is precisely the task that Addison ascribed to advertising when he wrote that 'the great Skill in an Advertizer, is chiefly seen in the Style which he makes use of. He is to mention *the universal Esteem, or general Reputation*, of Things that were never heard of' (*The Tatler*, No. 224, 1710). Advertisements especially, and the mass media in general, try to convince the consumer/reader that what s/he knows (and likes), or rather, should know (and like), is known (and liked) by everyone else already (cf. Helmstetter). Advertisements, once again, do not enable the observation of reality (which here would be the inherent qualities of the goods in question), but rather the (imaginary) observation of other observers:

> All Gentlemen may be Furnished with Cloaths, well made and fashionable at 3l.15s. per Suit of Drugget and Saggatee, and Spanish Dragget Suits lined with Durants at 4l.15s per Suit; Livery Suits with Shag Breeches at 4l.10s. per Suit, lace Liveries with Worsted Lace at 6l.10s per Suit; fine Cloath Suits at 7l. per Suit by Tho. Salkild [?] in Earls Court Bow-street, Covent Garden [...].[12]

'Fashionable' is indeed just another word for the fact that something is liked by others, even though one might not have heard about it. It is obvious that such an advertisement does not lead to rational-critical discourse in Habermas's sense, but does it leave no other option but passive-regressive consumption? What is the consumer to make of the compact impressions delivered by the mass media, made popular in the public sphere? Is s/he a mere victim of (hidden) capitalist persuaders?

Individuals

In Habermas's conception, individuals come together as private individuals with individual opinions who then form a consensual public opinion through rational discourse. Following Adorno, Habermas sees the mass media and their homogenizing tendencies ('uniform') as a threat to the individuality of individuals. For Luhmann, on the other hand, the apparent homogeneity of the mass media does not necessarily mean less individuality for the individual. On the contrary, standardization and individuality can be seen as two sides of the same coin, as Elizabeth Eisenstein assumes in her analysis *The Printing Revolution*: 'In this regard one might consider the emergence of a new sense of individualism as a by-product of the new forms of standardization. The more standardized the type,

---

[12]   *The Post Man*, No. 1876, 1710; again in June, September and November.

indeed, the more compelling the sense of an idiosyncratic personal self' (56). For Habermas, private individuals are endowed with diverse identities that they are able to, and have to, shed when they enter critical-rational debates, whereas for Luhmann, individuals are undifferentiated entities before they encounter mass media and consequently 'individualize'. Communication that aims at coercing people into forming a consensus can simultaneously signal to the addressee that s/he has the freedom to think differently about a certain topic. Only by realizing that they are asked to consent do individuals become aware of their power to disagree, and what has hitherto just been an idiosyncratic thought now becomes an individual opinion on a shared topic worthy of becoming the foundation of an individual identity. The public sphere, in this sense, does not facilitate consensus; it presents possibilities, a space to negotiate one's relation to a shared (imaginary) culture. Individuals are able to position themselves *vis-à-vis* this culture: 'Nothing defines our world more precisely and through nothing else do we become more individual than by the choice of our newspaper […] and the way in which we read it' (Baecker, 93; my translation).

However, the individual is at the same time positioned by the compact impressions through which (s)he distinguishes him-/herself. Mass media define those standards from which it becomes possible to deviate, the (limited and legitimated) possibilities from which to choose: 'You can have many opinions, but only within this spectrum and this horizon. And this is obviously invaluable for the behavioural security of humans' (Baecker, Bolz and Hagen, 127; my translation). Fashion enables a peculiarly modern – and it may even be doubtful whether there is any other – version of individuality and individual identity, which is actually a result of the proliferation of the mass media, rather than something needing to be defended against it:

> As a collective constraint, fashion actually left individuals with *relative* autonomy in matters of appearance; it instituted an unprecedented relation between individuals and the rule of society. Fashion's distinguishing feature was its imposition of an overall standard that nevertheless left room for the manifestation of personal taste. One must look like other people, but not exactly; one must follow trends *and* signal one's own taste. (Lipovetsky, 33; my emphasis)

Epilogue: Cultural Communications

Habermas's claim that consumption – of newspapers and informed by newspapers – is a passive, even 'regressive' act, replacing critically engaged conversations, has to be refuted. Surely, one cannot answer mass-mediated communications as one can in an interactional conversation, but there is still room for an active appropriation that Habermas denies and Luhmann ignores. The compact impressions that the mass media leave behind can be answered by another compact impression: consumers choose to wear these clothes and not those, they adorn themselves in what feels appropriate from the selection on offer. The mass media can, in turn, observe these compact impressions of individuals' positionings towards a shared (imaginary) culture in the form of trends and charts, which can then create new compact impressions that the consumers can appropriate anew. Such communication in the form of compact impressions is, of course, not a rational discourse; instead, it leaves room for affections, aversions and desires. The regulation of such communication works according to feedback loops, producing a sense of normality, and analyzing such exchanges becomes an equally endless task of deciphering highly dense, constantly changing images (pictorial as well as textual, but also various forms of design). However, I would like to state here that such communications via compact impressions are also part of the public sphere, and they should be taken into account when analyzing the culture of eighteenth-century Britain.

Chapter 10
Topography and Aesthetics: Mapping the British Identity in Painting

Isabelle Baudino

The first occurrence of the word 'topographer' in English is to be found in John Florio's 1603 translation of Montaigne's *Essays*, and this immediately puts the crossing of languages and the processes of cultural transfers in the scope of this study. All the more so as the word appears in Book I, Chapter XXX, entitled 'Of the Canniballes', and, to be more precise, in a passage in which Montaigne discusses the best method to give an accurate travel account:

> This narration of *Aristotle* hath no reference unto our new found countries. This servant I had, was a simple and rough-hewen fellow: a condition fit to yeeld a true testimonie. For, subtile people may indeed marke more curiously, and observe things more exactly, but they amplifie and glose them: and the better to perswade, and make their interpretations of more validitie, they cannot chuse but somewhat alter the storie. They never represent things truly, but fashion and maske them according to the visage they saw them in; and to purchase credit to their judgement, and draw you on to beleeve them, they commonly adorne, enlarge, yea, and hyperbolize the matter. Wherein is required either a most sincere reporter, or a man so simple, that he may, have no invention to build upon, and to give a true likelihood unto false devices, and be not wedded to his owne will. Such a one was my man; who besides his owne report, hath many times shewed me divers Mariners and Merchants, whom hee had knowne in that voyage. So am I pleased with his information, that I never enquire what Cosmographers say of it. We had need of Topographers to make us particular narrations of the places they have beene in. For some of them, if they have the advantage of us, that they have seene *Palestine*, will challenge a privilege, to tell us newes of all the world besides. I would have every man write what he knowes, and no more: not only in that, but in all other subjects. For one may have particular knowledge of the nature of one river, and experience of the qualitie of one fountaine, that in other things knowes no more than another man: who neverthelesse to publish this little scantling, will undertake to write of all the Physickes. From which vice proceed divers great inconveniences. (Montaigne, 203–4; my emphasis)

In this extract, Montaigne addresses key epistemological questions when he inquires into the various ways to acquire knowledge of 'new found countries'. For him, simple, rough fellows are to be trusted to give true testimonies of their whereabouts in previously unknown regions of the world, whereas more sophisticated people have a regrettable tendency to 'adorn', 'enlarge', and 'hyperbolize' their narrations. Contrary to what had been practiced in the Middle Ages, when imaginary travellers and real explorers had filled pages with fantastic visions of the Earthly Paradise, Montaigne declares he has a marked preference for less fictional accounts, that is for topographers over cosmographers, since the former write 'no more' than what they know. His demand for accuracy could be read as a materialist approach to travel writing: Montaigne turns away from cosmography, whose province is the general description of Heaven and Earth, verging sometimes on the apology of God, to favour topography, as it alone is capable of providing true, reliable knowledge of distant places.

An English contemporary of Michel de Montaigne, antiquarian and historian William Camden, took to improving the knowledge of his own country when he wrote a county-by-county description of it. This book, entitled *Britannia*, the first topographical survey of Great Britain, was originally published in Latin in 1586 and then, owing to its popularity, translated into English in 1610. Camden was a very well-educated schoolmaster, and he apparently shared Montaigne's demand for accuracy. He went to great lengths to collect and compile archives, spent his holidays travelling throughout England and kept up a lengthy correspondence with the 'the most skilfull observers' (n.p.), as he explained in his preface.

No doubt Camden was influenced by the philological endeavours of continental humanists, since he drew heavily on etymology and ancient sources (from Ptolemy to Roman and medieval English authors). Yet, after dedicating the first opening chapters to tracing the development of inhabitants from Roman times to the Norman period, his book consists, for the most part, in a description of each county in both England and Wales, of the Highlands and Lowlands in Scotland, of Ireland and even of the smaller islands, with a peculiar emphasis on the observation of landscape. In the wake of Camden, British topography could pride itself on this two-fold legacy – both empirical and textual in nature – when clergyman Edmund Gibson published an enlarged edition of *Britannia* in 1695; he revised it once more in 1722 and his improved version became the standard reference for eighteenth-century readers.

William Camden's father had been a member of the Worshipful Company of Painter-Stainers,[1] but as a topographer faithful to the Greek etymology of the word, and to its use by Montaigne, his son was primarily concerned with giving textual accounts of his surveys. However, telling others about places they have not seen inevitably triggers a need to give them analogues to one's collection of mental images resulting from visual observations; hence, communicating one's knowledge commands the production of visual representations to bridge the inter-semiotic gap. Interestingly enough, very early editions of Camden's work included engraved maps as well as reproductions of coins. The maps that were

---

[1]   The Company had been created in the thirteenth century and was one of the Livery Companies of the City of London. In 1581 it had been incorporated by royal charter and, like all such medieval guilds, it was primarily concerned with the protection of trades – of painters, in this particular case.

first appended to Camden's volumes reflected the cartographic standards of his day: they represented portions of the British Isles and bore a legend box with the scale. While meeting those scientific requirements, they also complied with a bird's-eye view aesthetic, showing relief and including many figurative signs picturing topographic details such as hills, trees, churches and castles, which should not have been visible had the scale been uniformly respected. Like Borges's cartographers, whose longing for perfection led them to draw maps that merged with the territory they were supposed to represent,[2] the authors of *Britannia*'s maps had resorted to variations of scale in order to increase the iconicity of their representation and to 'escape flatland'.[3]

The mountains, trees and monuments found scattered over these maps were not mere ornaments. They fitted in the overall topographical project, since they pointed to the real geographical or historical features described in the book. Whether natural or cultural, they were drawn in order of height (for hills and mountains) or size (for castles and monuments). They were highly evocative of the landscapes they referred to and they increased the verisimilitude of documents which would have otherwise appeared much more abstract. In their own unsophisticated mimetic way, they provided a very basic overview of vernacular identities; the distinctive local character of each county could be drawn from the specific distribution of trees, hills and monuments on the maps. Finally, they also functioned as a narrative incentive for the beholder, who was encouraged to comment on the qualities that made each county different from others.

Apart from being readers of Camden's *Britannia*, many eighteenth-century British painters were familiar with the questions arising from the depiction of landscapes on paper or canvas. For aesthetic, commercial and even political reasons, most British painters were forced to practise more than one pictorial genre. As they were working at developing and perfecting a native style, trying their hands and brushes at high and low genres alike, they were also involved in a debate about the arts which took the form of a reassertion of cultural categories. Due to the instability of classical forms and to the lack of a coherent British public to validate new aesthetic hierarchies, painters elaborated mixed genres and propped them up against social and political values. Although aristocratic in essence, the cult of land undoubtedly crossed social boundaries in the eighteenth century: land ownership was the main source of power and prestige and, as such, appealed to men of trade as well. But for even larger sections of the British population, as Linda Colley has shown, geography – and the simple fact that Great Britain was an island – underlay a marked sense of difference. In other words, from a geographical point of view, the land of Britain, in terms of its physical identity, its very shape and place on

---

[2] See the very short story entitled 'Of Exactitude in Science' in Borges, 131.

[3] I have borrowed the expression from Tufte, 12. The author draws on Edwin A. Abbott's novella *Flatland: A Romance of Many Dimensions* (1884) to introduce a most stimulating analysis of our ability to represent our experience of the world in 'the two-dimensionality of the endless flatlands of paper and video screen'.

the map, became the highest common denominator of otherwise disparate Welsh, English and Scottish populations (Colley 1996, 17).

This paper explores why topographical concerns ranked high among artistic circles, as well as to what extent painting British places meant sharing in Montaigne's ethics of trustworthiness. Benedict Anderson has demonstrated that maps are one of the three institutions which can profoundly shape the way in which people come to imagine their national domain (Anderson, 163–4). Anderson's very definition of a nation as 'an imagined political community' points to the cultural construction of nations and to the part played by cultural actors, such as painters, in this process. In their attempt at vindicating the very existence of a national school of painting and at federating a larger audience for the reception of their compositions, painters in Britain worked at increasing the plausibility of their visual creations. *Eikos* was an Ancient Greek rhetorical category combining both the objective meaning of probability and the subjective meaning of plausibility. However, as the Latin etymology of the latter points to, it aimed at making speeches more persuasive and at winning over the support of the audience.[4] Hence, in the context of eighteenth-century Britain, the search for collective approval and applause from viewers led painters to depict places or include distinctive local features in order to refer to a form of native physical truth and to lay future artistic developments on familiar national grounds.

Painting Places and the Search for Verisimilitude

From the outset of his career, William Hogarth drew his native city and included topographical elements in compositions which chronicled life in the Metropolis. His very first engravings all show accurately depicted London landmarks: the Monument and dome of St Paul's Cathedral in *The South Sea Scheme*, Burlington Gate in *Masquerades and Operas*. For all their exactness, his convincing viewpoints are not always flawless (for instance, Tom King's Coffee House was located on the south side of Covent Garden piazza and not on the west side, as pictured in *Morning*). Likewise, the buildings were not drawn without adjustments (the facade of Lord Burlington's house, shown in *Masquerades and Operas*, is surmounted by a statue of William Kent with the figures of Michelangelo and Raphael as slaves at his feet, and its Palladian pediment is inscribed with the mischievously Italianized words 'Accademy of Arts'). Yet they could be easily recognized by viewers, even by passers-by who might have caught a glimpse of Hogarth's prints as they walked by his shop. The strategy of mentioning specific places has been one of the most persistent ways of achieving verisimilitude since antiquity. In Hogarth's works, topographical quotes introduced elements of pictorial reportage and heightened the modernity of his so-called 'modern moral subjects'. They blurred the boundaries

---

[4]   For a comprehensive analysis of plausibility, see Schmitz.

between fictitious characters and the lifelike settings in which they moved, thus anchoring compositions which were mere works of fancy in contemporary life.

In the Progresses, both the Harlot and the Rake move about a great deal from place to place; their social journeys are spatialized and topography is one of the main threads connecting scenes together. Toponymy, for instance, is one potent narrative trigger in the first plate from *A Harlot's Progress*: as the York stagecoach is seen exiting to the left, it leaves behind a young girl who is immediately posited as a beautiful and naïve person freshly arrived from the distant Yorkshire countryside. It is primarily because she is one of those numerous rural migrants flooding the capital that she is bound to fall into prostitution. As the series unfolds, The Bell Inn, Cheapside, Drury Lane and Bridewell all line the path taken by Moll Hackabout. Likewise, The Rose Tavern in Drury Lane, St James's Palace, Marylebone Church, the Fleet Prison and Bedlam are milestones in Tom Rakewell's story, serving as literal landmarks in a world of fantasy. Identifiable places mark the distance between the eponymous heroes' dreams and the reality of their progression and, above all, of their fall and regression. Even when they can only be seen from the distance, monuments inform the viewer of the path taken by the characters. In the last plate from *Marriage A-la-Mode*, Old London Bridge can be seen through the window, indicating that the countess has left the elegant Palladian house where she lived in the West End. The medieval monument blocks off the horizon, like a gate shut on the alderman and his family, interrupting their climb up the social ladder and confining them in the area they should not have been so eager to leave.

In *The Four Times of Day*, time and space are the most potent diegetic factors. There are new characters on each plate and the anonymous frustrated spinster, Huguenot couple and deceived husband verge on stereotypes, even more so than Moll Hackabout or Tom Rakewell. As a consequence, time (morning, noon, evening, night) and place (London topography) are left to unify the narration. Each identifiable area of London (Covent Garden, Soho, Islington and Charing Cross) is not only the background to the action but a meaningful structural element in it. In his introduction to *Tom Jones*, Michel Baridon wrote that in the novel – the literary genre-in-the-making in general and this one by Fielding in particular – time and place are omnipresent, with a truly osmotic relationship between places and characters (Henry Fielding 2007, 22–3). Even though the journey had been a well-known motif in literature since *The Odyssey*, travelling became a literary framework in eighteenth-century British novels as well as in Hogarth's series. Hogarth accounted for all sorts of trajectories: forward, backward, and even circular. In *Industry and Idleness*, while wayward Tom Idle wanders in and out of London, the dutiful Francis Goodchild seems to be going round in circles; he is truthful to his middle-class smoothness, with his only adventurous move consisting in parading around the City of London in the Lord Mayor's state coach.[5]

---

[5]   Ronald Paulson has shown that the parallel structure of this complex series brings to the fore questions regarding Francis Goodchild's apparent triumph and Hogarth's production of a positive hero; see Paulson 1992, 294–302.

Fig. 10.1   Richard Earlom after William Hogarth (1697–1764), *Marriage A-la-Mode:
plate 6, The Lady's Death*. London: The British Museum, Department of
Prints and Drawings. © Trustees of the British Museum.

The significance of topography as a storytelling technique is best exemplified in the pair *Beer Street* and *Gin Lane*. Time has no real hold over the scene, which can be labelled either 'before and after' or 'after and before' depending on the optimistic or pessimistic stance adopted by the viewer. But Hogarth gave immediacy to his vision by setting it in two contrasting London districts: the spire of St Giles situates *Gin Lane* in notoriously poverty-stricken Bloomsbury, whereas St Martin-in-the-Fields fittingly rises in the background of prosperous *Beer Street*. The intermingling of real topographical elements with fictitious ones give the texture of everyday urban life to this mock London scene. Here, topography is treated exactly like a character, undergoing an evolution which parallels that of characters, reflecting their state of health or decay. In the same manner as the portraits of real-life Londoners included in the Progresses, topography was used to emphasize what Peter de Bolla called 'the reflective quality of the visual representation', mirroring the surface of the British society and thus triggering what Adam Smith called one's 'sympathetic imagination' (De Bolla, 76–7). Readily identifiable places consequently provided ekphrastic gateways, allowing spectators to engage in conversations about paintings and eventually to come closer to their pictorial nature.

If one draws on Pierre Bourdieu's sociological concepts and conceives the emerging British artistic field as a competitive arena in which the challenge to well-established standards was a prerequisite for the redistribution of symbolic capital without which British painters and British painting could not be recognized, then William Hogarth's play on topographical plausibility appears to be a truly heterodox stance. In the context of British resistance to French artistic domination, Hogarth's emphasis on verisimilitude aimed at stressing French artificiality and dependence upon conventions. Interestingly enough, his father-in-law, James Thornhill, had initiated a reflection on realism in painting for the decorations of the Royal Naval Hospital in Greenwich, where he had produced the one and only visual representation of two of the three founding events of modern Britain (the 'Glorious Revolution' and the Hanoverian Succession) between 1707 and 1718.

These two frescoes (respectively on the Lower Hall's ceiling and on the wall of the Upper Hall) were both painted in a mixed style combining idealism and realism. While the founding principles of the 'Glorious Revolution' and the new regime were presented under an allegorical guise, the new rulers (William III, Mary II, George I and the Prince of Wales) were portrayed in contemporary clothes as human, historical figures and not as timeless heroes in classical garb. To adorn the other walls, Thornhill chose to paint topographical variations on these two major events, namely the arrival of the two foreign-born princes in the British Isles. In the Upper Hall, Thornhill thus represented the landing of the Prince of Orange at Torbay and that of George I at Greenwich. The dates they landed upon British soil (5 November 1688 and 18 September 1714) become encapsulated in the places where they first set foot. The cartography of the events prevails over their chronology. The emphasis is laid on toponymy, and the two place-names function as tokens of legitimacy for kings whose authority was challenged by the

Fig. 10.2   James Thornhill, *George 1st Landing at Greenwich* (sketch for the decoration of the north wall of the Upper Hall), c. 1718–1725. London: The British Museum, Department of Prints and Drawings. © Trustees of the British Museum.

proponents of the natural Stuart line of succession. We know from sketches kept in the British Museum collections, and first brought to the attention of scholars by Edgar Wind's seminal study, that James Thornhill hesitated between historical truth and heroic grandeur for the glorification of the two monarchs (Wind, 116–27). Despite rejecting a matter-of-fact chronicle of the events and surrendering to a form of aesthetical correctness, Thornhill nonetheless chose to equate the political regime of the newly created nation with two English place names: Torbay and Greenwich.

Since William Hogarth confessed in his 'Autobiographical Notes' that his father-in-law's frescoes had left him with many enduring memories (Hogarth, 205), I would like to suggest here that he was particularly impressed by Thornhill's emphasis on spatial bearings as a means to counter-balance his masterly use of Baroque *trompe-l'œil* and to bypass French aesthetic authority. The reference to an extra-pictorial topographical reality allowed Thornhill to carry on the legacy of Raphael (who, through his realistic portrayals of characters and verisimilar depictions of places, was celebrated in London as the master of *decoro* for his ability to perfect the reality effect in painting) instead of being likened to continental painters who excelled in illusionistic decorations. Jonathan Richardson, Thornhill's friend and a fellow member of the Great Queen Street Academy – where the Raphael cartoons were copied, studied and commented upon – had drawn on Vasari's *Lives* to form his opinion of Raphael. He nonetheless departed from this major art-historical source to suggest that Raphael's greatest masterpieces were not in Rome but in the London periphery. Like Richard Steele before him (Addison and Steele, II.379),[6] Richardson considered the cartoons, restored and exhibited upon William III's orders, as the wonders of Hampton Court, and he wished all connoisseurs and artists to share in his pride (Jonathan Richardson 1725, 176, and 202). To this end, he constantly refers readers of his *Essay on the Theory of Painting* to the Raphael cartoons: allusions to them, as well as descriptions and assessments of them, are interspersed throughout his work. His belief that British painters should emulate their Roman elder led Richardson to issue the following edict: '*Being determined as to the History that is to be painted, the first thing the Painter has to do, is To make himself Master of it as delivered by Historians, or otherwise; and then to consider how to Improve it, keeping within the Bounds of Probability*' (ibid., 41).[7] The liberal artist, as Richardson saw it, was an articulate and learned painter whose primary aim was to present his contemporaries with representations that were credible. The method he outlines consisted in appropriating historical sources in order to improve them visually, but without 'hyperbolizing', to quote Montaigne. The subtext to most aesthetic principles from the Renaissance was Ancient

---

[6]   Like Jonathan Richardson and James Thornhill, Richard Steele was a member of the Great Queen Street Academy, where Raphael was invented as the ancestor of the English school.

[7]   Over the following two pages, Richardson presents the cartoon *Christ's Charge to Peter* as an illustration for this rule.

rhetoric; here Richardson's demanding concern with probability, or in other words his idea that painting had to conform to our sense of reality, was directly adapted from the notion of *eikos*. Plausibility in general and topographical verisimilitude in particular stemmed from the British fear of an aesthetic creativity running astray and from the Whig need to contain aesthetics within national boundaries. As a visual rhetorical device whose aim was persuasion, verisimilitude sought to establish on probable grounds a consensus between British artists and their public.

Going Local and the Emphasis on the Vernacular

In the first half of the eighteenth century, British painters ceaselessly sought to develop new visual forms of communication because they aimed at vindicating the very existence of such a thing as native painting and painters, a reality that was denied by the French and underestimated by British art collectors. Augustan connoisseurs were famed for their taste for idealized landscapes of the Roman Campania. Besides being colourful and atmospheric reminders of the Grand Tour sights, those paintings helped strengthen the parallel between Ancient Rome and the newly created nation, shedding a suffused, golden light on the political domination of Whig landowners. Members of the landed elite also appreciated topography, using the skills of surveyors and the knowledge of antiquarians as evidence of titles to land. In the later seventeenth century, they began employing Dutch and Flemish painters of topographical landscapes – such as Jan Griffier (c. 1646–1718) and Jan Siberechts (1627–1703) – to portray their country houses and estates. In the wake of the 'Glorious Revolution', English estates underwent major developments: previously small, enclosed gardens were opened up to include more and more of the landscape. With the extension of enclosures and the increasing size of properties, landowners worked at erasing the frontier between garden and nature, at least visually. The English painters and architects who were then employed to lay out gardens belonged to an artistic community-in-the-making whose members were anxiously concerned with their autonomy from French aesthetic rules and artistic supremacy. In gardening, as in painting or architecture, the path to English self-assertion was sinuous and involved the search for alternative models. In Europe, the most influential garden surrounded the villa built for the emperor Hadrian at Tivoli. English art collectors, who considered Claude Lorrain and Gaspard Dughet not as French artists but as interpreters of Ancient Rome, used their compositions as templates to recreate the atmosphere of classical antiquity on the English soil. Through the displacement of painterly tropes, they created a new symbolic language and purported that, in order to be seen, the English landscape required a process of translation whose rules were mastered by the educated classes. Not only did they acknowledge the expressive qualities of landscape but they also strived to make it more discursive and didactic. Their pictorialist approach extended their authority over the viewing of land and more firmly established their aesthetics of landscape capitalism.

In landscape painting as well, the British painters who aspired to aristocratic patronage produced either Italianate views of the English countryside or imitations of bird's-eye views of their patrons' properties; most of the time, they did both. However, in the first half of the eighteenth century, those members of the London artistic community who practised landscape developed new approaches to their subject through contact with foreign artists. Willem van de Velde, father and son, imported the lessons of Meindert Hobbema and Jacob van Ruisdael and also introduced the British to urban and marine variations on the *landskip*. In 1746, Canaletto, whose patrons were chiefly English collectors, moved to London, where he was, for a time, very successful. Through his cityscapes, British painters learnt the lessons of the Venetian topographical school. On the basis of these cross-influences, British painters were drawn to bring the features of London to light, thus focusing on the topicality of the capital's cityscapes. Welsh-born Richard Wilson inaugurated this movement while he was still practising portraits in his early London days. In 1737, he painted a conversation piece entitled *The Inner Temple after the Fire of 4th January 1737*, in which he recorded the devastation caused by the fire that had destroyed the area in the night between 3 and 4 January 1737. The theatrical smoking ruin looming in the background acts as a reminder of the wave of panic that had swept through Londoners, who feared a repetition of the Great Fire. In the foreground, however, Frederick, Prince of Wales, wearing the Garter, features prominently alongside a water pump. Though on a modest scale, this composition glorifies his action and, more particularly, his sending of the troops to help the inhabitants extinguish the blaze. Time and space overlap in this cityscape, offering a view which is precisely and explicitly dated by the state of the particular building it depicts, thus showing how landscape painting centred on topographical subjects could help localize pictorial memory.

Samuel Scott apparently shared the idea that topographical painting could become an art of memory when he made his *View of London Bridge Before the Late Alterations* in 1758. The massive medieval bridge appears standing in the background under a cloudbank and the darkening sky over it points to the impending demolition of its buildings due to decay. In the foreground, boats and ships metonymically allude to the necessary modernization of the thriving port of London. This painting was engraved by Pierre Charles Canot very shortly after Scott completed it, and it became extremely popular. In keeping with Benedict Anderson's argument, we tend to liken the circulation of engravings to that of newspapers in eighteenth-century Britain, thus envisaging the role played by such printed media in the framing of collective memory (Anderson, 24–5 and 37–46). In this particular instance, the original composition's accuracy and its great topographical qualities mainly account for the success of the engraved version, since Scott had painstakingly represented details of the buildings that were to be wiped out. The Great Stone Gateway, the group of houses in the middle, and, to the far left, the Piazza, a group of colonnaded shops, were all easily identifiable by his contemporaries. As was the case with maps, the texture of fine details was a key element in the storied accounts of the buildings represented. The Monument

Fig. 10.3   Richard Wilson, *The Inner Temple after the Fire of 4th January 1737*, 1737. London: Tate Britain. © Tate, London 2010.

Fig. 10.4   Samuel Scott, *A View of London Bridge Before the Late Alterations*, c. 1758. London: Tate Britain. © Tate, London 2010.

Fig. 10.5   Richard Wilson, *Westminster Bridge under Construction*, 1744. London: Tate Britain. © Tate, London 2010.

is visible in the distance through the ship's masts, standing like a commemoration-within-the-commemoration, reminding viewers that London landmarks passed down the memory of the events that had taken place (and time) in the capital.

It is therefore not surprising to see both Richard Wilson and Samuel Scott representing one of the events which brought a most dramatic change to the London cityscape, namely the building of Westminster Bridge between the years 1740 and 1750. Tellingly enough, even though there were four years between Wilson's *Westminster Bridge under Construction* and Scott's *The Building of Westminster Bridge*, both painters chose to emphasize the very notion of change by concentrating on the unfinished state of the bridge in their respective compositions. Whether depicted by Wilson from the north bank or by Scott from the south bank, both views outline a work-in-progress rather than a stable and fixed structure. Despite the opposition to the building of this new bridge – whose completion was delayed by Thames watermen, who sabotaged it repeatedly, fearing the decline of their activity – both painters set the event in a warm light reminiscent of paintings celebrating the glory of Venice or the legacy of Ancient Rome. The building of Westminster Bridge was indeed presented as proof of Britain's greatness and superior cultural achievements. Ever since Roman times, there had been only one bridge spanning the Thames in London; Scott pointed to its antiquity when he labelled it '*Old London Bridge*' and paired it with *The Building of Westminster Bridge* as yet another variation on the 'before and after' pattern. London Bridge materialized Roman ancestry and medieval legacy, whereas its companion signalled the advent of a new era. While Venice was celebrated for its past splendour and Rome as the cradle of Western civilization, Britain was a nation made for new horizons. Pointing a promising finger towards the new bridge, a young girl placed by Scott in the foreground of *The Building of Westminster Bridge* underlines the prospect (in every sense of the word) and epitomizes the British people's faith in the bright future that lay ahead.

For all their resonance with contemporary life, Wilson's and Scott's topographical views of the Thames could have amounted to no more than mere assertions of English metropolitan identity if they had not been paralleled in the topographical landscape of the English countryside, as well as that of Wales and Scotland. Samuel Scott, for one, produced many upstream as well as downstream views of the Thames. Wilson's and Scott's contemporary and fellow member of Hogarth's St Martin's Lane Academy, George Lambert, was the first British-born artist to devote himself to landscape, and he was famed for his views of English country houses. Because artists usually followed the basic English pattern of counties, topographical endeavours were dominated by the English. In Scotland, the county unit did not have the same administrative and historical presence, nor did it provide a basis for local identity. In Ireland, it was seen as an imposition and instrument of English colonization by the native Irish majority. The annexation of Wales in 1536 made it easier for the development of a topographical approach to the principality. Half a century before the bard was portrayed as the epitome of Welsh identity, topographical paintings first highlighted features which later became tokens of Welshness. In 1720, Peter Tillemans painted a pair of landscapes, respectively showing Chirk Castle and the Vale of Llangollen. Originally born in the Netherlands, Tillemans had immigrated in 1708 to England, where he had become a fixture in the London artistic community; he was a founding member of the Great Queen Street Academy in 1711. His artistic ability and his readiness to travel brought him many patrons and earned him a great reputation as a topographer. The two Welsh landscapes he painted in 1720 were chorographical in essence: this pair allows us to contemplate both the historical and the geographical sides of the same Welsh coin. His representation of Chirk Castle perfectly fitted in the traditional English topographical narrative, since this specific building, as well as other Welsh castles, had been described in William Camden's *Britannia*. Throughout the eighteenth century, Welsh castles were a favourite subject in topographical representations of the principality. Chirk Castle features again in the *Chorographica Britanniae* published in 1742 (engraved by William Henry Toms) and in a series of engravings by Samuel and Nathaniel Bucks specifically dedicated to Welsh castles. Even though Welsh-born artists such as Richard Wilson also practised castle painting, it nonetheless promoted an English viewing of Wales. Castles like Chirk had indeed been built in the late thirteenth century by Edward I to prevent rebellions in the principality he and his troops had subjugated in 1284, when he had imposed the Statute of Rhuddlan on them. These views of Welsh castles not only intensified the English political rule through its representation; they also repeated the visual control over Wales established by the English.

The 1720 pair by Tillemans also included a view of the vale of Llangollen, centred on what the Chinese held as the two basic components of landscape painting, namely mountains and rivers. Pictures of the depopulated countryside multiplied in the second half of the eighteenth century, when the inseparability of nature and culture was questioned and individuals felt freer to formulate their own responses to natural scenes. Until the 1760s, however, most representations of Welsh natural sites were draped in the clothing of Claude Lorrain or Gaspard Dughet. Before questions of aesthetic propriety were raised as to whether British themes should be treated in the manner of the Ancients or be presented on their own terms, Richard Wilson specialized in drawing pictorial analogies between Wales and Italy to make his compositions worthy of a connoisseur's appreciation. While in Rome in 1752, Wilson had portrayed painters being urgently drawn out of their studios by their need to capture the Italian dazzling light and warm colours in two very Gaspardesque views of Tivoli.[8] However, fiction prevailed over observation in the first Welsh landscape he composed upon his return from Italy: *Llyn Peris and Dolbadarn Castle* appears, indeed, as a very inaccurate topographical record of the castle as seen through a Claude glass. David Solkin argued that this was neither a 'compositional conceit' nor 'an inevitable result of

---

[8]   See Richard Wilson, *Tivoli: Cascatelli Grandi and the Villa of Maecenas* and its companion: *Tivoli: the Temple of the Sibyl and the Campagna*, both at the National Gallery of Ireland in Dublin.

Fig. 10.6   Pieter Tillemans, *Chirk Castle from the North*, c. 1720. Cardiff: National Museum of Wales.
© National Museum of Wales.

Fig. 10.7   Richard Wilson, *Llyn Peris and Dolbadarn Castle*, c. 1760. Cardiff: National Museum of Wales. © National Museum of Wales.

Wilson's Roman training', but 'a deliberate attempt to add serious intellectual meaning to an exercise in landscape topography' (Solkin 1982, 216). Wilson's focus on the palimpsestic nature of landscapes became more obvious when, two years later, he superimposed the same medieval Welsh fortress with the emblematic Lake Nemi in *The Lake of Nemi or Speculum Dianae with Dolbadarn Castle*.

Similarly Italianate views of the Scottish countryside had been made by James Norie and his sons, James and Robert, who specialized in creating pastiches of Italian and Dutch landscapes for the decoration of their wealthy patrons' castles or stately homes. James Norie Senior's *Classical Landscape with Architecture* appears to be a typical *capriccio* featuring Roman ruins. Yet these elements of architecture are set on the bank of an unmistakably Scottish loch. In Scotland, more than anywhere else in Britain, topography was a reminder of English rule, as the first Ordnance Surveys were carried out in 1747 when King George II commissioned a military survey of the Scottish Highlands following the Jacobite rebellion of 1745. Whereas the Lowlands were not considered as a subject fit for pictorial representation before the second half of the nineteenth century, the earliest representations of the Highlands were painted after Culloden. Jacob More, a Scottish painter who had trained under the Nories, broke new ground in 1770 when he composed three views of the impressive waterfalls on the stretch of the river Clyde above and below Lanark: Bonnington Linn, Corra Linn and Stonebyres Linn. More was to leave for Rome three years later, never to return to his native Scotland, but he had nevertheless infused his early Scottish views with classical and dignified serenity.

In the 1790s, William Gilpin's writings stimulated an aesthetic interest in nature at a time when the search for sublimity in landscapes renewed the appreciation of British scenery. Public language receded, clearing the way for private sensibilities, with travellers climbing the British mountains to discover untamed nature and new emotional grounds to visual experiences. Even though nature, the key concept of traditional aesthetics, was undermined, the topographical approach had encouraged artists to search for the vernacular character of the various regions of the British Isles. The titles of their compositions all pointed to specifically identified areas throughout Britain, thus marking a symbolic break, with a conspicuous verbal move away from foreign subjects. Moreover, the Italian prism encouraged the British to look backward as well as forward, as the parallel also highlighted the antiquity of their own countryside and launched the search for the 'genius of the place'. Hence, the falls of the Clyde, which became a popular viewpoint in the Grand Scottish Tour – Turner visited them in 1801 – were considered as a natural national monument on a par with Roman landscapes.

Fig. 10.8   Richard Wilson, *The Lake of Nemi or Speculum Dianae with Dolbadarn Castle*, c. 1764–1765. Bristol: City Museum and Art Gallery. © Bristol's Museums, Galleries and Archives.

Topography or History at Ground Level

It is precisely because they focused on topographical landmarks (both natural and cultural) that views of Britain that were either grossly inaccurate or contaminated by previous representations of foreign landscapes could still be labelled 'topographical'. During the Renaissance, landscapes had been revealed through a celestial eye that did not exist, whereas with the new British trend in painting, it was the landscape itself, seen through eighteenth-century British eyes, which did not exist. All deviations from a strict and accurate rendering of any given landscape could be ascribed to the painters' willingness to 'improve' their subjects, as Jonathan Richardson put it. In addition to being proof of artistic invention, they also pertained to the English topographical tradition in its broader sense, since it overlapped with what is nowadays commonly called 'local history'.

Still recalling Montaigne's materialistic stance, I would like to finally argue that while Whig historiography was finding its feet, British history began locally with topographical painting, at the layer of individual spatial experience – 'at ground level, with footsteps', to quote Michel de Certeau (129). Eighteenth-century landscape painters attempted to delineate how the past could be discerned in the existing landscape, therefore drawing on native topographical practise, which also involved writing about local places. The narrow focus on particular sites unearthed fragmentary and convoluted histories awaiting interpretation to make them fit within the grand national narrative. Given the dynamic interaction of politics, history and the visual arts, the representation of space also addressed global and collective issues. Moreover, in depicting spaces that conveyed a sense of history, the artists discovered a means to make history a part of the present. This spatial emphasis prompted a dynamic process which extended historiography to the recording of topical and modern events.

This topographical turn in painting allowed British artists to widen the scope of their landscapes and cityscapes. When pieced together they certainly did not reveal a perfect one-to-one map of Britain, but instead verbally or plastically conjured up a certain British reality. References to existing places increased the plausibility of paintings, thus solidifying the contract with the audience and enhancing the feeling of togetherness. Topographical landscapes were an exact account neither of the past nor of the present state of the kingdom in its different parts, but rather a vision, a vision which was the locus of shared ideological representations. In keeping with the theories of Benedict Anderson and Linda Colley, I would conclude that cultural artefacts in general – and landscape paintings in particular – served as powerful tools in the forging of the British nation, as through these media, Britain was imagined as a community in both time and space.

Chapter 11
The Panoramic Gaze:
The Control of Illusion and the
Illusion of Control

Michael Meyer

Linda Colley argues convincingly that the construction of the British 'patchwork' identity as Protestant, free, and economically and politically advanced in the long eighteenth century is less based on internal homogeneity than contingent and multiple relationships towards 'internal' and 'external' others. She singles out for closer analysis the fraught relationship between the English and the Scottish and the dominant conflict between the British and the French, which resulted in global wars for supremacy (1996, 5–17 and 122–40). While a residual English nationalism associated the Scots with the French, and the Scots retained a distinct national culture, Miranda Burgess claims, politics, economics, and English as the British vernacular tied the Scots to the imperial Union (88–90). Colley focuses on the impact of the acquisition and loss of the American colonies on the formation of British identity shared by the Scots and the English. She maintains that 'the second Empire would indeed be emphatically British' (1996, 153) but does not explore this issue in depth.[1] The current project historicizes landscape painting as a medium of national identity formation in the framework of the relationships between the Scots and the English as British, and the British and India in the late eighteenth century, which Colley neglects.

The 'Orient', and India in particular, are of special interest to the present project of mediated national identity because the increasing British appropriation of the Indian subcontinent is closely related to the rivalry with the French arch-enemy: the 'barbarian, Muslim Orientals' and the 'decadent, Catholic French' serve as a double foil for the 'enlightened, Protestant British'. The growing military and economic domination of India coincides with the development of more sophisticated techniques of representing space through mapping and the arts.[2] The encyclopaedic accumulation of knowledge about India certainly was

---

[1]   Colley addresses the geography of the nation rather briefly and uses historical paintings rather than landscapes in order to illustrate national identity.

[2]   According to Robert Colls, the 'first highly accurate, small-scale, geodetic mapping' (229) was performed in the post-rebellion Scottish Highlands between 1747 and 1755, the second in Bengal and Bihar between 1764 and 1755 with a view to control the land and its people. On the use of mapping, see Edney, 65–79, and Ludden, 78–9.

part of the imperial endeavour to assume power, but it would be far from the truth to suggest that British knowledge and colonial power in India were always in agreement, monolithic, and total.[3]

In *Landscape and Power*, W.J.T. Mitchell alerts us to the phenomenon that the interests in domestic and imperial landscape are intricately related to each other in terms of both the visual prospect and the prospective use of space (17). It has been noted that domestic conventions of viewing landscape have influenced the conception of nationality and the perception of imperial landscape. John Brewer argues that the English nation in the eighteenth century was conceived as represented landscape in spite of being cultivated nature in an increasingly urbanized nation, a landscape changed by enclosure and scientific agriculture. According to Robert Colls, the rising interest in landscape painting during the heyday of enclosures 'turned the countryside into just a view' (235), repossessing the meaning of the land. Private enclosures, he suggests, deprived the people of the fundamental use of the land and of social cohesion, undermining a sense of national identity (220–29). Brewer continues that travel writing turns into a patriotic experience of English landscape, its nature being 'evidently a cultural artefact' (632–3) and a nostalgic place of rest, harmony, virtue, and rusticity (ibid., 619). John Barrell (1983) would add that the detached view of harmonious Britannia in rural prospects, as in Thomson's *Seasons*, implies a detached subject, the 'disinterested', propertied, and retired gentleman, and a selective view, which embeds villages in trees and

---

Ludden, following Cosgrove, argues reductively that literature and the arts parallel mapping as the visible rendering of the world for the 'intellectual and material appropriation by English capitalism' (84).

[3]   In his Foucauldian polemic *Orientalism*, Edward Said has alerted us to the close relationship between imperialism and 'Orientalism as a Western style for dominating, restructuring, and having authority over the Orient' (3). In the late eighteenth century, Said remarks, a free-floating image of the Orient, which contained '[s]ensuality, promise, terror, sublimity, idyllic pleasure, intense energy' (118), was displaced by the project of the founding father of Orientalism, the polymath William Jones, to study and 'domesticate the Orient and thereby turn it into a province of European learning' (78). A.L. Macfie's *Orientalism* gives a concise and balanced version of Said's impact; Daniel Martin Varisco's *Reading Orientalism: Said and the Unsaid* is the most comprehensive overview to date. Ibn Warraq's detailed critique of Said in *Defending the West* delivers a polemical and one-sided counter-attack. In general, Said has been praised for his discussion of the politics of knowledge but criticized for fabricating a monolithic and essentialist Occident and Orient himself, reiterating stereotypes of poor research. Saree Makdisi claims that although 'Jones's knowledge of the colonial other and his participation in the colonial project are thoroughly intertwined, they are not quite coextensive' because not all of his knowledge directly served colonial rule (107). Said ignored the agency of the colonized and the fact that Orientalism was partly against imperialism and formed the basis of Indian nationalism (Macfie, 214–15; Warraq, 175 and 267; Burke and Prochaska, 20). As alternatives, Burke and Prochaska demanded to contextualize the relationship between the discourse of Orientalism and colonial culture (3); Maya Jasanoff stresses intercultural exchange and mutual change.

obscures towns by smoke (59–61).[4] The patriotic experience of – often picturesque – landscape scenes often seems to have glossed over differences of interest and instead offered an aesthetic identification of and with the country in compensation for the heavily curtailed common access to the land.

I would argue that British representations of Indian landscapes often function in similarly ambivalent ways, performing ideological work by specific selections, omissions, and combinations of views and motifs, which can express both the desire for 'the perfected imperial prospect and fractured images of unresolved ambivalence' (Mitchell, 10). John MacKenzie claims that imperialists have used 'art as a device to explain and justify their power, to express the mystique of rulers, and to illustrate their knowledge and command of the natural world' (296). 'India extended the range of British landscape' (ibid., 304) painting by recording Indian vegetation and architecture, but the picturesque view of the eighteenth century accommodated oriental landscape to British taste by toning down exotic elements. Picturesque as well as topographical renderings of landscape establish a privileged subject and a highly selective view at a distance. Barbara Maria Stafford juxtaposes the scientific, empirical gaze and the aesthetic, picturesque one. It is true that topographical truth is more immediately useful than the picturesque imagination, but concerning the formation of national identity, I would rather say that these views complement each other. Topographical pictures may produce aesthetic pleasure, and picturesque pictures may carry utilitarian implications (Stafford, 322–4).[5] For example, the Daniells hardly represent anyone at work in the numerous Indian landscapes they produced. Indian work is not only effaced because it would interfere with the aesthetic enjoyment of natural beauty,[6] but also because the omission suggests that the land could be easily appropriated and profitably used under colonial management.[7]

---

[4] Barrell would add that the exclusive prospect-view of landscape is complemented by an inclusive, economic model of society, which is based on 'the interdependence of its specialized labours' (1983, 66).

[5] In *Curiosity and the Aesthetics of Travel Writing, 1770–1840*, Nigel Leask points out that advocates of the picturesque aesthetic criticized the partiality of the colonial perspective, for example, in topographical views for military purposes (158–9), but maintains later that the female picturesque complements 'the "survey modality" of male empire-builders' (204). However, the inventor of the circular panorama, Robert Barker, stressed the topographical rendering of the picturesque as an achievement of his new technique (see below).

[6] Cf. Raymond Williams and John Barrell, who make similar claims for landscape in Great Britain (quoted in Mitchell, 15).

[7] In her impressive study *Picturing Imperial Power: Colonial Subjects in Eighteenth-Century British Painting*, Beth Fowkes Tobin maintains that India rarely figures 'as an arena for British economic and social action' in Anglo-Indian portraits (133), presenting 'the incorruptibility of the men who perform their duties in the public world of business and government' (121). One of the rare representations of Indian work in portraits, Arthur William Devis's painting *Arthur William Dent with his brother John and an Indian*

In order to understand the cultural function of landscape, Mitchell's 'dialectical triad' of space, place, and landscape is useful: 'If a place is a specific location, a space is a "practiced place", a site activated by movements, actions, narratives, and signs, and a landscape is that site encountered as image or "sight"' (Mitchell, x). As a space in the sense defined above, a place of action and a medium 'in which cultural meanings and values are encoded' (ibid., 14), the visible landscape is also subject to time. It is of great interest to explore how the use and interpretation of temporal space relates to the position of spectators invited by aesthetic representations of landscape, paying particular attention to the selection and construction of the scene as well as the distribution of perspectives *within* the given scene.

I would argue that in the late eighteenth century and the following decades, the panoramic gaze seems to perfect the illusion of visually controlling space and controlling the illusion of space as a medium conducive to forming national identities. The panoramic gaze assumes various forms, media, and ways of circulation:

(1) The visual, especially the topographical, prospect offers an exact copy of (a particular perspective on) the external world, an empirical, scientific grasp, an aesthetic experience, and the promise of equally sharing the same perspective on the domestic or imperial landscape, providing the opportunity of a communal experience and of forming a communal or even national identity. The copying of topographical paintings in etchings and their increasing circulation as prints promotes the consumption of shared images.

(2) The 360-degree panoramic painting (or its lesser 270-degree version) increases the reality effect of the topographical print and the communal experience due to its frameless appearance, the absence of a single centralizing perspective, and its display in an exhibition hall or a rotunda for mass consumption (relatively speaking, because the entry fee usually was one shilling). These huge panoramic paintings had a considerable social and cultural impact because of their popular and often sensational topics, their overwhelming size, the simulation of real experience rather than its imitation, and the dissemination of their views through the circulation of the paintings themselves (in major cities), their advertising and reviews, the discussion of their aesthetic merit among artists and connoisseurs, and their multiplication in the form of aquatints and prints.

Landlord, Anand Narain (1790) questions British domination, Tobin claims, in spite of the British building in the Indian landscape (132). I would add that the Indian landlord stands symbolically like an inscrutable statue in the very centre of the picture between the brothers and their mansion. It is very clear who is dominated: the dark farmer, bending down to work. However, none of the Indians seems to reciprocate and thus acknowledge the white perspective. The picture gives the lie to the civilizing mission the metropolitan imperialists proposed towards the end of the eighteenth century, and suggests that the colonial representatives at the periphery share the despotic economic system. Of course, the directors of the East India Company would profit from the Indian tax revenue, which was enhanced by transforming the *zamindars* into capitalist landlords in 1793 (Makdisi, 112), not by changing exploitation through modernization.

(3) Travel books and tour guides, especially illustrated ones, present panoramic views in the sense of an encyclopaedic accumulation of verbal and visual information.[8] Travelogues present a country as a particular place, space, and sight by exploring the geography, botany, society, economy, and culture of a particular region.

(4) The interplay between verbal and visual information, and between the spectator's view and the perspectives given within the picture, may complement or challenge each other, effacing differences of interest, allowing for an inclusive vision of differences within a whole (*e pluribus unum*) or presenting differences that question the common ground of a collective identity.

The representation of topographical prospects, large panoramas, and travelogues complement each other in the complex construction of British identity in relationship to national identity, race, class, and gender. In the scope of this article, a detailed discussion of picturesque tours of Great Britain is impossible and, in fact, unnecessary, since they have already received enormous coverage. The available space limits the analysis to a few significant examples.

The Ideology of Visual Technology

The monumental panorama appears in the context of an encyclopaedic amassment of knowledge of an increasingly visual nature, which is related to ideals of empiricism and enlightenment (see Stafford). The panorama develops the topographical prospect with its promise of visual pleasure, transparency, and objectivity to perfection (Mitchell, 16). In 1787, Robert Barker obtained a patent for the panorama under the name of 'La nature à coup d'œil' (Altick, 129). Oettermann argues that the patent recognizes this form of painting as an innovative technology of observation (7). Barker's advertisement in the *Diary: or Woodfalls Register* on 9 April 1789 makes clear that his project combines a truthful copy of nature and the picturesque, trying to buttress his claim to credibility as well as aesthetic pleasure:

> There is no deception of glasses, or any other whatever; the view being only a fair sketch, displaying at once a circle of a very extraordinary extent, the same as if on the spot; forming, perhaps, one of the most picturesque views in Europe. The idea is entirely new, and the effect produced by fair perspective, a proper point of view, and unlimiting the bounds of the Art of Painting. (Quoted in Hyde, 23–4)

The position of the panorama between art and science sparked debates about its aesthetic and epistemological value. Joshua Reynolds, the president of the Royal Academy of Arts, initially disapproved of the panorama in opposition to his fellow

---

[8]   Nigel Leask analyzes in an excellent way the 'integrative type' of illustrated travel books in *Curiosity and the Aesthetics of Travel Writing, 1770–1840*.

painter Benjamin West, who hailed the panorama as the greatest improvement in art (see Altick, 125, 132, and 135; see also Oettermann, 79). According to Reynolds, a good painting had to idealize nature and abstract from accidental particulars rather than mechanically mirroring reality (Ross King, 62). West's appraisal follows Henry Home's line of argument, which prefers the perfect 'representation to hide itself, to impose on the spectator, and to produce in him an impression of reality' (quoted in Schulte-Sasse, 114).

From the start, the panorama was a commercial enterprise that served to entertain and educate the masses. Oettermann points out that Barker's panorama can be regarded as the complement of Bentham's panopticon: the panoptical discipline of the employee's time at work is the dialectical opposite of the panoramic relief of the gaze at leisure, which, however, is also a discipline of the eye (Oettermann, 34–8). The illusion of the liberated gaze is deceptive because the gaze is imprisoned within the invisible frame of the representation (ibid., 18). The panorama forms the observer by simulating the total objective grasp of reality – with a specific bias (ibid., 19). The panorama can be understood as a democratic institution which opened new vistas, for example to those who could not afford to go abroad, but it also controlled the visitor's view by the choice of the subject matter, the points of view, and the guide map. In this respect, the panorama manipulates the spectators' illusion of reality (for the time being) and gives them the illusion of a visual control of the landscape; in the words of David Simpson, the panoramic 'subject is cast as the consumer of an already prefigured way of seeing' (quoted in Wood, 111). Gillen D'Arcy Wood argues persuasively: 'However absorbed in the thrill of the all-embracing view, the viewer remained aware of the spectacular, delusional nature of the panoramic image' (ibid.). What is more, spectators might have been aware of the notable omissions in the representation, the noise and movement of the traffic, and the change of the landscape or cityscape due to building projects; in other words, the agency of others beyond the scope of the present view. It is questionable whether the aesthetic awareness evident in the experience of both involvement and detachment corresponded to an ideological awareness of being interpellated by the panoramic construction of the subject in the sense of Louis Althusser.

Domestic Scenes

Domestic panoramas frequently depicted cityscapes or the picturesque countryside. Barker's first successful panorama (which was actually his second), entitled *London from the Roof of the Albion Mills*, was displayed from 1791 until about 1794 in London, followed by a second version that was on show until 1796 (Ross King, 60; Altick, 132; Hyde, 62). A copy of the panorama in the form of a Leporello could be bought at the entry under the name *Panorama of London and Westminster*. The factory, poetically named Albion and thus located firmly in the heart of 'olde' England, provides the central platform for the points of view and also dominates a considerable part of the canvas. This deplorable fact may be excused by the aim of faithful imitation, but it also foregrounds commercial enterprise because a scaffold could have been erected on top of the factory, avoiding the massive blocking of the prospect by the chimneys. Hyde suggests that the rotunda might have simulated the actual position on the roof of the mills by modelling the observation platform in order to enhance the reality effect (62). Barker's panorama of London strategically posits the economic centre of England and Great Britain between the landmarks of the religious and political forces, namely St Paul's Cathedral and Westminster. The four dominant chimneys without smoke and the rather clear sky, signifying that the view was taken on a Sunday, correspond to the situation of the onlookers, who visit the panorama during their leisure time. Instead of being spiritually elevated and provided with new insights at the church, the visitors have the illusion of being physically elevated and provided with new sights as a commodity offered for consumption.[9] The visitors' visual possession of the city could evoke a feeling of being part of a British collective that found its most modern expression in the dazzling capital.

How can we talk about the control of illusion if there was no single privileged perspective within the panoramic rotunda? The choice of a particular place and scene at the expense of others enabled information within an exclusive but invisible framework. The illusion of an almost tangible visibility was achieved by excluding all forms of atmospheric interference, such as clouds, haze, and fog, and the detailed verisimilitude of things both near and far. Circumstantial realism provided for individual discoveries and the recognition of everyday scenes, such as workmen repairing a road, a man rapping at a door, a woman calling from a window (Hyde, 64). However, the fact that the spectators were free to look at everything implied the possibility that some did not see the right things, did not know what they were looking at, or mistook the representation for reality. In other words, the visible has to be rendered legible in order to be recognized as a representation of a specific place. Paradoxically, the visual delusion had to be punctured in order to point out its superior mimetic quality. Therefore, the visitor received a map for 'looking by numbers' at the 'right' spots (see, for example, Oettermann, 79). The elevated point of view and the overwhelming mass of visual facts lead to feelings of vertigo in spectators, making them speechless and confounding their capacity for reflection (ibid., 9–12, 104–5). The visual overkill exceeded the spectators' verbal grasp, which was aided by the legends on the maps in order to stabilize the recognition of a space shared by the visitors. While the map indicated the important sights and institutions of power, spectators had to detect scenes of ordinary life on their own. Harking back to traditional notions of the body politic, the representation of ordinary people in this panorama suggests

---

[9]   In 1829, Thomas Hornor replaces the usual platform on a factory by one on the top of St Paul's Cathedral, literally displacing the faithful look upwards to the heavenly cupola by a faithful gaze downwards on the urban landscape.

that they, too, play their parts and have their share in running the capital of the nation, even if they do not necessarily understand the 'big picture'.

The cityscape of London as a point of identification for all Britons was complemented by the display of rural landscapes, which created a sense of regional diversity within the British Isles. The *South-western View from Ben Lomond and North-western view from Ben Lomond*, painted by John Knox in 1810, probably served as a study for the *Grand Painting of the View from Ben Lomond*, on exhibition in Edinburgh in 1811 (Hyde, 34–5 and 70). The picture clearly catered to the picturesque tourist. On the rocky peaks in the foreground, wanderers in pairs point out to each other the most interesting sights of the prospect, marking the relevance of sharing the aesthetic experience for both the wanderers in the picture and the spectators of the exhibition. The spectators are with a Scot, possibly a goatherd, with a skirt (and a gun?), who turns his back on the view and talks to the wanderer at rest in front of him. Three goats form a nice balance to three wanderers, contrasting a functional and aesthetic view of the land. The Scot seems to have been asked for directions and is now naming the sights. The Scottish painter, John Knox, marks the distance between the pragmatic use of the country made by the locals (the highlanders) and the picturesque interest of the tourists (and the lowlanders?) or the spectators in an exhibition. Knox himself popularizes the aesthetic appreciation of his country. The different attitudes of the tourists and the local inhabitants suggest both differences within Great Britain (or even Scotland) and the peaceful co-existence of its regional or national populations, since the aesthetic appreciation of landscape hardly seems to interfere with local interests, at least before the rise of mass tourism. The juxtaposed perspectives combine an ironic take at the rustic and backward ignorance of the modern picturesque aesthetic and nostalgia for a pastoral tradition that has been taken as a hallmark of national character but marginalized by modernization. The combination of panoramic views of metropolitan centres of commerce and picturesque representations of the countryside gives the impression that the British can enjoy the profits of modernization while also keeping traditions alive. However, it is also possible that the goatherd had been forced to graze his flock among the barren crags because he no longer had access to the richer pastures that reforms had turned into the private property of the Highland clan chiefs.[10] Therefore, the nostalgic picture can also be read as the 'conspicuous' effacement of a recent clash of economic interests (among the Scots) and the invention of a national pastoral tradition.

---

[10]   In *Romantic Imperialism*, Makdisi alerts us to the parallel capitalist development of private property in Scotland and India in order to maximize profit from landed property (112). He also reveals that James Mill takes Highland Scots and Hindus to be equally degraded and deceitful as opposed to cultivated and honest Britons (114–15).

Oriental Scenes

The panoramic representation of foreign countries in cityscapes and landscapes is not free from national interests, but is usually not as blatant as paintings of victorious battles against enemy forces.

It seems to be no accident that the first monumental panorama of an oriental city represents Constantinople: its geographical and symbolic juxtaposition of the 'Occident' and the 'Orient' is beautifully illustrated by the Bosporus as a zone of contact and division. Barker's topographical rendering of the city (sketched in 1799, on display from 1801–1802) places the observer on the European side of the city.[11] The view hardly differs from photographs taken half a century later, except for two remarkable features: Firstly, almost all of the ships are close to the European side, presumably due to reasons of navigation, but possibly also to demonstrate superior European naval power. Secondly, the single Christian church and its protruding steeple in the foreground are sunlit, as opposed to the roofs that surround it in the middle ground of the picture. The church on the European side of Turkey symbolizes the 'enlightened' but single Christian outpost in the 'darker' part of the world. The single church is outnumbered by several mosques on the oriental side of the divide in the background. The mosques are also in the light, stressing their significant number (and potential threat) but also their visibility in the eyes of the vigilant observer. The British spectator of this panorama might have felt assured that, close as the Asian continent may seem to the European side at the Bosporus, there still was a channel to protect the British from the Orient – just as the English Channel protected them from the French. From the perspective of the Protestant Britons, Turkish Muslims could hardly have presented a greater threat than the Catholic French in the Napoleonic wars. On the contrary: the Ottoman Empire was considered to form a bulwark against French and Russian imperial interests (Makdisi, 113). In the southern Indian theatres of war, however, the British – in India and at home – were seriously challenged by the combined powers of the French alliance with the two Muslim rulers of Mysore, a fact that I will come back to (Jasanoff, 9 and 149–67).

The artists Thomas and William Daniell had an enormous impact on the visual image of 'the Orient', and India in particular, from around 1800 onwards. They went on a long journey to India from 1785–1794 and produced no fewer than 144 splendid aquatints of great size in the six volumes of *Oriental Scenery and Antiquities* from 1795–1808, as well as oil paintings and prints based on their sketches. The volumes of *Oriental Scenery* and *A Picturesque Voyage to India by the Way of China* (1810) take advantage of recent printing technology and cater to the desire for visual information by publishing a series of annotated pictures rather than an illustrated travelogue. The artists claim that their visual art forms a narrative to the eye and an authentic 'transcript from nature' (Daniell and Daniell 1810, ii) free from errors of memory or fancy. They play down any military

---

[11]   The picture is represented and available in *Sehsucht* (133–4).

intervention for colonial power and the rapacious economic goals of the East India Company by praising the change from commercial to cultural interests at the end of the eighteenth century: 'Since this new era of civilization, a liberal spirit of curiosity has prompted undertakings to which avarice lent no incentive, and fortune annexed no reward' (ibid., i). The artists' claim of disinterested endeavour mirrors the redefinition of the second British Empire as a civilizing mission which nurtures, develops, and modernizes its colonies (Makdisi, 115–19). Here, they conceal their material investment and interest in India and (print-)capitalism along the ideology of the reformed Empire, but their metaphors give them away. After scientists, philanthropists, naturalists, and philosophers, artists should take their share in the 'guiltless spoliations' (Daniell and Daniell 1810, ii) of India. The martial terms of invading and plundering are not quite as ironic and metaphoric as they seem to be, since the scientists and scholars mentioned above depended on, shared in, and promoted colonization in indirect and direct ways (Said, 77–9). In a strangely dialogic phrase, Thomas and William Daniell admit that their innocent curiosity in the interest of humane progress is (mis-)understood as a violation of sacred customs and institutions: 'Curiosity has penetrated the veil of mystery [...] now exposed to the sacrilegious scrutiny of strangers' (Daniell and Daniell 1810, i). It remains to be seen to what extent their pictures and annotations register these divergent perspectives, which would result in discrepant auto- and hetero-stereotypes of national identities.

Thomas and William Daniell's representations of Calcutta serve as an interesting counterpart to London and Constantinople because the Indian city has grown from the encounter between East and West. In the second volume of *Oriental Scenery*, public life in Calcutta appears to be a free mixing of British civilians and military staff on horseback and in coaches with all sorts of Indians on foot, on animals, and on various exotic vehicles (Daniell and Daniell 1795–1808, vol. 2, plates 5 and 6). These scenes suggest a harmonious co-existence of Indians and the British, with diversity appealing to curiosity. However, Jasanoff explains that their depiction of Calcutta does not reveal that the British are far outnumbered by the Bengali population, crowded in an 'invisible' part of the city, and by Europeans of other nationalities within or outside the service of the East India Company: 'Calcutta, that most British of Indian cities, was a lot less British than images let on' (49).[12] The Daniells present Calcutta in a different, but not less British, light after the most powerful Indian enemy has been defeated in Mysore 15 years later. In their *Voyage to India* (1810), they adapt their pictures to the consolidation of British rule in India. In the 'View of Calcutta from the Garden Reach', one palanquin approaches a second one for a meeting at the shore, conveying leisure (Daniell and Daniell 1810, n.p.). The small oriental boats near the riverside in the foreground are contrasted with the big sailing ships in the middle ground, which,

---

[12] Jasanoff discusses an earlier panoramic sketch of Calcutta from 1768, which foregrounds commercial and military buildings to form an image 'as a merchant, a soldier, and a patriot would have liked to see it' (46).

like the huge cloud above, are driven by a powerful wind from the left (the West) towards the right (the East), and with the white panoramic silhouette of Calcutta at the horizon. The description that accompanies the picture stresses that life on the river is almost as varied as life in the streets of Calcutta, but the enumeration of architectural sights only singles out the hallmarks of British rule: Fort William, the Esplanade, the government house, and the new church. The 'Old Fort Gaut' is selected for an additional plate of Calcutta, offering a picturesque and peaceful view of oriental architecture, boats, and religious life, as Indians in colourful dress are waiting on the ghat or performing their ablutions in the river Ganges. The description gives a very different impression: Fort Gaut houses the infamous black hole, in which most of the British prisoners taken in 1756 perished from hunger and suffocation. The memory of oriental cruelty and horror is countered with a success story, since the British turned the insignificant village around the Muslim fort into a Western stronghold with palaces, hospitals, and colleges, 'the metropolis of British India, the seat of a powerful and prosperous Empire' (ibid.) about to disseminate enlightened law, liberties, arts, and knowledge. Next to the old fort, as an emblem of oriental tyranny that has been overcome, warehouses of the East India Company symbolize the economic basis and the future of the new ruling power, which seems to be tolerant of the religious Indian life in the foreground. However, meaning is in the eye of the beholder. The same picture can serve as evidence of a telling erasure of Indian competitors – and partners – in trade, or as evidence of the fact that plenty of Indian wealth ended up in British coffers, leaving the majority of ordinary Indians in poverty.[13]

In *Oriental Scenery*, Thomas and William Daniell do not commemorate the ugly story of conquest but suggest its desired result, the British guarantee of peace and stability. The artists almost always introduce the Union Jack wherever they depict remarkable sights of military significance. Indian hill-forts towering above impressive landscapes are dominated by the British flag, which is also displayed near historic monuments, such as the 'Gate of the Tomb of the Emperor Akbar in Agra' (Daniell and Daniell 1795–1808, vol. 1, plate 9). In a symbolic way, the British troops (and Indian sepoys) do not merely guard the site but succeed the grand Mogul empire. The selection of 'A Minar at Gour' and 'The Cuttub Minar' for plates in the last volume of *Oriental Scenery*, sites of surveillance and prayer, de Almeida and Gilpin argue, also recalls the previous conquest of India by Muslims, who are now replaced by the British (209).

The predilection for temples and ruins, or rather, temples in ruins, relegates the heyday of Indian culture to the past, implicitly justifying the Christian and enlightened British claim to cultural supremacy. The representations of contemporary religious worship in India stress the link to the past, in imperial terms to ancient superstition. 'The Waterfall at Puppanassum' may serve as an example (Daniell and Daniell 1795–1808, vol. 4, plate 2). The middle ground

---

[13] Sudipta Sen elucidates how British treaties were (ab)used to undermine Indian competition (136–54).

is taken by huge waterfalls and mist, framed by steep rocks; worshippers are standing, kneeling, or prostrate in adoration of rock carvings in the foreground. Can this picture be read along the lines quoted above – 'Curiosity has penetrated the veil of mystery [...] now exposed to the sacrilegious scrutiny of strangers' (Daniell and Daniell 1810, i)? It seems that Barbara Maria Stafford endorses the colonial myth of penetration and progress when she argues that the Daniells' pictures represent the modern form of vertical inspection, set off against a sympathetic, associative, and horizontal imagination, here exemplified by the Indian worshippers of spiritual nature (321–4). The British aggressive claim to knowledge, which can be shared by the spectators of the plate, is juxtaposed to the offence religious Indians would take at the intrusion on a holy site. These Indians do not necessarily serve as lead-in figures to the Western spectator. The Indian believers may focus on only a small part of what the invisible Western spectator takes in, but they may envision the whole universe in the part they worship. They may be denounced as superstitious, but their particular spirituality remains as inscrutable as the impenetrable mist rising from the bottom of the waterfall, which is hardly more than a whitish surface in the aquatint and can hardly be represented to the Western eye, let alone comprehended.[14] To the spiritual believers, British aesthetic, antiquarian, or economic interests might appear to be base. The faithful Indians may be oblivious to or even disrespectful towards the Western gaze, rejecting the colonial intrusion in the holy space. In retrospect, it seems that the British interest in and conservation of holy scriptures and sites triggered, or at least endorsed, Hindu cultural renaissance and provided a basis for Indian nationalism, which, ironically, ultimately lead to the demise of British rule. In pictures such as these, the panoramic Western gaze directed at the others and their land remains at the surface and does not penetrate the mystery, as the Daniells would have it.

Robert Ker Porter's monumental panoramic painting of *The Storming of Seringapatam* (1800) fills a gap in the picturesque *Oriental Scenery*. The panoramic recording of a decisive moment in a raging battle has obvious drawbacks concerning the perfection of illusion, but serves patriotic memory (Buddemeier, 49). Porter's monumental painting of a 270-degree prospect responds to the enormous public interest in the victorious battle for the capital of Mysore only several months earlier, which 'triggered off general patriotic rejoicing' (Hyde, 65). Given the massive press coverage, many spectators would have been aware of the imperial rivalry between the French and the British Indian Company in southern India since the 1740s, and the particular importance of these most powerful Muslim 'tyrants' to the 'enlightened' British self-image and imperial endeavour.[15] With the help of French personnel, technology, and tactics, Haider Ali and his son Tipu Sultan

---

[14]   Bernard S. Cohn shows that, in the 1760s, the Orientalist John Z. Howell already took issue with the superficial gaze of the Western traveller on religious Hindus, and recommended that travellers should first overcome their own ignorance and superstition before judging others, who can only be understood by learning their language (112–13).

[15]   See James, 124–7; Teltscher, 230–36; and Jasanoff, 153–66 and 174–5.

nearly annihilated the British in the Battle at Pollilur in 1780, and the impact of the news sobered British imperialists, who had already suffered from the loss of the American colonies (Colley 2002, 269–70). The British public would have been infuriated had they known of the panoramic 30-foot-long mural of Pollilur, which celebrates the victory of the masculine French and Indians against the feminized British and forms a worthy predecessor and counterpart to Porter's painting (ibid., 269–75).[16]

Porter's picture of the decisive battle commemorates a national event in the form of a spectacle simulating an eyewitness account of imperial power in action. The heroic historical painting helps to promote nationalism and benefits from its effect. The potentially topographical view of Seringapatam is obscured by realistic details of the battle. The visual effect of the scene results from the combination of visibility and obscurity, individual characters and weapons in the foreground, and plenty of smoke in the middle ground. Spectators could acquire a print with a key identifying the historical place and the characters involved (the descriptive reality effect of names), as well as a booklet that detailed the development of the battle (the narrative reality effect of succession in time).

An officer, who looks at the turmoil with a telescope from a safe position behind a big boulder to the right, serves as a lead-in figure for the spectator of the show. His perspective is juxtaposed to the one of an Indian (probably Tipu Sultan) in white dress and an adjacent figure in a French uniform on a tower of the fortification, looking down on the battle with rather helpless gestures. If we can believe Teltscher, only a small corps of 59 French soldiers took part in that battle, but here the symbolic function is more important than the military one (Teltscher, 238). The picture reveals how the national rivalry between the British and the French is carried on in the oriental theatre of war, a fact that brings the battle home to British spectators and adds national interest in what seems to be a rather remote area of the world, justifying the intervention of the British government in the business of the East India Company.

The picture foregrounds individual British officers and soldiers who have withdrawn from the battle to take care of their wounded comrades, revealing heroic struggle, national sacrifice, and brotherhood across the ranks. Guns and cannons in the foreground signify superior technology. The cannons have struck breaches into the ramparts in the middle ground, the centre of the fighting. British soldiers, including Scots in kilts and Indian sepoys, are fording a river, pushing up towards the breaches in wall formation, pitted against the defenders, scaling the ramparts, and sporting their flags on top. In the background, the spectators can observe the exotic towers of Seringapatam, identifying South Indian architecture and locating the contested space in a particular geographic place.

---

[16]   Jasanoff records that the British who actually saw it denigrated its artistic value, probably to compensate for the national humiliation, but also that Wellesley, in 'a kind of morbid fascination', restored it in 1799 (159).

Fig. 11.1   *The last effort of Tippoo Sultan, in defence of the Fortress of Seringapatam.*
Stipple engraving by J. Vendramini after Robert Ker Porter. Published by R.
Ker Porter and J.P. Thompson, London, 1801 to 1803. One of a set of three
stipple engravings, from the left part of the panoramic painting by R. Ker
Porter. Courtesy of the Council of the National Army Museum, London.

Fig. 11.2   *The Storming of Seringapatam, 1799.* One of a set of three stipple engravings by J. Vendramini, from the middle part of the panoramic painting by R. Ker Porter. Courtesy of the Council of the National Army Museum, London.

Fig. 11.3   *The Glorious Conquest of Seringapatam, 4 May 1799.* One of a set of three stipple engravings by J. Vendramini, from the right part of the panoramic painting by R. Ker Porter. Courtesy of the Council of the National Army Museum, London.

The spectators of the battle scene are invited to share the visual and the ideological points of view. Chaos and obscurity in an aesthetic and symbolic sense call for order and clarity. The throngs of warring soldiers suggest a contested and congested space and the need to displace one party. The movement from the outside to the inside and upward promises penetration, victory, and subsequent control via the restoration of peace and visibility, restoring the contested space to law and order and opening the closed space to British eyes and trade.

The centre of the picture is dominated by a triangular design that represents a hierarchy of nations, class, and race: officers with drawn sabres on the top of the triangle lead their troops to action; beneath them, British infantry with muskets and bayonets are about to engage in close combat with Muslim soldiers with sabres; at the very bottom of the triangle and in the shadowy foreground, two ragged men with muskets steal away from the broil. The triangle juxtaposes brave British officers engaging on the same level with the 'savage' enemy, a manly and fair fight with traditional sabres, and their soldiers as obedient followers, using their bayonets in hand-to-hand fighting rather than superior weapon technology. At the basis of the triangle, there are the cowardly and effeminate French deserters and British collaborators.

We see cannons in the hands of the British only, signifying superior Western technology in opposition to the historical fact of Tipu's strategic acquisition of European weapons and know-how. On the ramparts, the French officer stands next to the Indian leader, suggesting an egalitarian fraternity that is clearly marked off from the British, who bear the brunt of the battle, serving as a spearhead of the attack and being followed by their sepoys, who seem to be arriving at the scene after the British troops have already scaled the walls of the fortress and sported their flags on top. Thus, the picture represents temporalized space. The portentous moment of a narrative, which points to the near ransacking of the capital, inverts the fear of a French invasion of England by envisioning the storming of a fortress held with the support of the French. The picture implies the ultimate defeat of Napoleon, since the French officer is simply the dark shadow of a figure, which invites the spectators' projection of Napoleon onto the crumbling walls.[17]

The mutual and successful effort of the imperial British hierarchy serves as a model for the domestic hierarchy of the British class system, which is pitted against the egalitarian and revolutionary French. A problem might be that the sepoys are subordinate brothers in arms, who shed their blood with/for the British and therefore might have a claim to merit and acknowledgement, a claim that was voiced with verve much later, after the Indian support of the British in the two World Wars. The clear hierarchy of Porter's picture contains (in the sense of Michel Foucault) the potential claim to equality and establishes a decidedly masculine image of Britishness, combining traditional bravery and sophisticated technology.

---

[17]   Indeed, British and Indian letters of the time indicate that Tipu Sultan was waiting for more troops sent by Napoleon from Egypt; see Harlow and Carter, 40–48.

Conclusion

The scenes from Great Britain discussed above suggest that urban progress based on industry and trade is compatible with rural regional traditions based on agriculture, providing an inclusive – if simplified and distorted – version of Britishness. The representations of the Orient analyzed above map the conflicts that seem to be far away onto familiar ones, appealing to national interest in the context of the Napoleonic Wars and the traditional British construction of their identity in relationship to their arch-enemy across the Channel. Do the British panoramic representations of the Orient project a complementary image of the British and the (colonial) other, allowing for an integration of national identities under the umbrella of the Empire? The panorama of Constantinople draws a clear and apparently unchanging 'natural' divide between Christian Europe and the Muslim Orient, located on and symbolized by opposite continents. Imperial interventions abroad cross the divide and complicate the construction of collective identities. On the one hand, the imperial endeavour abroad strengthens the collective identity within Great Britain, because Britons from all regions shared in colonial conquest and its economic and symbolic profit. In addition, the picturesque representation of India often paints pictures of a peaceful, sparsely populated countryside or cultural sites under British 'protection'. Everyday work, the crafts, factories, and trade are largely omitted, suggesting an opposition between the 'lazy Oriental' and the diligent Briton, and a space of opportunity for the latter.[18] On the other hand, stepping into the footsteps of the powerful Mogul rulers runs the risk of corruption. Since the 1770s, the East India Company had been accused of ruthless and despotic 'oriental' practices, salient in the long impeachment process against Warren Hastings, governor-general of Bengal from 1772–1785 (see Harlow and Carter, 26–40, and Teltscher, 157–8). Two versions of imperial endeavour would help to dispel the spectre of corruption: the heroic defeat of the oriental despot Tipu Sultan, and sublimated aggression manifest as a civilizing mission, ultimately changing other cultural traditions, which are presented as being backward or on the decline.

The panoramic sequence of picturesque oriental scenes seems to render the exotic space as accessible as Ben Lomond to the tourist or armchair traveller. Nicholas Dirks argues that the picturesque rendering of India serves both 'the contradictory forces of idealization and possession' (228). It seems as if the stereotypically spiritual and simple Indians could be integrated in the British Empire as the traditional Scot had been in Great Britain. In *Oriental Scenery*, for example, the exotic others are used for the construction of an opposite British identity as enterprising, enlightened, and liberal, but these others do not welcome the British and endorse their self-fashioning, as some pictures imply and descriptions confirm. The aesthetic control of the visual illusion of the exotic

---

[18]   Compare Nochlin's argument on nineteenth-century Orientalist painting, discussed in Macfie, 66–8.

corresponds to an illusion of controlling the exotic (as 'inferior' natives), an impression that is destroyed by a closer look at the limits of representation and acceptance by the others. The panorama of the battle of Seringapatam serves as an instance of colonial resistance but affords the affirmation of traditional masculine values, which complement the pride taken in national traditions at home, revealed in nostalgic picturesque landscapes of rural pastorals and in national progress and power, which forms the topic and the condition of the urban panorama.

Chapter 12
Peripatetics of Citizenship in the 1790s

Christoph Houswitschka

Studies in recent years have demonstrated that in the early 1790s both state institutions and the loyal press on the one hand and the radical reform movement on the other created a highly complex web of various efforts to establish simplified ideological patterns of exclusion and inclusion. Suspicion was sufficient to justify prevention, and conspiracy theories prospered (Pfau). Going all the way from the Edinburgh Trial of 1793 to the unjustified accusations of high treason in 1794, the state tried everything to criminalize those in favour of reforms.[1] From a republican (and in many cases American or British left-wing) perspective this was described as a history of victimizing the reformers and their legitimate goals. Conversely, from the perspective of dominant British historiography, the radicals have been described as a danger for the monarchy, or too early in their strife for democratization and too close to the ideas from which the French Revolution was said to have emerged. Regardless of the political preferences of historians, the successful oppression of the radicals after 1795 made it inevitable to consider them as victims of the politics of Pitt and his Home Secretary, Dundas. Since the radicals never openly attacked the government using violence, 'opinion had to be the main object of repression' (Cobban, 21).

The prosecution of the publisher Daniel Isaac Eaton for seditious libel, to give but one striking example, had been represented by Thelwall

> in what had become, at least since the 1792 proclamations and the French declaration of war, the familiar terms of radical and opposition denunciations of the actions of the king and his ministers: the determined repression of aspirations to political reform; the bloodthirsty prosecution of an unjust and unnecessary war; the high level of taxation, falling disproportionately on the poor. (Barrell 2000, 105)

The government prosecuted the opposition on the basis of Acts against sedition (1793) and treason (1794). After the so-called *Two Gagging Acts*, oppression forced many reformers into seclusion to develop new forms of political participation that could not be prosecuted by the authorities. The city and the country became places

---

[1]   See the detailed account of Barrell 2000, 127–444, entitled 'Invention of Modern Treason, "A Conspiracy without Conspirators"' and Wharam's historical narrative of the High Treason Trials. For a collection of sources exploring the legal culture of the 1794 High Treason Trials, see Houswitschka 2004.

where new spaces of participation were defined. After the reform movement had been labelled as deviant, participation could only be facilitated from the margins. Therefore, the reformers had to construct new social spaces that would define them and their cause in a way that would make them recognizable as a group and protect them at the same time from more governmental repression and persecution.

Practicing the re-organization and re-definition of spaces could no longer define persons and objects in an exclusive way; rather their physical presence and their social practices would define those spaces in an inclusive manner. The highly volatile lives of reformers who used to be present and absent from the public, moving back and forth from the centre to the margins and from the city to the countryside, created democratic spaces in which a dynamic use of available knowledge in various social spaces was propagated. In the city the practice of walking the maze or labyrinth of streets and places defined an individual's taking his opinions to the places where the crowd would meet.

Moving from locations of the urban political public to those of the literary public, Thelwall, the author of *The Peripatetic* (1793), does not aim at quitting political activities but wants to politicize social activities and their locations.[2] In order to find these locations, reformers had to ideologically occupy spaces that belonged to their political adversaries. *The Peripatetic* introduces the 'the poet as wanderer [...], writer as sociological observer and political critic, poet as eccentric – wandering out of an established center' (Scrivener, 206). In the early nineteenth century, the phrase *pedestrian writing* 'signifies a writer walking over land populated by the disenfranchised, breaking free from the restrictions of established genres and commonplace perceptions', as Scrivener points out (ibid.). In the following argument, I will show how rural rambling is related to city strolling, since the latter is a social activity with a symbolic meaning while the rural rambler is both a literary motif and a social activity. In order to compare the act of walking in the city with the act of walking in the countryside, I will demonstrate how the reformers tried to politicize social spaces.

Thelwall learnt from Burke's successful propaganda in *Reflections on the Revolution in France* (1790) and tried to establish an autonomous literary space by drawing a borderline between rural culture and civilization from urban degeneration and oppression (Houswitschka 1997, 31–50). In his poetry, Thelwall institutionalized concepts of 'civiliz'd improvement' by working and writing in the country. He used a language that was different from the polite language of the city and was reminiscent of Wordsworth's statement in the *Preface* to present 'incidents and situations from common life' in a 'language really used by men' (Wordsworth and Coleridge, 244). Thelwall's literary constructions of rural spaces competed with Burke's classicist definition of the country. The radicals tried to adopt Burkean political rhetoric to dislocate the poetical spaces of the loyalists and the values associated with them.

There were already institutions and other institutionalized places, in both the country and the city, with specifically defined meanings. Thus the reformers tried

---

²   See Scrivener, 221, for Thelwall's retreat from the public in the summer of 1797.

to institutionalize social activities that would create new spaces that they could populate with their own ideas. Whether as alternative spaces in literature or as actual spaces in landscapes or cities, Thelwall and others sought to establish these spaces as sites of habitual social activity. They believed that these spaces could form a republic of letters and establish a sense of citizenship.

Walking has been thoroughly studied in recent years as both literary convention and social habit. The social meaning of walking might be explained best by comparing it to a different, more recent social practice, cross-country running. Speaking of how the two activities define space, John Bale distinguished walking from running, the latter of which developed only in the late 1900s:

> By running, the straight body was modelled, trained and educated in a container hall environment, and running was here a means of disciplining the "right" body poise, forming the straight backbone. The comparison of these different types of running and racing shows that sport is indeed not "natural", but a very specific staging of space and time. And it also shows that neither are space and time themselves "natural" and universal. (152)

Walking, as described by reformers such as Thelwall, was anything but sport in the modern sense. Particularly with respect to staging space and time, the exact opposite was true. Walking in the countryside was a counter-cultural activity meant to oppose the rationality behind the hegemony of landed property owners and of the government in the metropolis. The peripatetic's walking was not natural either, but claimed to be natural in order to legitimate its authority to speak for the nation. Following an ideological pattern first used by conservative authors, the reformers re-invented nature as a space of democracy and participation. Opposing this, institutions of modern states tried to re-establish control over their citizens' bodies – with the help of racing sports, for instance. Racing became an attempt to discipline and control the individual's body. The peripatetic's walking introduced an experience of space and time that formed a contrast to any form of standardization and institutionalization. Similar to forest racing in the late nineteenth century, walking put an emphasis on the variety and surprise of woods and trees, the curved paths and obstacles, the experience of smell and season, and the changes in landscape and nature. Space and time were not modelled to form a container appropriate for sports, nor were they constituted 'in the mainstream of societal common sense and social practice' (ibid., 149). Space was not seen as 'the framework that can and should be measured, structured and standardized, thereby fitting the functional needs of time-directed achievement production' (ibid.), but rather defined by participating in activities of creative imagination that allowed for contingency.[3] Robin Jarvis explored the relationship between

---

[3]   Recent studies on the sociology of space have changed our understanding of how social practices construct spaces and their meanings. While traditional concepts of space used to be essentialist, neither historians nor sociologists have tried to overcome the dominant cultural concept of space as a container. Sociologists such as Löw or Schroer

romantic writing and pedestrian travel. He analyzed the mentality and motives of early pedestrian travellers and discussed the influence of this cultural revolution on Romantic creativity. According to Jarvis, walking became not only an activity of self-enfranchisement but also a source of restless writing.[4]

In *The Tribune* (1795, no. 16), Thelwall described rural rambling as a political activity which opposed the normative definition of space by the ruling landed nobility:

> I have seen some of the lamentable consequences of the miserable ignorance, in which the governors of this country contrive to keep the people. *I have been rambling*, according to my wonted practice, *in the true democratic way, on foot*, from village to village, from pleasant hill to barren heath, *recreating my mind* with the beauties, and with the deformities of nature. *I have traced over many a barren track in that county (Surrey) which is called the Gentleman's county*; because, forsooth the beggarly sans culottes are routed out from it; their vulgar cottages, so offensive to the proud eye of luxury, are exterminated, and nothing but the stately domes of useless grandeur present themselves to our eyes. (1995a, 151–2; my emphasis)

For Thelwall, democratic rambling and 'democratic excursions' (see Scrivener, 209) were programmatic and highly political activities. In 'Shooter's Hill', a piece from *The Peripatetic*, Thelwall suggested the term 'Topographical Digressions' (2001, 185). John Thelwall introduced walking as a practice that defined and appropriated unoccupied spaces in the name of the democratic reform movement. Almost 30 years after publishing *The Peripatetic*, Thelwall wrote, in a work entitled 'On the Influence of the Scenery of Nature on the Intellectual and Moral Character, as well as on the Taste and Imagination':

> The true lover of Nature, indeed, is sure to be a pedestrian. Experience will soon teach him [...] that riding on horseback has more tendency to dissipate, and walking to energize his thoughts; as lounging in a carriage has, to a certain degree, or least, to lethargize his faculties and dispose to selfish inanity. (1822, 76)

---

have argued that social activities are not limited to certain places and closeness to them, but should rather be understood in relation to the persons who act and move inside and outside these spaces (Schroer, 26).

[4]   In a neo-Marxist reading, Langan showed that the conservative interpretation of walking as an inspirational habit for Wordsworth's imagination must be revised. This image can be found throughout his entire work. Before Langan's study, Wordsworth's observations of the picturesque beauty of nature, and descriptive sketches such as the account of his walking tour on the Continent, had been interpreted as acts of recollection and reflection. Langan showed that Wordsworth's peripatetic motion prefigured the liberal form of human society. Walking and freedom were regarded as tautological equivalents. Wordsworth helped shape an ideology of liberalism. The 'vagrant's' presence in society was a peripheral one. In a historical reading, Anne Wallace called Wordsworth's communal walking 'peripatetic walking'. Wallace's study of Wordsworth's poetry, such as *The Recluse* or *The Excursion*, suggested an influence by Thelwall's *The Peripatetic* (Wallace, 93).

In this essay Thelwall distinguished two forces that shaped the experience of travelling, one defining social actions and the other space itself. He occupied nature as a space attributing to him the authority he needed to proclaim his political programme. At the same time he construed nature as a space with democratic significance.

Rambling in nature was not just an aesthetic experience but also a political activity, a physical activity which took on the symbolic meaning of a political statement. Democratic forms of thinking, of opinion and decision-making were reified as rambling. They represented the intellectual appropriation of nature, suggesting constitutional terms and concepts: sovereignty and participation. Judith Thompson was the first to point out, in 'John Thelwall and the Enfranchisement of Literature', that the reformer managed to create an emblem of democracy in *The Peripatetic*:

> Profoundly committed to an ideal of free speech, open debate, and friendly conversation, Thelwall writes a text in which not only characters, but also genres interact, are questioned, challenged, undermined, and redefined. [...]. *The Peripatetic* amounts to an exercise in applied genre theory, which parallels and complements the explicit political theory development in Thelwall's pamphlets and speeches of the 1790s. (1998, 124)

The Peripatetic was a hybrid of various genres in which 'every one who has an interest' (Thelwall 2001, 140) found 'a voice also in the representation' (ibid.; see also Judith Thompson 2001, 36). Thelwall's 'quasi-novel' (Judith Thompson 2001, 11), with its lengthy title, *The Peripatetic or, Sketches of the Heart, of Nature and Society, in a Series of Politico-Sentimental Journals, in Verse and Prose, of the Eccentric Excursions of Sylvanus Theophrastus*, explored the relation between nature and society, between landscape and history. Literary forms such as the anecdote and the active appropriation of nature in sketches facilitated active participation. The peripatetic ramblers were individuals who envisioned political participation and democratic identity. The individual act of reading was compared to walking, an exploration of nature that teaches the participating mind to construct a social space of its own.

In 'Apology to the Critics', Thelwall defined anecdotal narratives and sketches, arguing that the contingent and individual take on a general and collective meaning. The literary form is not holistic, but pursues an approach that keeps the reader moving and his mind flexible, in a way quite different from 'any formal preface, introduction, or series of biographical memoirs that could possibly have been hereunto prefixed' (Thelwall 2001, 123). The continuous movement from centres to margins symbolized active minds that accumulated and distributed knowledge regardless of social belonging. On the road, the narrator felt more at home than in urban and rural spaces, which were occupied by the rich landowners and powerful urban elites:

> I felt a glow of health and vivacity, which the bustle and loaded atmosphere
> of the metropolis never yet afforded; and I could not but reflect, that from the
> *peripatetic habits of the ancient philosophers, and the attachment to rural life*
> *displayed by them all, in oppression to the practice of modern students, who are*
> *in some degree compelled, by the institutions of society, to bury themselves in*
> *large cities*, we might readily account for the apparent paradox, why the health
> of the latter should be so proverbially debilitated, while the former have been so
> pre-eminent for their longevity. (Ibid., 81; my emphasis)

Thelwall lends his voice to the narrator, Sylvanus Theophrastus, whose sketches
avoid holistic and absolutist concepts of literary order. The literary spaces that are
created in this manner match Thelwall's concept of nature, which is constituted
by a relativist-relational space. The various genre experiments must be discussed
before the background of Thelwall's politics, which united 'the different advantages
of the novel, the sentimental journal, and the miscellaneous collection of essays
and poetical effusions' (ibid., 72). In the terminology of a constructivist sociology
of space, Thelwall used genres like spaces, not as containers that were defined
as absolutist-substantial entities but as cognitive concepts inviting participation
and explicit criticism of political affairs: 'It will naturally be supposed, that these
anecdotes would lead us immediately into a consideration of the condition of the
labouring poor in this country; nor to those who are at all informed upon this
important topic [...]' (ibid., 350). The plurality of topics and perspectives that
could be found in these anecdotes (ibid., 353) also reflected upon the plurality of
ideas and opinions in a democratic society. The peripatetic activities in literature
and in social reality represented alternative patterns of thinking. They defined the
cognitive poetics of democracy.

Thelwall's *A Midnight Ramble* describes a person who wanders about during
the night and comes to a turning point in his intellectual development: 'In fact,
my mind was making its first painful efforts against the prejudices of education;
Reason was becoming importunate for the free exertion of her powers; and Faith
was no longer to be tamely held in the arbitrary chains of hereditary opinion'
(ibid., 108). The narrator rejected 'the system I had been taught' (ibid.). With the
help of reason, the narrator liberated himself from the cultural traditions he had
been educated and controlled by:

> The bigot phantoms of hereditary prejudice have vanished before the searching
> rays of investigation, and left in their place the pure and simple form of a milder
> persuasion, whose universal benevolence smiles endearment to the heart of
> Sensibility, whose cheerful precepts are founded on the convictions of reason;
> and which promises the perfection of Justice without the immolation of Mercy.
> – Yes, such has been the result of my enquiry: and these painful doubts shall
> disturb my peace no more. (Ibid., 110)

This 'midnight ramble' led the narrator out of the darkness of a false education. Rambling became a representation of citizenship.[5] Through walking from the city into the country and transgressing cultural and political boundaries, the reformers explored new spaces of democratic development and became citizens of the intellectual boroughs in the republic of letters the radicals had built for themselves. Walking and rambling in these spaces gave the peripatetic a democratic identity. Writing and reading about democratic habits and practices, the reformers helped to establish new cognitive instruments to develop what their contemporaries would have called a democratic taste.

While rambling through nature addressed concerns about the landowners' power to exclude the impoverished rural population from earning a modest living in the countryside, walking the streets of the city occurred in public spaces that were less exclusive and more diversified in the way they would be used. This way, rambling the countryside becomes a symbolic act of practicing the disenfranchisement of urban spaces. Applied to the city, the political meaning of rambling in the countryside could unfold only in a dialectic tension to the act of walking the streets of the metropolis. The streets and places of the city were linked to the institutions and spaces of power. This labyrinth connected everyone in a network of quite diverse relationships. The city encompassed social borders such as class hierarchies, economic differences, and various ways of including or excluding citizens. Seen from outside, the borderline was that of the city in opposition to the rest of the country. Crossing this border between two antagonistic cultural spaces is a sublime experience.

As an 'inhabitant of the metropolis', one of Thelwall's ramblers is overwhelmed by 'the aerial brow of this eminence, the vast majestic city, queen of commerce and of arts!' (Thelwall 2001, 296). In contrast to this rambler, the philosopher Sylvanus Theophrastus cannot accept these feelings for himself. Nothing appears to him more loathsome than 'the prospect of a great city': 'Turrets and thronging spires fill him with nothing but disgust, nor will he admit that there can be any pretensions to beauty in any landscape, in which even the prospect of the cupola of Saint Paul's, how distant soever, is intruded' (ibid.). The metropolis makes a strong impression on Wentworth, who comes back from the countryside after two months' absence:

> [...] no sooner did I behold the vast metropolis expanding beneath my feet, far to the right and to the left – see turrets, spires, and cupolas, thronging in pompous vassalage round yon still more magnificent dome, than wonder and delight rushed immediately upon my heart, and triumphed, for a while, over every other impression. (Ibid., 297)

---

[5]   The idea of a cultural policy based upon democratic citizenship goes back to Raymond Williams's ideas and was further developed by authors such as Nick Stevenson, who suggested a concept of 'common cultural citizenship' (6–9).

Wentworth admits that this is a superficial experience that cannot remove his doubts about the city that confuses him with her anonymity and the heterogeneous character of her crowds. His friends, for example, are 'scattered through this vast wilderness of population' (ibid.). They are exceptions in an urban world of corruption and negligence on the one hand and 'the fruits of its cultivation' (ibid.) and learning on the other.

In Thelwall's *The Peripatetic* ('Blackheath'), the rural rambler approaches the city and can only manage his conflicting feelings by analyzing its significance:

> Nor are the beauties of this extensive scenery a little heightened by the fine bird's eye prospect of London and its environs, whose spires and majestic buildings piercing the skies, and, above all, the magnificent dome of St. Paul's, rivet the eye in pensive admiration, and remind one of the power and opulence of the empire, whose narrow boundaries (I speak of the natural boundaries of the parent state – the only *profitable* territory of any empire) can maintain the waste and riotous consumption of so immense a capital. (Ibid., 150)

By relating the nation and the empire to the Metropolis in terms of a process of accumulation and concentration of capital and resources, Thelwall tries to explain the fascination with London. At the same time, he makes sure to address the relationships of power, exploitation, and oppression which are made possible by this process of accumulation of people and money. In the expression 'the waste and riotous consumption', we find a key topic of urban studies and early literature on the urban crowd. The crowd cannot be controlled because of the contingency that is inherent in consumption.

Thelwall is an urban intellectual, as Scrivener puts it (226).[6] Scrivener, however, does not try to define how Thelwall's concept of rural rambling reflects on walking in the city. The spaces in which this 'riotous consumption' takes place are the streets, places, and buildings of the city, where people interact with but also observe one another. This is done in a fashion which is typical of big cities and which would not be possible in the countryside, since everybody would know each other. The anonymity of the city streets that Wordsworth describes in the fifth book of his *Prelude* created the position of the observer who watches people doing their business without being known themselves. As Godwin claimed in *Thoughts On Man* (1831), 'I go forth in the streets, and observe the occupations of other men' (1993, 67). Like Thelwall, Godwin emphasizes the density of economic activities in the streets:

> I remark the shops that on every side beset my path. It is curious and striking, how vast are the ingenuity and contrivance of human beings, to wring from their fellow-creatures, "from the hard hands of peasants" and artisans, a part of their earnings, that they also may live. We soon become feelingly convinced, that we also must enter into the vast procession of industry [...]. (Ibid.)

---

6   'Thelwall also pays attention to the literacy and cultural quality of each place he visits, noting the presence, and more often absence, of libraries, reading rooms, and book shops' (Scrivener, 226).

Godwin praises the economic power of the city and introduces the city's life as a source of social activity and prosperity. But Godwin also acknowledges the city's dark side, the individual's fear of being watched and persecuted. In *Caleb Williams* (1794), the narrator tells us the following, a story of violence and oppression of the individual:

> I proceeded along the streets with considerable caution. I looked before me and behind me, as well as the darkness would allow me to do, that I might not again be hunted in sight by some man of stratagem and violence without my perceiving it. I was not as before beyond the limits of the town, but considered the streets, the houses and the inhabitants as affording some degree of security. (Godwin 1982, 285)

Throughout the eighteenth century the streets could take people to the open places of demonstrations or the criminal no-go areas of the city, such as The Seven Dials. 'Each district was comparatively isolated', we learn from Jonathan Richardson:

> [T]he state of isolation produced peculiarities and the peculiarities corroborated the isolation, [...]. The precincts and purlieus of Westminster Abbey were unknown to those who inhabited within half a mile of them! The ramifications of the Seven Dials [...], was to the timid and respectable very properly a perfect terra incognita. (1856, 3–4)

While studies of Romantic rambling are also interested in the psychological significance of walking, Jacobin authors were more concerned with the mental formation of these social spaces and the representations they offered in relation to citizenship. Scrivener confirms Vernon O. Grumbling's reading that the 'actual revolutionary theme which dominates *The Peripatetic* is democracy' (Scrivener, 211).

In *The Tribune* (1795, no. 17), John Thelwall draws comparisons between the poverty in the city and that in the very surroundings of the capital, London, where people live like 'slaves for the higher orders of society' (1995b, 180) because no money is spent to cultivate these 'waste lands': 'Go even into the neighbourhood of this metropolis; where manure is abundant; where the means of cultivation are easy; go which way you will; turn to the east, the west, the north or south; – see what tracks of land lay bare and desolate' (ibid.). People escape the countryside and arrive in the city, where these social injustices create counter-spaces of swarming streets where many diverse activities define citizenship:

> The modern city has been the stage for all types of public demonstrations. In fact, the promise of incorporation into modern society included not only the city and consumption but also the polity. Images of the modern city are in many ways analogous to those of the modern liberal-democratic polity, consolidated on the basis of the fiction of a social contract among equal and free people, which has shaped the modern political sphere. (Caldeira, 126)

The streets are transitory places that bring people of various walks of life together and lead them back into their separated quarters, which are sometimes very exclusive and forbidding to others. De Quincey, for example, associates London in *Confessions of an Opium Eater* (1821) with *terrae incognitae* (48). In contrast, De Quincey mentions Oxford Street many times as a space where everybody would have gone. For this reason, the city is less a place for symbolizing the poetic or philosophical mind of the individual, but rather the place of the urban crowd. And while walking rural areas has been studied quite thoroughly in romanticist studies, walking the streets of the big cities is rather associated with Benjamin's interpretation of Baudelaire's essay on Poe's man of the crowd as a flaneur.

While the flaneur seeks pleasure and takes his private voice into the streets, the crowd represents both a public and a collective voice that allows for the flaneur to observe the crowd and be part of it at the same time. The flaneur might appear the mid-nineteenth-century urban equivalent of the late eighteenth-century rural peripatetic. In opposition to the rural radical of the 1790s, however, he walked about in a completely different social and economic environment. The flaneur is attracted by the crowd and at the same time he wants to distance himself from it. According to Benjamin's reading, the flaneur 'becomes their [the crowd's] accomplice even as he dissociates himself from them. He becomes deeply involved with them, only to relegate them to oblivion with a single glance of contempt' (Benjamin, 172). This is not to suggest that Benjamin's concept of the flaneur, which has been criticized 'as a myth supporting his one-sided understanding of modernity as involving self-loss, alienation, and fetishization' (Lauster, 139), should be applied to a late eighteenth-century urban situation. Rather, it supports Lauster's reading that journalistic sources help to re-define the flaneur as a literary concept that supports 'an understanding of modernity in terms of a dynamically growing public sphere' (ibid.). Benjamin sees the delight of the flaneur as 'immersing oneself in the crowd, the object of observation, and on the other hand, being viewed with suspicion' (Lauster, 140). Lauster contrasts Benjamin's concept of the flaneur 'as someone who has abandoned his private space' with the 'dwindling of privacy', a concept which helps one to better understand the 'social processes and methods of observation' during the 1830s and 1840s. Lauster's concept of the flaneur seems to address aspects closer to the urban peripatetic of the reform movement in the 1790s, when the French Revolution had made it obvious that politics had invaded the private sphere seeking overall control.

Lauster's reading of Benjamin suggests introducing a different type of urban peripatetic or city stroller that could be understood as the 'ancestor' of the flaneur in the streets of London at the end of the eighteenth century. The flaneur is both a post-revolutionary and post-Romantic concept. The crowd had existed as a civic consciousness that frustrated the government's desire to control the rioting classes throughout the eighteenth century. After the revolution, however, the crowd comes into being as a historical force powerful enough to topple the entire social and political order of a nation and to jeopardize the private sphere of any person. As Edmund Burke brilliantly remarked: 'Then the greatest changes which could be rationally foreseen could have but little effect on the domestick happiness of mankind – now no man's fireside is safe from the Effects of a political Revolution' (Edmund Burke 1968, 64).

The flaneur inherits this power from the crowd, but, according to Benjamin's interpretation, he is disclaiming it. He is no longer like the rural peripatetic, who walks the ground of the big landowners claiming intellectual property of their land, but does nothing to actually jeopardize their power. Rather, the city stroller observing the crowd from a distance is part of it at the same time, claiming participation and citizenship. Raymond Williams regards these activities as corresponding to 'a wide range of new kinds of activity in the extraordinary commercial expansion of the city' (104). In the case of the figure of the 'city stroller', the analogy 'is a correspondence of observational perspective, and thence of literary stance, in different social and literary forms'. Raymond Williams suggests that 'the plausibility of the relation depends not only on a formal analysis of the historical social process but on the consequent deduction of a displacement or even an absence'. This absence is framed in the term homology (see Williams, 104–5). It is this kind of correspondence or homology that transforms the absence of the radical city stroller in political institutions into participation while moving in the streets and public spaces of the metropolis.

The post-revolutionary city stroller becomes a medium of political ideas and political power competing with other media, such as literature, in creating structures that analyze these historical social and political processes. John Plotz speaks of the 'enormous changes in the rules of public speech and public behavior between 1800 and 1850 [that] make crowds, variously defined, into a potent rival to the representational claims of literary texts themselves' (2). Therefore 'every text centrally concerned with crowds proves interested in establishing the role of literature itself within a public discursive space at least partially defined by those very crowds' (ibid.). As the place where the crowd gathers, the city, in part or as a whole, embodies this space.

The streets, however, guide the crowd, limit its activities, and give it specific meanings. While 'public speech and public behavior' find their articulation in public places, it is the streets of the city that bring individuals and smaller groups together. The closer individuals get to public places, the more they give up their individuality and merge into the crowd. The streets are like arguments leading to a specific activity of the crowd that is represented in the public speech and its effect on that crowd. The streets shape the crowd as much as the speech. The audience consists of all the individuals who arrive at the public place; the public speech represents all their voices, attracting and uniting them.

For the authorities, the crowds, like the orators who address them, are dangerous and uncontrollable. In *The Tribune* (1795, no. 47), Thelwall is well aware of these representational claims of the crowd when he opposes the authorities' accusations:

> While ministerial hirelings post me about the streets as a *miscreant*, and that scandalous and profligate paper called the *"Times"*, accuses me with hiring the mob that committed the tumults of Thursday, I am informed that the poor, infatuated, deluded people, at the east end of the town, who in the present hour of distress throng about the shops to buy for themselves the garbage and offal formerly consigned to dogs, and pay 4d a pound for bullock's liver, will turn sometimes indignantly away, and after first cursing the wicked administration that brought them into such miseries, will accuse me of preventing them, by my pacific doctrines, from redressing their grievances. (Thelwall 1995c, 326)

Thelwall sympathizes with the crowd, which consists of impoverished people living in the East End who are said to have rioted because of Thelwall's speech. While the authorities seek to make Thelwall responsible for the crowd's actions, the orator claims to have merely voiced their grievances. Thelwall defends his activities, pointing out that streets are a place for the distribution of knowledge and for political participation. The example he allegedly follows in this is no less the philosopher than himself. Thelwall, who had a classical education, would later disguise topical material with examples from Roman history as a means of addressing an urban audience in the years of political persecution and oppression. Defending his public speeches in the second part of *The Rights of Nature, Against the Usurpations of Establishments* (1796), he pointed out that according to one of his biographers (Cullen's life of Socrates), Socrates had taught 'his fellow *citizens* wisdom and virtue. In the open streets, in the public walks and baths, in private houses, in the *workshops of artists*, or wherever he found men whom he could make better, he entered into conversation with them, explained what was right and wrong, good and evil, holy and unholy, &c.' (1995e, 400). Thelwall calls this street activity an 'intrepid zeal for the promotion of truth, and the assertion of human liberty' (ibid.).

According to Thelwall, the streets will quickly become dangerous when the exchange of opinions fails. Over and over again he refers to France, where the streets turned red with blood, in order to distinguish this uncontrolled violence from what he called the democratic rights of citizens. It is this belief in citizenship, political participation, and social improvement that distinguishes Thelwall from romantic writers and friends such as Samuel Taylor Coleridge and William Wordsworth. Both regard London as a monster of commerce that turns most people into consumers rather than creative human beings, that is, producers. Coleridge writes to Thomas Poole, for example:

> There is no instance in the World in which a Country has ever been regenerated which has had so large a proportion of its [*sic*!] Inhabitants crowded into its [*sic*!] metropolis, as we in G. Britain. […] So enormous a metropolis imposes on the Governors & People the necessity of Trade & Commerce – these become the Idols – and every thing that is lovely & honest fall[s] in sacrifice to these Demons. (Coleridge, 720–21)

Wordsworth appreciates neither the crowds nor the hectic, anonymous life of London, as we know from his treatment of London in 'Residence in London', Book VII, ll. 149–63, of the *Prelude*:

> Rise up Thou monstrous ant-hill on the plain / Of a too busy world! Before me flow, / Thou endless stream of men and moving things! / Thy every-day appearance, as it strikes – / With wonder heightened, or sublimed by awe– / On strangers of all ages; the quick dance / Of colours, lights, and forms; the deafening din; / The comers and the goers face to face, / Face after face; The string of dazzling wares, / Shop after shop, with symbols, blazoned names, / And all the tradesman's honours overhead. (225–6)

Both poets, when they walk the city's streets, see only shop after shop and an anonymous crowd. They do not see the individuals in the crowd as citizens, but rather as a threat to their longing for individual privacy. In spite of the fact that Wordsworth, in writing his *Excursions*, was influenced by Thelwall, there

> is nevertheless a difference in emphasis between Thelwall's and Wordsworth's depictions of memory. Thelwall's are in a sprawling, multivoiced novel whose social meanings are prominent, whereas Wordsworth's representations of memory are emphatically private in *The Prelude*, the great epic of individualism. (Scrivener, 214)

Scrivener shows that the reader 'is constructed as an antibourgeois' (215). Wordsworth's vision of the tumultuous city is more benevolent, however, than Browning's, whose 'Juan is transported to a "pinnacle" above St. Mark's Square in Venice, from which he views the crowd below with disgust until he decides to take the humanistic option of diving in among them' (Baker, 164).

In de Certeau's terminology, Coleridge and Wordsworth view the crowd from the panoptical above. Coleridge and Wordsworth view 'the panorama-city' as a 'theoretical (that is visual) simulacrum, in short a picture, whose condition of possibility is an oblivion and a misunderstanding of practices' (de Certeau, 112). De Certeau calls the person who views the city from this position a 'voyeur-God' (ibid., 112). Wordsworth and Coleridge make a habit of this view and do not lose it while walking the streets of the metropolis. Their city is the concept-city that cannot be changed by walking the streets.

This panoptical view differs from that of Thelwall, who explores the city and gives a voice to its impoverished and uprooted classes who suffered under the social and economic order Wordsworth and Coleridge despised. 'The act of walking is to the urban system what the speech act is to language or to the statements uttered', says de Certeau (114). In a similar way, Thelwall walking the metropolitan streets and visiting places such as inns and debating clubs represents a pedestrian speech act that signifies a specific political attitude. Like de Certeau's city stroller,

> [h]e thus creates a discreteness, whether by making choices among the signifiers of the spatial "language" or by displacing them through the use he makes of them. He condemns certain places to inertia or disappearance and composes with others spatial "turns of phrase" that are "rare", "accidental" or illegitimate. But that already leads into a rhetoric of walking. (De Certeau, 115)

The multitude of activities and things available make the phrasing of the pedestrian speech act highly volatile and contingent. The heterogeneity of opinions and printed texts available demonstrates the diversity that the metropolitan walker encounters. The 'waste and riotous consumption of so immense a capital' might be frightening to the rural peripatetic, but on the level of intellectual diversity it is rather a gain than a loss, as Thelwall explains in *Sober Reflections on the Seditious and Inflammatory Letter of the Right Hon. Edmund Burke* (1796) when he speaks about reading:

> Mankind now read too many books to be permanently injured by any. Whatever mischief is to be apprehended, must be rather from the *stagnation* than the *nature* of their enquiries: and, perhaps, the best advice that can be given them, is to read every thing that comes their way, from a Grub-street ballad to a Royal proclamation. (1995d, 335–6)

The urban 'peripatetics' of reading consume everything 'that comes their way'. It is contingency that controls the selection, since no one can read everything. The labyrinth of the streets will lead citizens to their proper aim as long as they participate actively in urban life. Walking the streets is an economic as much as an intellectual activity because everyone has to make choices. In *Rights of Nature, Against the Usurpations of Establishments* (1796), Thelwall draws the analogy between reading and running:

> Even in that small proportion of the people of Britain, whom he [Burke] calls 'the British public', there is a still smaller subdivision (men of complete leisure, and of trained political education) whom he regards as the initiated few, and who, of course, may be expected to catch up, and put together, many of the loose disjointed hints, scattered here and there, with such studied carelessness as to escape the observation of those who 'read as they run'. (1995e, 396)

Those who 'read as they run' represent the democratic crowd. The late eighteenth-century city stroller is the orator and pamphleteer who guides the crowd through the streets of knowledge and commerce, making them participate in the diversity and creativity of urban consumption. Thelwall couples the modern urban experience with a political and intellectual life in which similar ideas and values had emerged.

In contrast to studies on the meanings of walking in the countryside, this essay is rather concerned with the question of how the citizen as walker constructed democratic spaces. These spaces should not be mistaken for social reality; they are representations of specific cognitive concepts such as freedom or democracy.

While studies of Romantic rambling are interested in the psychological significance of walking, Jacobin authors were more concerned with the mental formation of these social spaces and the representations they offered in relation to citizenship.

Presence was no longer a requirement of participation, but a subtle and dialectic relationship between presence and absence, which helped in defining new spaces and media. Labelled criminal and acting from the margins, reformers constructed democratic identity as a dynamic process, thus changing the political structures of social spaces in the centre. The tension between remoteness and closeness asks for various means of organizing mobility and distribution. This applies to mobility of both persons and products. In the case of the reformers, these products are pamphlets and literature; in other words, they distribute various products of intellectual property for political reasons and for a living. Operating from the margins of society, the reformers thus appropriated symbolic capital from the elite in the centre of society. Using their own bodies as a medium, they walked from the designated marginal places in society to the spaces of the political and cultural centre, representing the arrival of their political ideas in an oppositional political and, eventually, social context.

Mediating identities in this sense was a cognitive exercise in constructing an alternative urban world. Walking created these alternative spaces, either as literary representation or as physical performance. This way, the body became a medium for attributing meaning to unoccupied spaces in literature and society, by representing alternative realities which could be constructed by democratic ideas of participation, appropriation, and advancement. Lacking political power, the reformers re-defined presence and absence, selfness and otherness, inclusion and exclusion, and acceptance and deviancy – all in terms of moving from one place to the other.

While participation is traditionally understood in terms of proximity, the reformers developed various practices to define their identity in a dynamic change from positions of closeness to those of remoteness, either by approaching – and thus provoking – the centre or by creating exclusive places of closeness and communal living at the margins of society. The democratic identity was mediated by the creative capacity of citizens to establish individual activities. These activities and their spaces, however, are either individual refuges, such as Wordsworth's cottage in the Lake District, Thelwall's retreat in the countryside, or the urban spaces of the city stroller, who explored spaces of participation and citizenship – an 'ancestor' of the nineteenth-century flaneur, but one who envisioned the purpose of public spaces as being to gather various opinions of citizens in a political demonstration.

Chapter 13
Critical Responses

Rainer Emig, Hans-Peter Wagner, Christoph Heyl

Literature and the Discursive Construction of Identities (Rainer Emig)

Thresholds, a term highlighted by Katharina Rennhak in Genette's writings, is the common theme of all the projects in this section. Thresholds are essential for the concept of mediating, but they are not stable and essential entities in themselves. They are also subject to the effects of mediating and therefore part of the discourses that they help organize – and not their ontological take-off point.

In the projects presented above, one encounters in Isabel Karremann's contribution on Defoe social, political, and corporeal thresholds that help distinguish fully functional white male bourgeois bodies against sick, dying, and dead ones, but also thresholds of emerging literary genres – between factional reportage and clearly fictional texts. In the same eighteenth-century text we are also pointed towards a threshold between the text's content and its meta-level as a reading instruction on contemporaneous British ideology (cf. Womersley, 237–56). In Franz Meier's contribution we encounter a threshold between the pornography of the soul in Sentimentalism and the pornography of the body in *Fanny Hill*. Thresholds between texts for children (however they might be defined at the time) and adults (whatever they might be considered to be), as well as between already established literature and its cheap and trivialized variety in chapbooks, become apparent in Anja Müller's project.[1] Returning to Katharina Rennhak's contribution, we see thresholds of texts and paratexts, of author and narrator – and narrator and implied reader as well as author and reader in texts by female novelists of the period.

Thresholds enforce positionings. They also seduce, perhaps even entrap, and certainly contribute to shaping the reader – as a voyeur in Defoe's *Journal of the Plague Year* and *Fanny Hill*, as a joint authority together with the narrator in children's texts, as a male judge on female writers and their personae, as a collaborator in a fictionally constructed female community (of narrator and implied readers, or perhaps author and readers), or, finally, as part of a dominantly male community of authors and readers of pornography.[2]

---

[1] Compare the approaches in Immel and Witmore.

[2] How complex this relationship can become is discussed – with reference to German eighteenth-century literature – in Schindler, 66–80.

Yet these positionings are never simple and unambiguous. Can the same text mediate an ideal of manliness and challenge its cultural authority in the process? Why does pornography privilege a feminine narratorial perspective while catering mainly to a male readership? How can children's literature in the form of narrative fiction with a limited cultural value claim authority? Why do women writers invent female narrators (and even identify themselves with them) if they simultaneously have to acknowledge their limited power?

My suggested answer to this is twofold, and historical as well as structural. Historically speaking, in fictional prose we are dealing with a scenario in which rules of genre and media are still being worked out. It is anachronistic to talk about the emergence or even dominance of realism in the fiction of the eighteenth century if it is yet undecided when a 'true history' is true and when it is an entertaining and exciting story. The proximity of narrative prose to its old model, the romance, is still too close to permit any claims to an unbiased, objective, narratorial perspective. Nonetheless, the new bourgeois narrators clearly insist on presenting themselves as different from the privileged and largely aristocratic narrators of romances, who could rely on their audiences sharing their tastes and views, something that the new narrators have yet to ascertain.

In the literary examples used in this section, what I therefore propose as a structural concept is the careful and troublesome establishment of a kind of contract between author and reader, as well as between narrator and implied reader. This is why prefaces simultaneously need to address the status of the speaking voice and the status of the readers of their statements.[3] This is why texts for children (a new genre for a new and as yet undefined readership) need to assert their right to truths that supersede established ones – such as those of common superstition. This is why a text on the plague can claim an authority that it would normally have to share with official declarations, medical texts, and hearsay.

The problem of the contract, however, is indeed again that of mediation, since it needs to posit partners in the exchange as well as their position and status. But, as Deconstruction suggests, this produces a paradox because, in order to enter a contract, you need an implicit contract to start with (cf. Derrida 1987, 128–49).

The all-female community of writer, narrator, implied reader, and reader in women's fiction rests on the assumption that writer and narrator are female (which is not the case in *Moll Flanders* or *Pamela*) and that implied reader and reader also share the same sex (which is, again, clearly not generally the case). The observant reader of the spectacular account of the plague by Defoe is also not as certain as the text wishes to posit. Will he be a he, and if yes, will he know the plague from rumours, stories, or first-hand experience? Any of these positions will make him (or her) a different reader of the text. Will the reader of *Pamela* and *Fanny Hill* be suitably sympathetic or aroused or both – and if yes, for the right reasons? Will the reader of an eighteenth-century children's book be a child or an adult, a child reading on its own, a child reading to an adult (to prove his or her skills),

---

[3]   The problem is pinpointed in West, 105–23.

a child reading to other children (a frequent scenario in these books), an adult reading to a child (in which case, the commentaries of the texts turn him or her into a ventriloquist), or perhaps an adult reading on his or her own (as is the case with *Harry Potter* today)?

What my problematization of the *contrat fictional* intends to show is that fictionality is indeed identical with the mediating that forms the core of the project whose results are presented here. In terms of media, we merely have to deal with one form: the printed text. However, we have to face plenty of genres, many of which have not yet been defined (see Starr, and McDowell 2006). Similarly, the subject positions of the participants in this exchange are also undefined. In the examples presented above we find all the aspects of identity that twentieth- and twenty-first-century scholars have been trained to discover in texts: gender, class, and national identities, but we also find those of adults and children, so crucial to so-called Enlightenment thinking.

We see in these examples that these identities are being negotiated rather than posited. They are being tried out, that is, and not merely in the texts – in the shape of characters and narrators – but also between the texts and their audiences. This is where texts become the media of identity – on the double level that Isabel Karremann explores in her paper on Defoe, on the double level with which Franz Meier regards Sentimentality and pornography as two sides of the same coin,[4] on the double level that Katharina Rennhak sees as the simultaneous workings of narratorial fiction and the fiction of narrating, and on the double level on which adult texts become children's texts, and vice versa, in Anja Müller's project.

Fiction, to put it in a nutshell one last time, is one of the means through which identity is mediated in the eighteenth century. This is hardly surprising. At the same time, however, the shape, the genres, and the cultural value of fiction in the eighteenth century and beyond are themselves mediated, negotiated, and to a large degree shaped by this mediation. In other words: the identity of fiction itself is also at stake.

Perhaps this is the reason why eighteenth-century texts frequently encounter an unwilling audience today, why students, for example, but also many colleagues, find them troublesome, opaque, alien, and strange. The safety of established genre boundaries, realistic conventions, and narratorial rules is not yet firmly established in them. They are still in flux in these respects. Yet in this flux we may also recognize a historically distant echo of the fluent ways in which our modern Western patriarchal white identities come about. We may also recognize in them the contradictions and *aporias* that this constitution entails – and the manifold prices to be paid for eradicating or perhaps merely obscuring them.

---

4   As does Nussbaum 2006, 63–9.

The Multiple Spaces of Identity Construction in Eighteenth-Century England (Hans-Peter Wagner)

Concerned with the discursive construction of identities in the long eighteenth century, the contributions by Anna-Christina Giovanopoulos, Anette Pankratz, and Christian Huck claim to take a double focus – they explore the act of mediating as well as its results. Rather than responding to each article separately, I should like to comment on some issues that remain problematic precisely because the key terms of analysis are themselves still under debate. Along the way, I shall illustrate my arguments with some engravings by William Hogarth. In this way, I hope to be able to shed some light on critical areas of research in the sense explained by J. Hillis Miller in his magisterial study of what happens when you focus.[5] My playground will be the ramifications of the key terms 'public', 'identity', and 'discourse'. I hope to show that, far from being solid entities fit for critical analysis, they appear to be what Lacan once termed *points de capiton*, desperate attempts in critical debates to control the dissemination and diversification of contradictory and paradoxical meaning.[6]

Let me begin with the terms 'public' and 'public sphere'. The contributors are agreed that Habermas's concept of the latter – a somewhat homogeneous community of enlightened citizens entering into a rational discourse – might never have existed as such in eighteenth-century England.[7] Thus, Giovanopoulos acknowledges (with Tim Harris) the importance of popular politics outside Parliament and their influence on political decision-makers (112) as well as the existence of multiple public spheres, which Habermas disregarded. Sometimes, they were restricted to established or emerging social strata (one hesitates to use the term 'class' in the absence of class consciousness), but more often than not the separating lines, if they can be drawn at all, ran across the élite and the

---

[5]   See J. Hillis Miller, *Illustration*. Using engraved works of William Hogarth, I am of course fully aware of the fact that they do not represent eighteenth-century reality (in the sense of being the equivalent of photographic snapshots), but that they represent a biased, satirical, and hence distorted view of English customs and manners, even if (or, perhaps, just because) they operate with the reality effect. See my discussion of this problem of reading and using Hogarth's visual discourse in Wagner 1996 and Wagner 2001b.

[6]   Literally, a *point de capiton* is an upholstery button pinning down stuffing in a mattress or piece of upholstered furniture and stopping it from moving around. It has also been translated as 'anchoring point' in the sense that it unifies an ideological field and provides it with an identity in the presence of a plurality of meaning. What is at issue is precisely the *point de caption*, for it quilts the ideological field and imposes the (personal, ideological) meaning of the speaker or writer (see Lacan, 268–9). In what follows, my implicit criticism, for instance, is that the contributors, like Habermas, operate with an élitist, bourgeois (*avant la lettre*) notion of public and identity that knots the signified and the signifier together in a quilting project that does not allow the plebeian voice to be heard.

[7]   See, especially, Huck's persuasive critique of Habermas in the wake of recent challenges of his presuppositions (for example, Downie 2005, discussed by Huck).

popular/plebeian. The problem is not only Habermas's concern with a 'reasoning public' that obstructs our view of the importance of other, equally important public spheres, but also the tendency of the critics of Habermas to operate with notions of homogeneous, class-bound (or at least socially limited) spheres.

A brief look at visual representation may highlight the problem. While even Habermas's critics accept the fact that the so-called 'reasoning public' was constituted by the patrons (almost exclusively male) of coffee-houses, clubs, or salons, one needs to point out that both the patrons (how many of them, for example, were literate?) and the locations deserve more of our attention in terms of what I like to call the holy trinity in English studies – class, gender, and race. True, the educated tended to meet in the newly fashionable coffee-houses. One may recall the story of Richard Hogarth, William Hogarth's sadly unsuccessful father, who in early 1704 ran an advertisement in the *Post Man* for what seemed a new line of business:

> At *Hogarth*'s Coffee House in St Johns Gate [...] there will meet daily some Learned Gentlemen, who speak Latin readily, where any Gentleman that is either skilled in that language, or desirous to perfect himself in speaking thereof, will be welcome. The Master of the House, in the absence of others, being always ready to entertain Gentlemen in the Latin Tongue. There is likewise design'd a Society of Trades to meet every Monday night in the Great Room over the Gateway, for the promoting their respective Trades. (Quoted in Paulson 1991, 14)

The advertisement specifically addresses itself to 'Gentlemen', a term that by 1700 included non-titled citizens (merchants, for example), silently excludes women and those below the rank of gentleman, and combines intellectual with commercial interests. We still know very little about these meeting places.[8] What we do know is that by 1700 London had over 2,000 such houses that were becoming increasingly specialized, as a 'wide range of social types, to various professions and educational backgrounds, gathered here [...] to drink coffee, tea, cocoa, and exchange news, gossip, opinions, and stocks' (Paulson 1991, 15). Given this social variety, one wonders about the homogeneity of the patrons. Richard Hogarth's intellectual-economic venture, incidentally, came to nothing and he ended up in the debtors' prison. In addition, while the coffee-houses had the reputation for free conversation, they were also put down by some moralists as places of 'blasphemous dispute [...] where God could be denied in an afternoon, and the Church destroyed in the intercourse of a week' (ibid., 17). Indeed, Hogarth's visual renderings of coffee-houses and similar meeting places (for example, gambling houses) – even if one considers the caveat that they are not realistic renderings but satirical attacks on social vices – provide impressions of citizens far from reasoning and debate. In *A Midnight Modern Conversation* (1733), for instance, he gives us a private view of St John's Coffee-house in Shire Lane, Temple Bar, while satirizing the term 'conversation' in both senses: as an exchange of observations, opinions, and ideas, and as a conversation picture.

---

[8]   For studies of coffee-houses, see Ellis and Lillywhite.

Fig. 13.1   William Hogarth, *A Midnight Modern Conversation*, 1733. Private collection of the author.

Instead of reasoning citizens, we see men in various stages of drunkenness. The print seems to warn against this as much as against the political discussions that might have taken place before alcoholic intoxication set in. As some of the contributors to this volume note, newspapers were always available in coffee-houses – in Hogarth's print, we notice that the man at the far right (setting fire to his ruffle) has the *London Journal* and *The Craftsman* sticking out of his pocket, both propaganda journals of Walpole and the Opposition, respectively (Paulson 1989, 84–5). Such coffee-houses were competing with other locations, some of them more restricted (as the above advertisement shows, a social selection was always at work). One of these was the club, another the gambling house – Hogarth gave us equally disturbing views of rather unreasonable citizens (gentlemen) in plate 6 of *A Rake's Progress* (1735), a scene that alludes to such locations in Covent Garden as well as to the notorious White's gambling house in St James's Street (of which we see a visual allusion in plate 4 of the series).

The rake, it would seem, is the typical 'gentleman' addressed by the advertisement quoted above – the spendthrift son of a miserly merchant, he finds himself between classes, and in his social behaviour apes those above him, with disastrous consequences. Hogarth's visual evidence suggests that if the situation in regular coffee-houses was at times rather 'unreasonable', the private clubs were even worse.[9]

However, there were public spheres competing with the already relatively genteel coffee-house. Again, Hogarth's visual satire provides some interesting evidence. In *Beer Street* (1751; revised in 1759), the companion piece of his triptych *manqué*, *Beer Street and Gin Lane*, Hogarth gave an answer to the increase of gin houses that, together with the help of Fielding, led to the passing of the Gin Act in the summer of 1751.[10] The scene (or sphere) here is the outside of an alehouse, indicated by the signboard showing a barley mow in a farmyard. What is interesting for our context is the fact that the plebeians in the picture would probably not be those addressed by Richard Hogarth's advertisement meant for gentlemen – they are members of the labouring class (today's working class). We see a fat butcher, a blacksmith or cooper, fishwives, and servants, among others, while an overweight gentlewoman is carried by in the background. Like the gentlemen in the coffee-house, these plebeians also constitute a public sphere – Hogarth's visual representation even suggests that they enter into 'reasoning', as we notice various forms of discourse read and ignored. On the table beside the

---

[9]   See, for example, his painting entitled *Sir Francis Dashwood at His Devotions*, c. 1750, private collection. One might, of course, argue that the very blasphemy of the members of the Hell-Fire Club and similar aristocratic clubs was an attempt by 'reasonable citizens', although from the upper class, to spread Enlightenment atheism in a country totally controlled by religion. But my point is that the conversation that took place there was not of the kind imagined by Habermas.

[10]   For a discussion of the dissemination of the great wealth of ambiguous signifiers in the print, including the reality effect (realistic details), see Wagner 1997.

Fig. 13.2   William Hogarth, *A Rake's Progress: plate 6*, 1735. Private
collection of the author.

butcher are displayed *The Daily Advertiser* and the King's Speech of 29 November
1748, while the fishwives are reading (or perhaps one, being literate, is reading to
the other) *A New Ballad on the Herring Fishery*. Simultaneously, at right, we are
shown the kinds of discourse that do not find favour with these people. Destined
For Mr Pastem the Trunk maker are, in a hamper, *Modern Tragedys*, *Hill on
Royal Societies*, *Turnbull on Ancient Painting*, *Politicks vol. 9999*, and *Lauder on
Milton*. This is, in other words, reading matter for gentlemen, and of no interest
to those people shown in the engraving. Reading matter is aligned with social
stratum (again, I hesitate to use the term 'class'), as the engravings make it a
satirical point.[11] Still, what the engraving reminds us of is the fact that there were
public spheres outside and beyond the one discussed by Habermas and his critics
in this volume – and this public, still largely illiterate in the eighteenth century, was
no doubt also important for the construction of (national) identity. If this sphere

---

[11]   For a discussion of the reading matter, see Paulson 1989, 146–7 and Wagner 1994.

(and especially the illiterate) has been ignored, it is mainly because we, as intellectuals, have been more interested in the intellectuals of the long eighteenth century, in our counterparts rather than in those lower down on the social scale.

This brings me to the issue of identity, a term that lies at the heart of Pankratz's study of eighteenth-century comedy. While it seems to me that what separates the Restoration comedy from its successor in the eighteenth century is social stratum (aristocracy versus emerging middle class), there were again spheres for dramatic and theatrical discourse that went on outside the theatre attended by gentlemen (and ladies). Hogarth's *The Laughing Audience* (1733) provides a satirical view not only of a contemporary theatre audience, but, more important, of how identity – as discussed by Pankratz – might have been constructed in this sphere:

> At bottom is the orchestra [...]; next is the pit, separated from the orchestra by a row of spikes, in which the commoners are violently enjoying the play. Only one of them is sourly restrained, presumably a critic (at that time critics sat in the pit). At the top is the box with two foppish gentlemen completely inattentive to the play that is convulsing the populace; they are making advances, one to an orange girl, the other to a lady; and a second orange girl is trying to catch the attention of the first of these gentlemen. (Paulson 1989, 86)

My point here is less the inattentiveness of the upper social stratum to theatrical discourse than the mixed reaction of the audience. In fact, some other engravings by Hogarth suggest an influence of theatrical discourse across social borders and in some ways not discussed by Pankratz. In his early, heavily moralistic *Masquerades and Operas* (1724), Hogarth attacks the fashion of contemporary ballad operas while conceding that they were extremely popular with commoners and aristocrats alike.[12] Yet it is Hogarth's *Southwark Fair* (1734) that should alert us to a public sphere where identities were constructed and re-confirmed – independent of the social background of the spectators, and also independent of their being literate or illiterate.

This was the sphere provided at fairs by the popular plebeian theatre, of which we see some examples in the picture.[13] Among other performances, we witness the staging of Elkanah Settle's *The Siege of Troy* beneath the church tower, *Punches Opera*, and the Fall of Adam and Eve from the Scriptural puppet-show, *The Old Creation of the World*. Another competing company, at left, announces 'Ciber and Bullock's' *The Fall of Bajazet* as the stage metaphorically collapses, and there are various other shows (exhibitions and the prototype of a peep show), artists, jugglers, and musicians to entertain the mixed audience. It was precisely at such public performances, and literally in such a public sphere, that plays could appeal to the knowledge of the educated in religion, mythology, and literature while the illiterate could still follow, since they did not have to read. In other words, if we

---

[12] For a brief discussion of the print see Paulson 1989, 47–9; also see Hogarth's *Masquerade Ticket* of 1727.

[13] Details are discussed in Paulson 1989, 86–9.

Fig. 13.3   William Hogarth, *Southwark Fair*, 1734. Private collection of the author.

discuss the formation of English identities, we must not ignore these events and what is left of them as written or visual evidence. The public sphere was important because it brought together aristocrats and day labourers, gentlewomen and servant-maids, and they all took part in the consumption of a cultural discourse we may have underestimated. The public sphere of the fairs also allows a fresh look at a problem indicated by Huck: the notion and meaning of the popular. Until recently, the popular in the eighteenth century would be associated with the common or plebeian people, but the fairs, as well as the equally fashionable puppet theatres (attended by adults and children), were truly classless, attended and appreciated as they were by people from all walks of life and all social strata. This sphere, in other words, remains to be explored *vis-à-vis* its impact on mentalities and identities.

Finally, a word about the discourse involved in identity construction. As we saw with Hogarth's *The Laughing Audience*, any given discursive form might provoke different reactions, depending on the social background of the spectators, ranging from total absorption to utter boredom or disinterest. My final visual example is from Hogarth's series *A Rake's Progress*, which relates the tragic story of a newly rich heir and wastrel. Like Moll Hackabout in the *Harlot* series, in which the fault of the heroine consists in her wish to live the life of a lady, the rake is constantly surrounded by human vultures and by seductive discourse he cannot resist. The power of this socio-economic (and hence ultimately ideological) discourse across social strata, and even across ages, is perhaps best demonstrated in plate 4.

Destitute through gambling again, and beset by his creditors, the rake is saved once more by his lover, Sarah Young, whom he abandoned after inheriting his father's money. Below the rake we see some boys engaged in half-criminal activities, the print suggesting that the whole of English society is already infected by the disease of making money illegally (gambling and politics). There is one little boy at the left of the group who is shown reading *The Farthing Post*. This was a piratical paper vending gossip, news, and politics at low cost by evading the stamp tax. While contributing to the theme of piracy in the series, the scene within the scene also suggests something about the construction of identity through what might be termed official discourse in the 1730s. Totally absorbed in a cheap, sensational newspaper (the equivalent of today's *The Sun*), the picture suggests that – like the rake – the boy will become a victim of what he is seeing and reading. He will follow the examples about whom he is reading; his identity, the print suggests, is constructed in a way that could not be more disastrous. It is such popular discourse that deserves more of our critical attention as we engage in the reconstruction of both the formation of identity and the impact of discursive forms in eighteenth-century England.[14]

---

[14] I made some tentative gestures in that direction in Wagner 1991; but it seems that very few scholars have the time or courage to descend into the allegedly less interesting world of eighteenth-century English popular writing (for example, sensational newspapers aiming at a mass market, pastoral letters, penny pamphlets, and, of course, popular visual satire).

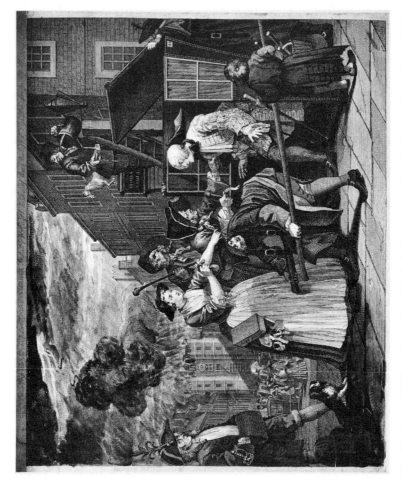

Fig. 13.4   William Hogarth, *A Rake's Progress: plate 4, Arrested for Debt*, 1735. Private collection of the author.

Panoramic and Peripatetic Modes of Identity Construction in Eighteenth-Century England (Christoph Heyl)

The nexus between space and identity can safely be regarded as a ubiquitous element of cultures throughout history. It has always been used by people in order to make sense of themselves and of their surroundings. This is done by treating space as a signifying structure, by inscribing it with meaning, and by relating this meaning to individual or shared identities. It can reasonably be assumed that the link between space and identity has always, in various shapes and forms, been part of English culture. However, in the course of the long eighteenth century, this phenomenon became, in many respects, much more prominent than it had been before. It also acquired new characteristics. This can be observed in both the private and the public spheres.

A momentous change was at work in the private sphere: there was a new awareness among the middle classes that domestic space could be used as a visible manifestation of one's identity. Growing affluence and the expansion of the market for consumer goods meant that one had more options than ever before to pick and choose material objects. Domestic space was increasingly used as a signifying structure, as a stage furnished with props chosen for both comfort and effect. Middle-class men began to play a range of roles in different social contexts. These roles were all tied to specific spaces – you could be a loving *paterfamilias* at home, a merchant in the city, a member of a club, and perhaps a man about town at night. Although the role played in one's domestic sphere was frequently described as one's true identity, you could, in fact, have a number of space-specific sub-identities.

The new thing about all of these eighteenth-century developments linking spaces and identities was the increasing importance and influence of various media in this context. Countless texts and images formed part of an ongoing debate about identity and the private sphere. It became a routine practice to characterize both fictional characters and real people by descriptions or depictions of their domestic surroundings. The nexus between space and identity kept cropping up in an endless number of conduct books. Cabinetmakers and interior decorators published pattern books from which you could choose ready-made props for any identity you might aspire to (cf. Heyl, 109–304 and 413–43).

Similar developments can be observed in the realm of the public sphere. Again, the most striking new development during the long eighteenth century was the importance and influence of various media when it came to negotiating the nexus between spaces and identities. This increasing importance of the media is reflected in the papers by Michael Meyer and Christoph Houswitschka.

Michael Meyer's paper deals with self-perception and perception of the 'other'. Again, media – in this case the topographical prospect, the panorama and illustrated travel books and tour guides – played a key role in the construction of national, regional, and imperial identities. The question of how works of art depict certain places, spaces, and landscapes is linked to the issue of the controlled gaze, or, to be more precise, to the dialectic of the controlling and the controlled gaze. In Robert Ker Porter's *Storming of Seringapatam*, the controlling gaze surveys the act of controlling a foreign enemy. Interestingly enough, national identity-building seemed to require an 'other' in the shape of something French again, so we get a glimpse of a French military adviser on the enemy side. Tipu Sultan, the sultan of Mysore, had indeed received French republican envoys and had planted a French tree of liberty in Seringapatam.[15] The French were probably also involved in making the famous sculpture known as Tipu's Tiger, a life-size wooden tiger devouring a soldier of the British East India Company which was fitted with a barrel organ.[16] All of this was widely publicized at the time (cf. Marshall, 57–74). This panorama was therefore not only about the colonial 'other', it was also about the fear of post-revolutionary France and its world-wide influence.

Robert Barker's remarkable panorama of London is another interesting case. The building – or at least the ghost of the building – in which Barker and his son displayed their famous panoramic view of London is still there. In 1865, the huge cylindrical structure, which was just off Leicester Square, was converted into a French Catholic church. Although the church had to be rebuilt after severe war damage, the original dimensions and the scheme of the circular plan were retained. It is therefore still possible to get a good impression of the monumental dimensions of this panorama.

The most intriguing feature of Barker's London panorama must be the intrusive prominence of the roof of Albion Mills in this depiction of the metropolis. Why does this building dominate the canvas to the extent of blocking out much of the prospect? Albion Mills (see Wheatley and Cunningham, 18–19) was London's first great steam-powered flour mill. Built in Lambeth in 1786, it was the most visible embodiment of the Industrial Revolution in the metropolis at the time. Its advent changed the character of Lambeth; soon, the area was populated by unskilled factory hands earning very low wages, and thus became a slum. Albion Mills was destroyed by a fire in 1791. When this happened, the fire was openly celebrated in a number of satirical prints,[17] and Luddite arsonists were suspected, probably rightly so. The factory was not rebuilt, and the burned-out shell of the building remained in place for 18 years. This hugely conspicuous ruin just opposite Blackfriars Bridge was London's best-known and most infamous urban eyesore of this period.

The Panorama opened more than half a year after the destruction of Albion Mills, in the autumn of 1791. This means that the building which formed the visual core of this image was in fact no longer there. It only existed as a ruin associated

---

15   Relations between Tipu Sultan and the French are discussed in Sheik Ali, 1–18.

16   After the battle of Seringapatam, Tipu's tiger was taken to London, where it was displayed in the East India Company's museum. It is now part of the Victoria & Albert Museum's collection (No. 2545 [15]).

17   For instance *The Baker's Glory, or, The Conflagration* (London, 1791), British Museum Prints & Drawings (Reg. No. 1868, 0808.6017) and *The Albion Mills on Fire* (London, 1791), British Museum Prints & Drawings (Reg. No. 1868.0808.6016).

Fig. 13.5   Notre Dame de France Church, Leicester Place, London. Photograph by Christoph Heyl.

with social unrest and Luddite arsonist attacks. Surely this must have had implications for contemporary reactions to this panorama. I would like to suggest that the destruction and factual absence of Albion Mills as shown in the panorama provided this image with a powerful sub-text. It is haunted by an invisible spectre, the spectre of social unrest. Maybe it is not so much about control but about loss of control, and not so much about capitalist enterprise but about the spectacular downfall of capitalist enterprise.

The much-feared spectre of social unrest and revolutionary tendencies brings me to Christoph Houswitschka's article. It was precisely this fear which polarized the political discourse of the period and led the government to implement drastic measures against the radical opposition. Once again, the related spectre of revolutionary France loomed large in the background. Therefore, the French are in the picture again, much as they were in the two other papers. Reformers like John Thelwall insisted that their political stance was in accordance with ancient Germanic law, that is, with the old, pre-Norman status quo. Thelwall presented himself as defending the ancient liberties of the Britons against the modern version of the Norman Yoke.

Christoph Houswitschka's paper presents yet another approach to the nexus between spaces and identities. His findings once again point to the increasing importance of print media when it came to negotiating identities in relation to various spaces. He shows how the opposition created places of their own, how they tried to gain ground – in a literal sense – by re-defining the political topography of urban and rural locations. All of this could only work because the radical reformers succeeded in publicizing their doings through a wide range of texts. So, as in Michael Meyer's paper, we can see the crucial importance of various media when it came to establishing links between spaces and identities. This also applies very much to the practice of rural walking and the formation of democratic spaces. These walks only made sense because meaning was attached to them by means of texts. Space was not appropriated by means of walking but by means of writing about one's walk.

Even during the early phase of Romanticism, and only a few years before the famous tours of Wordsworth and others, the concept of walking tours must have appeared extremely strange to most English people. When Karl Philipp Moritz decided to go on a long walking trip in England in 1782, most people he met regarded his mode of travelling as extremely bizarre and downright suspicious. Innkeepers refused to put him up at night.[18] Authors of travel books kept ridiculing Moritz, pointing out that anyone doing a walking trip in England would be regarded as more than just a little bit strange (Büsch, 97). This indicates that, at that time, walking was still unusual enough to be taken up as a radical gesture.

---

[18] 'Ein Fußgänger scheint hier ein Wundertier zu sein, das von jedermann, der ihm begegnet, angestaunt, bedauert, in Verdacht gehalten und geflohen wird [...].' ('A pedestrian seems to be a chimera here, being admired, pitied, suspected and shunned by whoever he encounters'. Moritz, 75).

Thelwall's labelling of this politicized type of rambling as *peripatetic* is interesting. On the one hand, rambling is conceived as a radical practice, something done by marginalized people in marginal areas. On the other hand, the very word implied an appropriation of elite culture. It indicated that its users were acquainted with Greek culture, especially with Aristotle's περίπατος, that is, the peripatetic school of philosophy. This claim is reinforced by the persona used by Thelwall in his text entitled *The Peripatetic*. The name of this persona is 'Sylvanus Theophrastus'. Theophrastus was a close friend of Aristotle and became the head of the peripatetic school of philosophy.

The Name 'Sylvanus' was likely to trigger yet another association: the pseudonym traditionally used by the editors of the vastly influential *Gentleman's Magazine* was 'Sylvanus Urban' (see Heyl, 378–9). If you invented a persona called 'Sylvanus Theophrastus', you indicated that you had peripatetic tendencies and that you could do without the labels 'gentleman' and 'urban'. Here we can once more observe the nexus between spaces and identities.

There is yet another important background to the radical practice of rambling that is worth mentioning. Rambling was, in fact, a protest against the enclosure movement. The thousands of enclosure acts that passed during the late eighteenth century did away with commons and rights of way. From a radical perspective, the enclosure movement was a prime example of the despotic rule exercised by landowners. It was regarded as closely related to the practices introduced by the Normans, as a contemporary form of the Norman Yoke. Radical ramblers would, depending on your perspective, trespass on private land *or* assert age-old rights of way. Two opposing topographical constructions of identity were bound to collide. On the one hand, there was the radical identity claiming access to the land in defence of ancient liberties. On the other hand, there were the landowners deriving their status – and hence much of their identity – from the land they owned.

The tradition of radical rambling lived on. Societies for the protection of ancient footpaths were formed in the early nineteenth century (Darby, 130). In 1935, the Ramblers' Association was formed. It is still very active, and just like its early predecessors, it pursues a political agenda, campaigning for open access to the land and against the claims of landowners.[19] Thus, peripatetic political action is still very much alive in Britain today.

---

[19] See the Association's website: http://www.ramblers.org.uk [9 May 2008].

Bibliography

Addison, Joseph (1713), *Cato: A Tragedy*, 2nd edn (London: J. Tonson).

Addison, Joseph and Richard Steele (1965, 1711–1714), *The Spectator*, Donald Bond (ed.), 5 vols (Oxford: Clarendon).

The Albion Mills on Fire (1791), (London: British Museum Prints & Drawings), Reg. No. 1868.0808.6016.

Althusser, Louis (2001), 'Ideology and Ideological State Apparatuses', in Vincent B. Leitch, et al. (eds), *The Norton Anthology of Theory and Criticism* (New York and London: Norton), 1483–1509.

Altick, Richard D. (1978), *The Shows of London* (Cambridge, MA: Belknap).

Anderson, Benedict (1991), *Imagined Communities: Reflections on the Origin and Spread of Nationalism*, rev. edn (London: Verso).

Baecker, Dirk (2005), *Kommunikation* (Leipzig: Reclam).

Baecker, Dirk, Norbert Bolz, and Wolfgang Hagen (2005), 'Über das Tempo der Massenmedien und die Langsamkeit ihrer Beobachter', in Wolfgang Hagen (ed.), *Warum haben Sie keinen Fernseher, Herr Luhmann? Letzte Gespräche mit Niklas Luhmann* (Berlin: Kadmos), 109–44.

Bailey, Margery (ed.), (1951), *Boswell's Column: being his Seventy Contributions to The London Magazine under the pseudonym The Hypochondriack* (London: William Kimber & Co.).

Baker, John Haydn (2004), *Browning and Wordsworth* (Madison: Fairleigh Dickinson University Press).

The Baker's Glory, or, The Conflagration (1791) (London: British Museum Prints & Drawings), Reg. No. 1868, 0808.6017.

Bale, John (2004), *Running Cultures: Racing in Time and Space* (New York: Routledge).

Balibar, Etienne (2006), 'My *Self* and My *Own*: One and the Same?', in Bill Maurer and Gabriele Schwab (eds), *Accelerating Possession: Global Futures of Prosperity and Personhood* (New York: Columbia University Press), 21–44.

Bannet, Eve Tavor (2000), *Domestic Revolution: Enlightenment Feminisms and the Novel* (Baltimore: Johns Hopkins University Press).

Barker, Jane (1713), *Love Intrigues: or, The History of the Amours of Bosvil and Galesia as Related to Lucasia, in St Germains Garden. A Novel. Written by a Young Lady* (London: E. Curll and C. Crownfield).

——— (1723), *A Patch-Work Screen for the Ladies; or, Love and Virtue Recommended: in a Collection of Instructive Novels. Related after a Manner Intirely new, and Interspersed with Rural Poems, Describing the Innocence of a Country-Life* (London: E. Currll and T. Payne).

Barker, Robert (1988, 1792), *London from the Roof of the Albion Mills* (Etching by Frederick Birnie), in Hyde, 18–19.

——— (1993, 1799), 'Constantinople', in *Sehsucht*, 133–4.

Barker-Benfield, G.J. (1996), *The Culture of Sensibility: Sex and Society in Eighteenth-Century Britain* (Chicago: University of Chicago Press).

Barrell, John (1983), *English Literature in History, 1730–80: An Equal, Wide Survey* (London: Hutchinson).

——— (1989), '"The Dangerous Goddess": Masculinity, Prestige, and the Aesthetic in Early Eighteenth-Century Britain', *Cultural Critique* 12: 101–31.

——— (2000), *Imagining the King's Death: Figurative Treason, Fantasies of Regicide, 1793–1796* (Oxford: Oxford University Press).

Benedict, Barbara M. (1994), *Framing Feeling: Sentiment and Style in English Prose Fiction 1745–1800* (New York: AMS).

Benjamin, Walter (1968), 'On Some Motifs in Baudelaire', in *Illuminations*, trans. Harry Zohn (New York: Schocken), 155–200.

Benwell, Bethan and Elizabeth Stokoe (2006), *Discourse and Identity* (Edinburgh: Edinburgh University Press).

Blackstone William (1979, 1765–1769), *Commentaries on the Laws of England*, Stanley N. Katz (ed.), 4th edn (Chicago: University of Chicago Press).

Böker, Uwe (2002a), 'Angelsächsische Geltungsgeschichten der frühen Neuzeit: Die Legitimierung der *Ancient Constitution* und das Prinzip der *Rule of Law*', in Gert Melville and Hans Vorländer (eds), *Geltungsgeschichten: Über die Stabilisierung und Legitimierung institutioneller Ordnungen* (Köln: Böhlau, 2002), 203–41.

——— (2002b), 'Institutionalized Rules of Discourse and the Court Room as a Site of the Public Sphere', in Uwe Böker and Julie Hibbard (eds), *Sites of Discourse – Public and Private Spheres – Legal Culture* (Amsterdam: Rodopi), 35–66.

Borges, Jorge Luis (1975, 1954), *A Universal History of Infamy*, trans. Norman Thomas Di Giovanni (London: Penguin).

Boswell, James (1770), 'Remarks on the Profession of a Player', *London Magazine* 39 (August–October).

Boulukos, George (2008), *The Grateful Slave: The Emergence of Race in Eighteenth-Century British and American Culture* (Cambridge: Cambridge University Press).

Bourdieu, Pierre (1984), *Distinction: A Social Critique of the Judgement of Taste* (London: Routledge).

Braithwaite, Alfred W. (1962/1964), 'Early Friends' Experiences with Juries', *Journal of the Friends' Historical Society* 50: 217–27.

——— (1972), 'Three Hundred Years Ago: The Penn-Meade Trial and Its Sequel', *Quaker History* 61: 3–15.

Braudy, Leo (1970), '*Fanny Hill* and Materialism', *Eighteenth Century Studies*, 4: 21–40.

Brewer, John (1997), *The Pleasures of the Imagination: English Culture in the Eighteenth Century* (London: HarperCollins).

Brissenden, R.F. (1974), *Virtue Rewarded: Studies in the Novel of Sentiment from Richardson to Sade* (London: Macmillan).

British Trials, 1660–1900 (1993), microfiche edition (Cambridge: Chadwyck-Healey).

Brodsley, Laurel (1993), 'Defoe's *Journal of the Plague Year*: A Model for Stories of Plagues', in E.S. Nelson (ed.), *AIDS: The Literary Response* (New York: Twayne), 11–22.

Brooke, Frances (1997, 1777), *The Excursion*, Paula R. Backscheider and Hope D. Cotton (eds) (Lexington: University Press of Kentucky).

Brooks, David (1992), 'Daniel Defoe's *A Journal of the Plague Year*', in Peter Hinton (ed.), *Disasters: Image and Context* (Sydney: Sydney Studies), 167–85.

Brunken, Otto (1988), 'The Novel as Controversial Reading Material for Young People in the 16th, 17th and 18th centuries', *Phaedrus* 13: 40–48.

Buddemeier, Heinz (1970), *Panorama, Diorama, Photographie: Entstehung und Wirkung neuer Medien im 19. Jahrhundert* (Munich: Fink).

Burgess, Miranda (2009), 'Nationalism in Romantic Britain and Ireland: Culture, Politics, and the Global', in Jon Klancher (ed.), *A Concise Companion to the Romantic Age* (Oxford: Blackwell), 77–98.

Burke, Edmund (1968), *The Correspondence: January 1792–August 1794*, vol. VII, P.J. Marshall and John A. Woods (eds) (Cambridge: University Press).

—— (1993, 1790), *Reflections on the Revolution in France*, L.G. Mitchell (ed.) (Oxford: Oxford University Press).

Burke, Edmund III and David Prochaska (eds) (2008), *Genealogies of Orientalism: History, Theory, Politics* (Lincoln: University of Nebraska Press).

Burke, Helen (2003), *Riotous Performances: The Struggle for Hegemony in the Irish Theater, 1712–1784* (Notre Dame: University of Notre Dame Press).

—— (2005), 'Eighteenth-Century Theatrical Touring and Irish Popular Culture', in Nicholas Grene and Christopher Morash (eds), *Irish Theatre on Tour* (Dublin: Carysfort Press), 219–32.

—— (2007), 'Acting in the Periphery: The Irish Theatre', in Jane Moody and Daniel O'Quinn (eds), *The Cambridge Companion to British Theatre, 1737–1830* (Cambridge: Cambridge University Press), 219–32.

[Burney, Frances] (1990, 1793), 'Brief Reflections Relative to the Emigrant French Clergy', in Claudia L. Johnson (ed.), '*Considerations on Religion and Public Education' [Hannah More] and 'Brief Reflections […]'* (Los Angeles: University of California Press).

Burtt, Shelley (1992), *Virtue Transformed: Political Argument in England, 1688–1740* (Cambridge: Cambridge University Press).

Büsch, J.G. (1786), *Bemerkungen auf einer Reise durch einen Teil der Vereinigten Niederlande und Englands* (Hamburg: Bohn).

Butler, Judith (1993), *Bodies that Matter: On the Discursive Limits of 'Sex'* (New York: Routledge).

——— (1999), *Gender Trouble: Feminism and the Subversion of Identity*, 2nd edn (London: Routledge).

Caldeira, Teresa P.R. (1999), 'Fortified Enclaves: The New Urban Segregation', in James Holton (ed.), *Cities and Citizenship* (Durham: Duke University Press), 114–38.

Calhoun, Craig (ed.) (1996), *Habermas and the Public Sphere*, 4th edn (Cambridge, MA: MIT Press).

Camden, William (1637, 1586), *Britain* (London: Andrew Hee).

Chetwood, W.R. (1749), *A General History of the Stage, from its Origin in Greece down to the Present Time* (London).

Claeys, Gregory (ed.) (1995), *Politics of English Jacobinism: Writings of John Thelwall* (Philadelphia: Pennsylvania State University Press).

Cleland, John (2001, 1749), *Fanny Hill; or: Memoirs of a Woman of Pleasure*, Peter Wagner (ed.) (London: Penguin).

Clery, Emma (2004), *The Feminization Debate in Eighteenth-Century England* (Houndmills: Palgrave Macmillan).

Clive, Catherine (1753), *The Rehearsal: or, Bays in Petticoats* (Dublin).

——— (1763), *Sketch of a fine Lady's Return from a Rout* (LA220), Larpent Collection, Henry E. Huntington Library, San Marino, CA.

——— (1765a), *The Faithful Irish Woman* (LA247), Larpent Collection, Henry E. Huntington Library, San Marino, CA.

——— (1765b), *Every Woman in Her Humour* (LA174), Larpent Collection, Henry E. Huntington Library, San Marino, CA.

——— (1973, 1744), *The Case of Mrs Clive* (Los Angeles: William Andrews Clark Memorial Library).

Cobban, Alfred (ed.) (1960), *The Debate on the French Revolution, 1789–1800* (London: A. and C. Black).

Cohn, Bernard S. (2008), *Genealogies of Orientalism: History, Theory, Politics* (Lincoln: University of Nebraska Press), 102–53.

Coleridge, Samuel Taylor (1956), *Collected Letters*, vol. 2, 1801–1806, Earl Leslie Griggs (ed.) (Oxford: Clarendon).

Colley, Linda (1996), *Britons: Forging the Nation, 1707–1837*, 3rd edn (London: Vintage).

——— (2002), *Captives: Britain, Empire and the World, 1600–1850* (London: Cape).

Colls, Robert (2002), *Identity of England* (Oxford: Oxford University Press).

Copeland, Edward W. (1972), 'Clarissa and Fanny Hill: Sisters in Distress', *Studies in the Novel* 4: 343–52.

Crane, David (1989), 'Introduction', in Sheridan 1989 (London: A & C Black): ix–xxvi.

——— (1995), 'Satire and Celebration in *The Critic*', in James Morwood and David Crane (eds), *Sheridan Studies* (Cambridge: Cambridge University Press), 87–95.

Crary, Jonathan (1998), 'The camera obscura and its subject', in Mirzoeff, 245–52.

Crook, John (1701), 'The Cry of the Innocent for Justice', in *The Design of Christianity, with other Books, Epistles, and Manuscripts, of that Ancient Faithful Servant of Christ Jesus, John Crook. To which is Prefixed a Short Account of His Life Written by Himself* (London), 146–211.

———— (1993, 1692), *The Cry of the Innocent for Justice: being a Relation of the Tryal of John Crook, and others, at the General Sessions, held in the Old Bayley, London* [...] *Published for no other end but to prevent Mistakes, and to satisfie all moderate Enquirers, concerning the Dealings and Usages that the said J.C. and others met withal, from the beginning of the said tryals to the end*, in *British Trials, 1660–1900*, no. 628.

Crowley, Patrick (2003), 'Paul Ricoeur: The Concept of Narrative Identity, the Trace of Autobiography', *Paragraph: A Journal of Modern Critical Theory* 26.3: 1–12.

Cunningham, Hugh (1995), *Children and Childhood in Western Society Since 1500* (London: Longman).

Curtis, T.C. and Arthur William Speck (1976), 'The Societies for the Reformation of Manners: A Case Study in the Theory and Practice of Moral Reform', *Literature and History* 3: 45–64.

Daniell, Thomas and William Daniell (1795–1808), *Oriental Scenery*, 6 vols (London: Longman, Hurst, Rees, Orme, and Brown).

———— (1810), *A Picturesque Voyage to India by the Way of China* (London: Longman, Hurst, Rees, Orme, and Brown).

Darby, Wendy Joy (2000), *Landscape and Identity. Geographies of Nation and Class in England* (Oxford: Berg).

Darton, F.G. Harvey (1982), *Children's Books in England: Five Centuries of Social Life*, 3rd rev. edn (Cambridge: Cambridge University Press).

Davies, Thomas (1780), *Memoirs of the Life of David Garrick, Esq.* (2 vols, London).

De Almeida, Hermione and George H. Gilpin (2005), *Indian Renaissance: British Romantic Art and the prospect of India* (Aldershot: Ashgate).

De Bolla, Peter (2003), *The Education of the Eye: Painting, Landscape and Architecture in Eighteenth-Century Britain* (Stanford: Stanford University Press).

De Certeau, Michel (1985), 'Practices of Space', in Marshall Blonsky (ed.), *On Signs* (Oxford: Blackwell), 122–45.

De Mause, Lloyd (ed.) (1976), *The History of Childhood* (London: Souvenir Press).

De Quincey, Thomas (1985), *Confessions of an English Opium-Eater and Other Writings*, Grevel Lindop (ed.) (Oxford: Oxford University Press).

Defoe, Daniel (1970, 1722), *The Complete English Tradesman: Directing him in the several Parts and Progressions of Trade*, 2 vols (repr. New York: Burt Franklin).

———— (1994, 1719), *Robinson Crusoe* (London: Penguin).

—— (2003, 1722), *A Journal of the Plague Year*, Cynthia Wall (ed.) (London: Penguin).

Derrida, Jacques (1987), 'Devant la loi', trans. Avital Ronell, in Alan Udoff (ed.), *Kafka and the Contemporary Critical Performance: Centenary Readings* (Bloomington: Indiana University Press), 128–49.

—— (2004), *Dissemination*, trans. Barbara Johnson (London: Continuum).

Dirks, Nicholas B. (1994), 'Guiltless Spoliations: Picturesque Beauty, Colonial Knowledge, and Colin Mackenzie's Survey of India', in Catherine B. Asher and Thomas R. Metcalf (eds), *Perceptions of South Asia's Visual Past* (New Delhi: American Institute of Indian Studies, et al.), 211–32.

Douglas, Mary (1966), *Purity and Danger* (New York: Praeger Publishers).

Downie, James Allan (1993), 'Periodicals and Politics in the Reign of Queen Anne', in Robin Myers and Michael Harris (eds), *Serials and their Readers, 1620–1914* (Winchester: St. Paul's Bibliographies), 45–61.

—— (2005), 'Public and Private: The Myth of the Bourgeois Public Sphere', in Cynthia Wall (ed.), *A Concise Companion to the Restoration and Eighteenth Century* (London: Blackwell), 58–79.

Duncan, Kathryn (2009), *Religion in the Age of Reason: A Transatlantic Study of the Long Eighteenth Century* (New York: AMS Press).

Dunn, Kevin (1994), *Pretexts of Authority: The Rhetoric of Authorship in the Renaissance Preface* (Stanford: Stanford University Press).

Dussinger, John A. (1974), *The Discourse of the Mind in Eighteenth-Century Fiction* (The Hague: Mouton).

Eaves, T.C. Duncan and Ben D. Kimpel (1971), *Samuel Richardson: A Biography* (Oxford: Oxford University Press).

Edney, Matthew H. (2003), 'Bringing India to Hand: Mapping an Empire, Denying Space', in Felicity A. Nussbaum (ed.), *The Global Eighteenth Century* (Baltimore: Johns Hopkins University Press): 65–79.

Eger, Elizabeth, Charlotte Grant, Clíona Ó Gallchoir, and Penny Warburton (2001), 'Introduction', in Elizabeth Eger et al. (eds), *Women, Writing and the Public Sphere: 1700–1830* (Cambridge: Cambridge University Press), 1–23.

Eisenstein, Elizabeth L. (1983), *The Printing Revolution in Early Modern Europe* (Cambridge: Cambridge University Press).

Elias, Norbert (1993–1994), *Über den Prozeß der Zivilisation*, 2 vols (Frankfurt/ Main: Suhrkamp).

Ellis, Aytoun (1956), *The Penny Universities: A History of the Coffee-houses* (London: Secker & Warburg).

England and Wales, Parliament: A collection of some memorable and weighty transactions in Parliament in the year 1678 and afterwards in relations to the impeachment of Thomas, Earl of Danby (1695) (London).

Erickson, Amy (1993), *Women and Property in Early Modern England* (London and New York: Routledge).

Esposito, Elena (2004), *Die Verbindlichkeit des Vorübergehenden: Paradoxien der Mode*, trans. Allesandra Corti (Frankfurt/Main: Suhrkamp).

Etherege, George (1982), *The Plays of Sir George Etherege* (Cambridge: Cambridge University Press).

An Examination of the Impartial State of the Case of the Earl of Danby in a Letter to a Member of the House of Commons (1680) (London).

Faller, Lincoln B. (1993), *Crime and Defoe: A New Kind of Writing* (Cambridge: Cambridge University Press).

Feldmann, Doris (1995), 'The Modern "Art of Puffing": Theatrical and Political Discourses in Richard Brinsley Sheridan's *The Critic*', *QWERTY* 5: 87–97.

[Fenn, Eleanor] (c. 1782), *School Occurrences* (London).

——— (1784), *The Female Guardian* (London).

Fielding, Henry (1980, 1742 and 1741), *'Joseph Andrews' and 'Shamela'*, Douglas Brooks-Davies (ed.) (Oxford: Oxford University Press).

——— (1988, 1751), *An Enquiry into the Causes of the Late Increase of Robbers*, Malvin R. Zirker (ed.) (Oxford: Clarendon Press).

——— (2004), *Plays. Volume I: 1728–1731* (Oxford: Clarendon Press).

——— (2007), *Histoire de Tom Jones, enfant trouvé*, Michel Baridon (ed.) (Paris: Gallimard).

Fielding, Sarah (1749), *The Governess; or, Little Female Academy* (London: A. Millar).

Fischer-Lichte, Erika (1990), *Geschichte des Dramas: Epochen der Identität auf dem Theater von der Antike bis zur Gegenwart*, 2 vols (Tübingen: Francke).

——— (2004), *Ästhetik des Performativen* (Frankfurt/Main: Suhrkamp).

Fletcher, Loraine (2001), *Charlotte Smith* (Houndmills: Palgrave).

Fludernik, Monika (1996), *Towards a 'Natural' Narratology* (London: Routledge).

Flynn, Carol Houlihan (1990), *The Body in Swift and Defoe* (Cambridge: Cambridge University Press).

Foote, Samuel (1974), *The Works* (repr. Hildesheim: Olms).

Foucault, Michel (1979), *Discipline and Punish* (New York: Vintage).

Fox, Christopher (1982), 'Locke and the Scriblerians: The Discussion of Identity in Early Eighteenth Century England', *Eighteenth-Century Studies* 16: 1–25.

Fraser, Nancy (1989), 'Rethinking the Public Sphere', in Calhoun, 109–42.

Freeman, Lisa (2002), *Character's Theatre: Genre and Identity on the Eighteenth-Century English Stage* (Philadelphia: University of Pennsylvania Press).

Friedman, Lawrence M. (1975), *The Legal System: A Social Perspective* (New York: Russell Sage Foundation).

Frushell, Richard C. (1968), 'An Edition of the Afterpieces of Kitty Clive' (Diss. Duquesne University).

——— (1970), 'The Textual Relationship and Biographical Significance of Two Petite Pieces by Mrs. Catherine (Kitty) Clive', *Restoration and 18th-Century Theatre Research* 9.1 (May): 51–8.

Garside, Peter, James Raven, and Rainer Schöwerling (eds) (2001), *The English Novel 1770–1829: A Bibliographical Survey of Prose Fiction Published in the British Isles*, 2 vols (Oxford: Oxford University Press).

Genette, Gérard (1997), *Paratexts: Thresholds of Interpretation*, trans. Jane E. Lewin (Cambridge: Cambridge University Press).

Godwin, William (1982, 1794), *Caleb Williams*, David McCracken (ed.) (Oxford: Oxford University Press).

——— (1993, 1831), 'Thoughts On Man, His Nature, Productions and Discoveries. Interspersed with Some Particulars Respecting the Author', in Mark Philp (ed.), *Political and Philosophical Writings of William Godwin; vol. VI: Essays* (London: William Pickering), 31–292.

——— (2001, 1805), *Fleetwood: or, The New Man of Feeling*, Gary Handwerk and A.A. Markley (eds) (Peterborough: Broadview).

Goulemont, Jean Marie (1994), *Forbidden Texts: Erotic Literature and its Readers in Eighteenth-Century France*, trans. James Simpson (Cambridge: Polity).

Greaves, Richard L. (1990), *Enemies under His Feet: Radicals and Nonconformists in Britain, 1664–1677* (Stanford: Stanford University Press).

Green, Thomas Andrew (1985), *Verdict According to Conscience: Perspectives on English Criminal Trial Jury, 1200–1800* (Chicago: University of Chicago Press).

Greenblatt, Stephen (1980), *Renaissance Self-Fashioning: From More to Shakespeare* (Chicago: University of Chicago Press).

Greene, John C. and Gladys L.H. Clark (1993), *The Dublin Stage, 1720–1745: A Calendar of Plays, Entertainments, and Afterpieces* (Bethlehem: Lehigh University Press).

Gregg, Stephen (1999), 'Godly Manliness: Defoe's Men in Bad Times', in Andrew P. Williams (ed.), *The Image of Manhood in Early Modern Literature: Viewing the Male* (Westport, CT: Greenwood), 141–59.

——— (2009), *Defoe's Writings and Manliness: Contrary Men* (Farnham: Ashgate).

Gregory, Jeremy (1997), 'Homo Religiosus: Masculinity and Religion in the Long Eighteenth Century', in Hannah Barker and Elaine Chalus (eds), *Gender in Eighteenth Century England: Roles, Representations and Responsibilities* (London: Longman), 85–111.

Grenby, Matthew O. (2002), 'Adults Only? Children and Children's Books in British Circulating Libraries, 1748–1848', *Book History* 5: 19–38.

Habermas, Jürgen (1962), *Strukturwandel der Öffentlichkeit: Untersuchungen zu einer Kategorie der bürgerlichen Gesellschaft* (Neuwied: Luchterhand).

——— (1974, 1964), 'The Public Sphere: An Encyclopedia Article', trans. Sara and Frank Lennox, *New German Critique* 3: 49–55.

——— (1989), *The Structural Transformation of the Public Sphere*, trans. Thomas Burger (Cambridge: Polity Press).

Hall, Stuart (1979), 'Culture, the Media and the "Ideological Effect"', in James Curran (ed.), *Mass Communication and Society* (London: Edward Arnold), 315–48.

——— (2000), 'Who needs 'identity'?', in Paul Du Gay, Jessica Evans, and Peter Redman (eds), *Identity: A Reader* (London: Sage), 15–30.

———— (2005), 'Thinking the Diaspora: Home-thoughts from Abroad', in Gaurav Desai and Supriya Nair (eds), *Postcolonialisms: An Anthology of Cultural Theory* (New Brunswick: Rutgers University Press), 543–60.

Hammond, Brean S. (1997), *Professional Imaginative Writing in England 1670–1740: Hackney for Bread* (Oxford: Clarendon Press).

The Harcourt Papers (1880–1905), E.W. Harcourt (ed.) (13 vols, Oxford: Parker).

Hargrave, Francis (ed.) (1777), *A Complete Collection of State-Trials, and Proceedings for High-Treason, And other Crimes and Misdemeanors*, vol. 5, 4th edn (London: T. Wright), 339–83.

Harlow, Barbara and Mia Carter, (eds) (1999), *Imperialism and Orientalism: A Documentary Sourcebook* (Oxford: Blackwell).

Harris, Michael (1986), 'Introduction: The Seventeenth and Eighteenth Centuries', in Michael Harris and Alan Lee (eds), *The Press in English Society from the Seventeenth to Nineteenth Centuries* (London: Associated University Press), 19–24.

Harris, Susan Cannon (2007), 'Mixed Marriage: Sheridan, Macklin, and the Hybrid Audience', in Michael Cordner and Peter Holland (eds), *Players, Playwrights, Playhouses: Investigating Performance, 1660–1800* (Basingstoke: Palgrave), 189–212.

Harris, Tim (2001), 'Understanding Popular Politics in Restoration Britain', in Alan Houston and Steve Pincus (eds), *A Nation Transformed: England After the Restoration* (Cambridge: Cambridge University Press), 125–53.

Harvey, Karen (2004), *Reading Sex in the 18th Century: Bodies and Gender in English Erotic Culture* (Cambridge: Cambridge University Press).

Haywood, Eliza (2000, 1719/1729), *Love in Excess; or, The Fatal Inquiry*, David Oakleaf (ed.), 2nd edn (Peterborough: Broadview).

Helmstetter, Rudolf (2007), 'Der Geschmack der Gesellschaft: Die Massenmedien als Apriori des Populären', in Christian Huck and Carsten Zorn (eds), *Das Populäre der Gesellschaft: Systemtheorie und Populärkultur* (Wiesbaden: VS-Verlag), 44–72.

Hentzi, Gary (1993), 'Sublime Moments and Social Authority in *Robinson Crusoe* and *A Journal of the Plague Year*', *Eighteenth-Century Studies* 26.3: 419–34.

Herrup, Cynthia B. (1985), 'Law and Morality in Seventeenth-Century England', *Past and Present* 106: 102–23.

Heyl, Christoph (2004), *A Passion for Privacy: Untersuchungen zur Genese der bürgerlichen Privatsphäre in London, 1660–1800* (Munich: Oldenbourg).

Heywood, Colin (2001), *A History of Childhood* (Cambridge: Polity).

Hillis Miller, J. (1992), *Illustration* (London: Reaktion Books).

The History of Little Goody Two-Shoes; Otherwise called, Mrs. Margery Two-Shoes (1766) (London).

Hoadly, Benjamin (1710), *An Explanation of some Hard Terms now in Use: For the Information of all such as Read, or Subscribe Addresses* (London).

Hogarth, William (1955), *The Analysis of Beauty*, Joseph Burke (ed.) (Oxford: Clarendon).

Holmes, Geoffrey (1993), *The Making of a Great Power: Late Stuart and Early Georgian Britain 1660–1722* (London: Longman).

Hoppit, Julian (2000), *A Land of Liberty? England 1689–1727* (Oxford: Oxford University Press).

Horle, Craig (1988), *The Quakers and the English Legal System 1660–1688* (Philadelphia: University of Philadelphia Press).

Houswitschka, Christoph (1997), '" […] where Culture spreads luxuriant" – John Thelwall's Poetical Relocation of Burkean Values', in Jürgen Kamm (ed.), *The City and the Country: Proceedings from the Sixth British and Cultural Studies Conference Dresden 1995* (Essen: Die Blaue Eule), 31–50.

——— (ed.) (2004), *Freedom – Treason – Revolution: Uncollected Sources of the Political and Legal Culture of the London Treason Trials (1794)* (Frankfurt/ Main: Lang).

Huck, Christian (2007), 'Calico Bill and the Calico Madams: Fashion, Print, and the Public', in Sabine Volk-Birke and Julia Lippert (eds), *Anglistentag 2006 Halle: Proceedings* (Trier: WVT), 53–63.

——— (2010), *Fashioning Society, or, the Mode of Modernity: Observing Fashion in Eighteenth-Century Britain* (Würzburg: Königshausen & Neumann).

Hyde, Ralph (1988), *Panoramania! The Art and Entertainment of the 'All-Embracing' View* (London: Trefoil & Barbican Art Gallery).

Immel, Andrea and Michael Witmore (eds) (2006), *Childhood and Children's Books in Early Modern Europe, 1550–1800* (London: Routledge).

An Impartial State of the Case of the Earl of Danby in a Letter to a Member of the House of Commons (1679) (London).

Innes, Ionna (1990), 'Politics and Morals: The Reformation Manners Movement in Later Eighteenth-Century England', in Eckhardt Hellmuth (ed.), *The Transformation of Political Culture: England and Germany in the late 18th Century* (Oxford: Oxford University Press), 57–118.

Isaacs, Tina (1982), 'The Anglican Hierarchy and the Reformation of Manners 1688–1738', *Journal of Ecclesiastical History* 33: 391–411.

Iser, Wolfgang (1994a), *Der implizite Leser: Kommunikationsformen des Romans von Bunyan bis Beckett*, 3rd edn (Munich: Fink).

——— (1994b), *Der Akt des Lesens: Theorie ästhetischer Wirkung*, 4th edn (Munich: Fink).

Jackson, Mary V. (1989), *Engines of Instruction, Mischief, and Magic: Children's Literature in England from its Beginnings to 1839* (Lincoln: University of Nebraska Press).

James, Lawrence (1998), *The Rise and Fall of the British Empire* (London: Abacus).

Janeway, James (1763), *A Token for Children: Being An Exact Account of the Conversion, Holy and Exemplary Lives and Joyful Deaths of several Young Children. In Two Parts* (London).

Jarvis, Robin (1997), *Romantic Writing and Pedestrian Travel* (New York: St. Martin's Press).

Jasanoff, Maya (2005), *Edge of Empire: Conquest and Collecting in the East, 1750–1850* (London: Fourth Estate).

Jefferies, J. (1750), *The Virtuous Novelist; or, Little Polite Court Tales; Compos'd Originally for the Education of a Young French Prince; by the Universally admir'd Author of Telemachus with other Ingenious Fictions &c. Abridg'd for the Amusement & Instruction of our British Youth of Both Sexes* (London).

Joncus, Berta (2005), '"His Spirit is in Action Seen": Milton, Mrs. Clive and the Simulacra of the Pastoral in *Comus*', *Eighteenth-Century Music* 2.1: 7–40.

Jones, Robert W. (2002), 'Sheridan and the Theatre of Patriotism: Staging Dissent During the War for America', *Eighteenth-Century Life* 26.1: 24–45.

Juengel, Scott (1995), 'Writing Decomposition: Defoe and the Corpse', *Journal of Narrative Technique* 25: 139–53.

Kames, Henry Home Lord (1774–1775), *Sketches of the History of Man. In four volumes*, vol. I (Dublin), Eighteenth Century Collections Online, Gale Group, http://galenet.galegroup. com/servlet/ECCO (1.12.2007).

Karremann, Isabel (2008), *Männlichkeit und Körper: Inszenierungen eines geschlechts-spezifischen Unbehagens im englischen Roman des 18. und frühen 19. Jahrhunderts* (Königstein: Taunus).

Kelley, Hugh (1766), *Thespis, or, a critical examination into the Merits of All the Principal Performers Belonging to Drury-Lane Theatre* (London).

Keupp, Heiner (ed.) (1993), *Zugänge zum Subjekt: Perspektiven einer reflexiven Sozialpsychologie* (Frankfurt/Main: Suhrkamp).

——— (ed.) (2002), *Identitätskonstruktionen: Das Patchwork der Identitäten in der Spätmoderne*, 2nd edn (Reinbek: Rowohlt).

Keymer, Thomas and Peter Sabor (eds) (2001), *The Pamela Controversy: Criticisms and Adaptations of Samuel Richardson's* Pamela, *1740–1750*, 6 vols (London: Pickering & Chatto).

Kibbie, Anne Louise (1991), 'Sentimental Properties: *Apela* and *Memoirs of a Woman of Pleasure*', *ELH* 58: 561–77.

[Kilner, Mary Ann] (c. 1785), *The Adventures of a Whipping-Top* (London).

King, Kathryn R. (1995), 'Of Needles and Pens and Women's Work', *Tulsa Studies in Women's Literature* 14.1: 77–93.

King, Ross (1993), 'Wordsworth, Panoramas, and the Prospect of London', *Studies in Romanticism* 32: 57–73.

King, Thomas A. (2004), *The Gendering of Men, 1600–1750*, 2 vols (Madison: University of Wisconsin Press).

Kinservik, Matthew J. (1996), 'Garrick's Unpublished Epilogue for Catherine Clive's *The Rehearsal: or, Bays in Petticoats* (1750)', *Etudes Anglaises* 49.3: 320–26.

Knights, Mark (2005), 'History and Literature in the Age of Defoe and Swift', *History Compass* 3: 1–20.

Knowles, Murray and Kirsten Malmkjaer (1996), *Language and Control in Children's Literature* (New York: Routledge).

Knox, John (1988, 1810), *South-western view from Loch Lomond and South-western view from Ben Lomond*, in Hyde, 40.

Koschorke, Albrecht (1999), *Körperströme und Schriftverkehr: Mediologie des 18. Jahrhunderts* (Munich: Fink).

Kubek, Elizabeth (2003), 'The Man Machine: Horror and the Phallus in *Memoirs of a Woman of Pleasure*', in Patsy S. Fowler and Alan Jackson (eds), *Launching Fanny Hill: Essays on the Novel and Its Influences* (New York: AMS Press), 173–95.

Lacan, Jacques (1993), *The Seminar. Book III. The Psychoses, 1955–56*, trans. Russell Grigg (London: Routledge).

Lamb, Mary and Charles Lamb (1995, 1809), *Mrs Leicester's School* (Poole: Woodstock Books).

Lamoine, George (ed.) (1992), *Charges to the Grand Jury 1689–1803* (London: Royal Historical Society).

Landes, Joan (ed.) (1998), *Feminism, the Public and the Private* (Oxford: Oxford University Press).

Langan, Celeste (1995), *Romantic Vagrancy: Wordsworth and the Simulation of Freedom* (Cambridge: Cambridge University Press).

Laqueur, Thomas (1990), *Making Sex: Body and Gender from the Greeks to Freud* (Cambridge: Harvard University Press).

Lauster, Martina (2007), 'Walter Benjamin's Myth of the Flaneur', *The Modern Language Review* 102.1: 139–56.

Leask, Nigel (2004), *Curiosity and the Aesthetics of Travel Writing, 1770–1840* (Oxford: Oxford University Press).

Leavy, Barbara Fass (1992), 'The Historical and Ethical Significance of Defoe's *Journal of the Plague Year*', in Barbara Fass Leavy, *To Blight with Plague: Studies in a Literary Theme* (New York: New York University Press), 21–39.

Leeds, Thomas Osborne, Duke of; Tewksbury, Henry Capel, Lord Capel of (1678), *Articles of impeachment of high treason and other hgih* [sic] *crimes, misdemeanours and offences against Thomas, Earl of Danby, Lord High Treasurer of England as they were delivered in to the House of Lords in the name of the Commons of England, by Sir Henry Capel, December 23, 1678, together with a letter of the lord treasurers to Mr. Montague, late embassador in France* (London).

Lesnik-Oberstein, Karín (1999), 'Essentials: What is Children's Literature? What is Childhood?', in Peter Hunt (ed.), *Understanding Children's Literature: Key Essays from the International Companion Encyclopedia of Children's Literature* (London: Routledge), 15–29.

Leujeune, Philippe (1975), *Le pacte autobiographique* (Paris: Seuil).

The Life of Mr. James Quin, Comedian. With the History of the Stage from his Commencing Actor to his Retreat to Bath (1766) (London).

Lillo, George (1965, 1731), *The London Merchant* (London: Arnold).

Lillywhite, Bryant (1963), *London Coffee-Houses: A Reference Book of Coffee-Houses of the 17th and 18th centuries* (London: Allen & Unwin).

Linebaugh, Peter (1992), *The London Hanged: Crime and Society in the Eighteenth Century* (Cambridge: Cambridge University Press).

Lipovetsky, Gilles (1994), *The Empire of Fashion: Dressing Modern Democracy*, trans. C. Porter (Princeton: Princeton University Press).

Little Master's Miscellany. Or Divine and Moral Essays, in Prose and Verse, Adapted to the Capacities and Deign'd for the Improvement of the Youth of both Sexes (1748), 2nd edn (Birmingham).

Lloyd, David (1990), *Ireland After History* (Cork: Cork University Press).

Lloyd, Geneviève (1984), *The Man of Reason: 'Male' and 'Female' in Western Philosophy* (London: Methuen).

Locke, John (1988, 1689), *Two Treatises of Government*, Peter Laslett (ed.) (Cambridge: Cambridge University Press).

——— (2000, 1693), *Some Thoughts Concerning Education*, John W. and Jean S. Yolton (eds) (Oxford: Clarendon).

Lord, Edward (1724), *A Sermon Preached to the Societies for Reformation of Manners [...] The Thirtieth Account of the Progress made in the Cities of London and Westminster, and Places adjacent, By the Societies for the Promoting a Reformation of Manners; By Furthering the Execution of Laws against Prophaneness and Immorality, and other Christian Methods* (London).

Love, Harold (1993), *Scribal Publication in Seventeenth-Century England* (Oxford: Oxford University Press).

Löw, Martina (2007), *Raumsoziologie*, 5th edn (Frankfurt/Main: Suhrkamp).

Ludden, David (2008), 'Orientalist Empiricism: Transformations of Colonial Knowledge', in Edmund Burke III and David Prochaska (eds), *Genealogies of Orientalism. History, Theory, Politics* (Lincoln and London: University of Nebraska Press), 75–101.

Luhmann, Niklas (1989), 'Individuum, Individualität, Individualismus', *Gesellschaftsstruktur und Semantik: Studien zur Wissenssoziologie der modernen Gesellschaft*, vol. 3 (Frankfurt/Main: Suhrkamp), 149–258.

——— (1990), 'Gesellschaftliche Komplexität und öffentliche Meinung', *Soziologische Aufklärung*, vol. 5 (Opladen: Westdeutscher Verlag), 170–82.

——— (1997), *Die Gesellschaft der Gesellschaft*, 2 vols (Frankfurt/Main: Suhrkamp).

——— (1998), *Gesellschaftsstruktur und Semantik*, 5 vols (Frankfurt/Main: Suhrkamp).

——— (2000), *The Reality of the Mass Media*, trans. Kathleen Cross (Stanford: Stanford University Press).

——— (2004), *Die Realität der Massenmedien*, 3rd edn (Wiesbaden: VS Verlag).

Macfie, A.L. (2002), *Orientalism* (London: Longman).

MacKenzie, John (1996). 'Art and the Empire', in Peter James Marshall (ed.), *The Cambridge Illustrated History of the British Empire* (Cambridge: Cambridge University Press), 296–317.

Mackie, Erin (1997), *Market à la Mode: Fashion, Commodity, and Gender in* The Tatler *and* The Spectator (Baltimore, London: Johns Hopkins University Press).

Maclean, Marie (1991), 'Pretexts and Paratexts: The Art of the Peripheral', *New Literary History* 22: 273–9.

Maese, Sarah (1766), *The School* (London).

Mainwaring, Arthur (1975, 1711), 'An Excellent New Song, Called Mat's Peace, Or, The Downfall of Trade', in F.H. Ellis (ed.), *Poems on Affairs of State*, vol. 7 (New Haven, CT: Yale University Press), 504–13.

Makdisi, Saree (1998), *Romantic Imperialism: Universal Empire and the Culture of Modernity* (Cambridge: Cambridge University Press).

Malcolmson, Robert W. (1973), *Popular Recreations in English Society 1700–1850* (Cambridge: Cambridge University Press).

Marshall, J.P. (1993), *Trade and Conquest: Studies on the Rise of British Dominance in India* (Aldershot: Variorum).

Maus, Katharine Eisaman (1995), *Inwardness and Theater in the English Renaissance* (Chicago: Chicago University Press).

Mayer, Robert (1990), 'The Reception of *A Journal of the Plague Year* and the Nexus of Fiction and History in the Novel', *ELH* 57.3: 529–55.

McDowell, Paula (1998), *The Women of Grub Street: Press, Politics, and Gender in the London Literary Marketplace 1678–1730* (Oxford: Clarendon Press).

——— (2006), 'Defoe and the Contagion of the Oral: Modeling Media Shift in *A Journal of the Plague Year*', *PMLA* 121.1: 87–106.

McLane, Maureen (2001), 'Ballads and Bards: British Romantic Orality,' *Modern Philology* 98.3: 423–43.

McLynn, Frank (1989), *Crime and Punishment in Eighteenth-century England* (London: Routledge).

Meehan, Johanna (ed.) (1995), *Feminists Read Habermas: Gendering the Subject of Discourse* (New York, London: Routledge).

Meißner, Karin (1994), *Au Lecteur: Studien zu den französischen Romanvorworten des 17. Jahrhunderts* (Frankfurt/Main: Lang).

Mellor, Anne K. (2000), *Mothers of the Nation: Women's Political Writing in England 1780–1830* (Bloomington: Indiana University Press).

Melton, James van Horn (2001), *The Rise of the Public in Enlightenment Europe* (Cambridge: Cambridge University Press).

Memoirs of the Extraordinary Life, Works, and Discoveries of Martinus Scriblerus. Written in Collaboration with the Members of the Scriblerus Club (1988), Charles Kerby-Miller (ed.) (New York: Oxford University Press).

Miège, Guy (1703), *The New State of England, Under Our Sovereign, Queen Anne, in three parts*, 5th ed. (London).

Miller, Louise M. (1995), 'Invasion as Theatrical Appropriation in *The Critic*', *QWERTY* 5: 99–104.

Milne, Anne (2008), *'Lactilla Tends Her Fav'rite Cow': Ecocritical Readings of Animals and Women in Eighteenth-Century British Labouring-Class Women's Poetry* (Lewisburg, PA: Bucknell University Press).

Mirzoeff, Nicholas (ed.) (1998), *The Visual Culture Reader* (Routledge: New York).

Mitchell, W.J.T. (2002), *Landscape and Power*, 2nd edn (Chicago: Chicago University Press).

Montaigne, Michel de (2006), *Essays*, Book I, trans. John Floriot, 3 vols (London: The Folio Society).

Moore, Benjamin (1992), 'Governing Discourses: Problems of Narrative Authority in *A Journal of the Plague Year*', *The Eighteenth Century: Theory and Interpretation* 33.2: 133–47.

Moore, Lisa (1997), *Dangerous Intimacies: Toward a Sapphic History of the British Novel* (Durham: Duke University Press).

Morash, Christopher (2002), *A History of Irish Theatre 1601–2000* (Cambridge: Cambridge University Press).

Moritz, Karl Philipp (2000), *Reisen eines Deutschen in England im Jahre 1782* (Frankfurt/Main: Insel).

Morley, David (1992), *Television, Audiences and Cultural Studies* (London: Routledge).

Muir, Percy (1954), *English Children's Books, 1600 to 1900* (London: B.T. Batsford).

Müllenbrock, Heinz-Joachim (1997), *The Culture of Contention: A Rhetorical Analysis of the Public Controversy About the Ending of the War of the Spanish Succession, 1710–1713* (Munich: Fink).

Müller, Anja (2006), 'Spectatorship and Performance in Eighteenth-Century Periodicals', in Frédéric Ogée and Peter Wagner (eds), *Representation and Performance in the Eighteenth Century* (Trier: WVT), 191–207.

——— (2009), *Framing Childhood in Eighteenth-Century English Periodicals and Prints, 1689–1789* (Aldershot: Ashgate).

Mulvey, Laura (1975), 'Visual Pleasure and Narrative Cinema', *Screen* 16.3: 6–18; repr. in Leo Braudy and Marshall Cohen (eds) (1999), *Film Theory and Criticism: Introductory Readings* (Oxford: Oxford University Press), 833–44.

Naumann, Peter (1976), *Keyhole and Candle: John Cleland's "Memoirs of a Woman of Pleasure" und die Entstehung des pornographischen Romans in England* (Heidelberg: Winter).

Nenner, Howard (1995), *The Right to be King: The Succession to the Crown of England, 1603–1714* (Basingstoke: Macmillan).

Neumann, Fritz Wilhelm (2008), 'Spying the Innumerable Attractions and Distractions of the Metropolis: The London Leisure Industry in the Early Eighteenth Century', *EESE* 3, http://webdoc.gwdg.de/edoc/ia/eese/eese.html.

Newman, Donald J. (2005), 'Introduction', in Donald J. Newman (ed.), *The Spectator: Emerging Discourses* (Newark: University of Delaware Press), 11–38.

Nicholson, Marjorie Hope (1976), *Science and Imagination* (Hamden, CT: Archon Books).

Nixon, Cheryl L. (2002), '"Stop a Moment at this Preface": The Gendered Paratexts of Fielding, Barker and Haywood', *JNT: Journal of Narrative Theory* 32.2: 123–53.

Nodelman, Perry (2000), 'Pleasure and Genre: Speculations on the Characteristics of Children's Fiction', *Children's Literature* 28: 1–14.

Novak, Maximilian E. (1977), 'Introduction', in Maximilian E. Novak (ed.), *English Literature in the Age of Disguise* (Berkeley, CA: Yale University Press), 1–14.

——— (1992), 'Defoe and the Disordered City', in Paula R. Backscheider (ed.), *Daniel Defoe: A Journal of the Plague Year* (New York: Norton), 301–18.

Nussbaum, Felicity (2003), *The Limits of the Human: Fictions of Anomaly, Race, and Gender in the Long Eighteenth Century* (Cambridge: Cambridge University Press).

——— (2006), 'Naughty Pamela's "Sweet Confusion"', in Lisa Zunshine and Jocelyn Harris (eds), *Approaches to Teaching the Novels of Samuel Richardson* (New York: Modern Language Association of America), 63–9.

O'Brien, John (2005), 'Genre, Gender, Theater', in Cynthia Wall (ed.), *A Concise Companion to the Restoration and Eighteenth Century* (London: Blackwell), 183–201.

O'Connell, Michael (2000), *The Idolatrous Eye: Iconoclasm and Theatre in Early Modern England* (Oxford: Oxford University Press).

O'Malley, Andrew (2003), *The Making of the Modern Child: Children's Literature and Childhood in the Late Eighteenth Century* (New York: Routledge).

O'Toole, Fintan (1997), *A Traitor's Kiss: The Life of Richard Brinsley Sheridan* (London: Granta).

Oettermann, Stephan (1980), *Das Panorama: Die Geschichte eines Massenmediums* (Frankfurt/Main: Syndikat).

Ogden, Daryl (2005), *The Language of the Eyes: Science, Sexuality, and Female Vision in English Literature and Culture, 1690–1927* (Albany, NY: SUNY).

Old Bailey Proceedings Online (2003–2008), http://www.oldbaileyonline.org/ (5 December 2008).

Ong, Walter J. (2002), *Orality and Literacy: The Technologizing of the Word* (London: Routledge).

Orme, Nicholas (2001), *Medieval Children* (New Haven: Yale University Press).

Outhwaite, Richard B. (2006), *The Rise and Fall of the English Ecclesiastical Courts, 1500–1860* (Cambridge: Cambridge University Press).

Owen, Susan J. (1996), *Restoration Theatre and Crisis* (Oxford: Clarendon).

Pateman, Carole (1988), *The Sexual Contract* (Cambridge: Polity).

Paulson, Ronald (1989), *Hogarth's Graphic Works* (London: The Print Room).

——— (1991), *Hogarth*, vol. I: *The 'Modern Moral Subject'* (New Brunswick: Rutgers University Press).

——— (1992), *Hogarth*, vol. II: *'High Art and Low'* (New Brunswick: Rutgers University Press).

Peakman, Julie (2003), *Mighty Lewd Books: The Development of Pornography in Eighteenth-Century England* (New York: Macmillan).

[Penn, William] (1670), *The Peoples Ancient and Just Liberties asserted, in the Tryal of William Penn, and William Mead, at the Sessions held at the Old-Bailey in London, the first, third, fourth and fifth of Sept. 1670. against the most Arbitrary Procedure of that Court*, repr. in *Phenix XI* (1670?), in *British Trials 1660–1900*, no. 4 (10/1) and no. 5.

Penn, William (1794), *The People's Ancient and Just Liberties Asserted* [...] (Sheffield).

Pfau, Thomas (1997), 'Paranoia Historicized: Legal Fantasy, Social Change, and Satiric Meta-Commentary in the 1794 Treason Trials', in Stephen C. Behrendt (ed.), *Romanticism, Radicalism, and the Press* (Detroit: Wayne State University Press), 30–64.

Phillips, Nicola (2006), *Women in Business, 1700–1850* (Woodbridge, Suffolk: Boydell Press).

Pincus, Stephen (1995), '"Coffee, Politicians Does Create": Coffeehouses and Restoration Political Culture', *Journal of Modern History* 67: 807–34.

Plotz, John (2000), *The Crowd: British Literature and Public Politics* (Berkeley: University of California Press).

Plumb, J.H. (1982), 'The Commercialization of Leisure', in Neil McKendrick, John Brewer, and J.H. Plumb (eds), *The Birth of a Consumer Society* (Bloomington: Indiana University Press).

Pocock, J.G.A. (1975), *The Machiavellian Moment: Florentine Political Thought and the Atlantic Republican Tradition* (Princeton: Princeton University Press).

—— (1985), *Virtue, Commerce, and History: Essays on Political Thought, Chiefly in the Eighteenth Century* (New York: Cambridge University Press).

Pollock, Linda (1983), *Forgotten Children: Parent-Child Relations from 1500 to 1900* (Cambridge: Cambridge University Press).

Porter, Robert Ker and John Vendramini (1800), *The Storming of Seringapatam*, in Hyde, 65.

Porter, Roy (1982), 'Mixed Feelings: The Enlightenment and Sexuality in Eighteenth-Century Britain', in Paul-Gabriel Bouce (ed.), *Sexuality in Eighteenth-Century Britain* (Manchester: Manchester University Press), 1–27.

Pratt, Mary Louise (1992), *Imperial Eyes: Studies in Travel Writing and Transculturation* (London: Routledge).

Ragussis, Michael (2000), 'Jews and Other "Outlandish Englishmen": Ethnic Performance and the Invention of British Identity under the Georges', *Critical Inquiry* 26 (Summer): 773–97.

Rambuss, Richard (1989), '"A Complicated Distress": Narrativizing the Plague in Defoe's *A Journal of the Plague Year*', *Prose Studies* 12: 115–31.

Raymond, Joad (2003), *Pamphlets and Pamphleteering in Early Modern Britain* (Cambridge: Cambridge University Press).

Reinfandt, Christoph (1997), *Der Sinn der fiktionalen Wirklichkeiten: Ein systemtheoretischer Entwurf zur Ausdifferenzierung des englischen Romans vom 18. Jahrhundert bis zur Gegenwart* (Heidelberg: Winter).

Rennhak, Katharina and Virginia Richter (2004), 'Einleitung', in Katharina Rennhak and Virginia Richter (eds), *Revolution und Emanzipation* (Cologne: Böhlau Verlag), 5–13.

The Renowned History of Primrose Prettyface, who By her Sweetness of Temper and Love of Learning, was raised from being the Daughter of a poor Cottager, to great Riches, and the Dignity of Lady of the Manor (1782) (London, n.d.).

Richards, Sandra (1993), *The Rise of the English Actress* (London: St. Martin's Press).

Richardson, Jonathan (1725, 1715), *Essay on the Theory of Painting* (London: Bettesworth).

——— (1856), *Recollections, Political, Literary, Dramatic and Miscellaneous of the Last Half-Century* (London: C. Mitchell).

Richardson, Samuel (1980, 1740), *Pamela; or, Virtue Rewarded*, Peter Sabor (ed.) (London: Penguin).

——— (1986, 1753), *Sir Charles Grandison*, Jocelyn Harris (ed.) (Oxford: Oxford University Press).

——— (2004, 1747), *Clarissa; or, The History of a Young Lady*, Angus Ross (ed.) (London: Penguin).

Richetti, John (1992), 'Epilogue: *A Journal of the Plague Year* as Epitome', in Paula R. Backscheider (ed.), *Daniel Defoe:* A Journal of the Plague Year (New York: Norton), 295–301.

Ricoeur, Paul (1991), 'Narrative Identity', *Philosophy Today* 35.1: 73–81.

——— (1992), *Oneself as Another* (Chicago: Chicago University Press).

Roach, Joseph (2003), 'Celebrity Erotics: Pepys, Performance, and Painted Ladies', *Yale Journal of Criticism* 16.1: 211–30.

——— (2007), *It* (Ann Arbor: University of Michigan Press).

Ronksley, William (1712), *The Child's Weeks-work: or, A Little Book, so nicely Suited to the Genius and Capacity of a Little Child, Both for Matter and Method, That it will infallibly Allure and Lead him on into a Way of Reading With all the Ease and Expedition that can be desired* (London).

Rosenthal, Laura (2006), *Infamous Commerce: Prostitution in Eighteenth-Century British Literature and Culture* (Ithaca: Cornell University Press).

Rousseau, George S. (1968), 'Nerves, Spirits, and Fibres: Towards Defining the Origins of Sensibility', in *Studies in the Eighteenth Century: Papers Presented at the David Nichol Smith Memorial Seminar, Canberra, 1966* (Toronto: University of Toronto Press), 137–57.

Said, Edward (1994), *Orientalism* (New York: Vintage Books).

Schabert, Ina (1997), *Englische Literaturgeschichte: Eine neue Darstellung aus der Sicht der Geschlechterforschung* (Stuttgart: Kröner).

Schindler, Stephan K. (1996), 'The Critic as Pornographer: Male Fantasies of Female Reading in Eighteenth-Century Germany', *Eighteenth-Century Life* 20.3: 66–80.

Schmitz, Thomas A. (2000), 'Plausibility in the Greek Orators', *American Journal of Philology* 121: 47–77.

Schoenfeldt, Michael C. (1999), *Bodies and Selves in Early Modern England: Physiology and Inwardness in Spenser, Shakespeare, Herbert, and Milton* (Cambridge: Cambridge University Press).

Scholz, Susanne (2000), *Body Narratives: Writing the Nation and Fashioning the Subject in Early Modern England* (Houndmills: Macmillan).

Schröder, Hans-Christoph (2006), 'Die Geschichte Englands bis 1945', in Hans Kastendiek and Roland Sturm (eds), *Länderbericht Großbritannien* (Bonn: Budrich), 14–51.

Schroer, Markus (2006), *Räume, Orte, Grenzen: Auf dem Weg zu einer Soziologie des Raums* (Frankfurt/Main: Suhrkamp).

Schulte-Sasse, Jochen (1990), 'Aesthetic Illusion in the Eighteenth Century', in Frederick Burwick and Walter Pape (eds), *Aesthetic Illusion: Theoretical and Historical Approaches* (Berlin: De Gruyter), 105–21.

Scrivener, Michael Henry (2001), *Seditious Allegories: John Thelwall and Jacobin Writing* (University Park: Penn State University Press).

Sehsucht: Das Panorama als Massenunterhaltung des 19. Jahrhunderts (1993), Kunst- und Ausstellungshalle der BRD (ed.) (Frankfurt/Main: Stroemfeld).

Seigel, Jerrold (2005), *The Idea of the Self: Thought and Experience in Western Europe since the Seventeenth Century* (Cambridge: Cambridge University Press).

Sen, Sudipta (2004), 'Liberal Government and Illiberal Trade: the Political Economy of "Responsible Government" in Early British India', in Kathleen Wilson (ed.), *A New Imperial History. Culture, Identity, and Modernity in Britain and the Empire, 1660–1840* (Cambridge: Cambridge University Press), 136–54.

Shaftesbury, Anthony Ashley Cooper (1900, 1711), *Characteristics of Men, Opinions, Times*, John M. Robertson (ed.), 2 vols (London: Richards).

Shavit, Zohar (1990), 'Cultural Notions and Literary Boundaries: On the Creation of the Systemic Opposition between Children's Literature and Adult Literature in the Eighteenth Century', *Proceedings of the XIIth Congress of the International Comparative Literature Society* (Munich: Iudicum), 416–22.

Sheik Ali, B. (1999), 'French Relations with Haidar Ali and Tipu Sultan', in K.S. Mathew and S. Jeyaseela Stephen (eds), *Indo-French Relations* (Delhi: Pragati Publications).

Sheridan, Richard Brinsley (1979, 1777), *The School for Scandal* (London: A & C Black).

——— (1989, 1779), *The Critic* (London: A & C Black).

Shoemaker, Robert B. (1998), *Gender in English Society, 1650–1850* (London: Longman).

Shuger, Debora (2000), 'Life Writing in Seventeenth-Century England', in Patrick Coleman, Jayne Lewis, and Jill Kowalik (eds), *Representations of the Self from the Renaissance to Romanticism* (Cambridge: Cambridge University Press), 63–78.

Smith, Charlotte (1794), *The Banished Man: A Novel*, 4 vols (London: T. Cadell, Jr., and W. Davies).

―――― (1796), *Marchmont: A Novel*, 4 vols (London: Sampson Low).

―――― (1993, 1792), 'Preface to the Sixth Edition [of *Elegiac Sonnets and Other Poems*]', in Stuart Curran (ed.), *The Poems of Charlotte Smith* (New York: Oxford University Press), 4–6.

―――― (1997, 1792), *Desmond*, Antje Blank and Janet Todd (eds) (London: Pickering & Chatto).

―――― (1999, 1798), *The Young Philosopher*, Elizabeth Kraft (ed.) (Lexington: University Press of Kentucky).

Solkin, David H. (1982), *Richard Wilson: The Landscape of Reaction* (London: The Tate Gallery).

Sommerville, C. John (1972), 'Bibliographic Note: Toward a History of Childhood and Youth', *Journal of Interdisciplinary History* 3.2: 439–47.

―――― (1972), *The Discovery of Childhood in Puritan England* (Athens: University of Georgia Press).

―――― (1981), 'Breaking the Icon: The First Real Children in English Books', *History of Education Quarterly* 21.1: 51–75.

―――― (1989), 'Puritan Humor, or Entertainment, for Children', *Albion: A Quarterly Journal Concerned with British Studies* 21.2: 227–47.

Speck, W.A. (1970), *Tory & Whig: The Struggle in the Constituencies, 1701–1715* (London: Macmillan).

―――― (1994), *The Birth of Britain: A New Nation 1700–1710* (Oxford: Blackwell).

Stafford, Barbara Maria (1984), *Voyage into Substance: Art, Science, Nature, and the Illustrated Travel Account, 1760–1840* (Cambridge, MA: MIT Press).

Stallybrass, Peter and Allon White (eds) (1986), *The Politics and Poetics of Transgression* (Ithaca: Cornell University Press).

Stanton, Judith Phillips (1988), 'Statistical Profile of Women Writing in English from 1660 to 1800', in Frederick M. Keener and Susan Lorsch (eds), *Eighteenth-Century Women and the Arts* (New York: Greenwood), 247–54.

S[tarling], [Sir] S[amuel] (1671), *An Answer To the Seditious and Scandalous Pamphlet, Entituled, The Tryal of W. Penn and W. Mead, at the Sessions held at the Old Baily, London, the 1, 3, 4, 5 of Sept., 1670* [...] (London).

Starr, G. Gabrielle (2004), 'Objects, Imaginings, and Facts: Going beyond Genre in Behn and Defoe', *Eighteenth-Century Fiction* 16.4: 499–518.

Staves, Susan (1990), *Married Women's Separate Property in England, 1660–1833* (Cambridge, MA: Harvard University Press).

Steel, David (1981), 'Plague Writing: From Boccaccio to Camus', *Journal of European Studies* 11: 88–110.

Steele, Richard (1987, 1709–1711), *The Tatler*, Donald Bond (ed.), 3 vols (Oxford: Clarendon).

―――― (1968, 1722), *The Conscious Lovers* (London: Arnold, 1968).

Steffen, Lisa (2001), *Defining a British State: Treason and National Identity* (Basingstoke: Palgrave).

Stevenson, Nick (2003), *Cultural Citizenship: Cosmopolitan Questions* (Maidenhead: Open University Press).

Straub, Kristina (2009), *Domestic Affairs: Intimacy, Eroticism, and Violence between Servants and Masters in Eighteenth-Century Britain* (Baltimore: Johns Hopkins University Press).

Taylor, Charles (1989), *Sources of the Self: The Making of Modern Identity* (Cambridge, MA: Harvard University Press).

Teltscher, Kate (1995), *India Inscribed: European and British Writing on India, 1600–1800* (New Delhi: Oxford University Press).

The Theatrical Bouquet: Containing an Alphabetical Arrangement of the Prologues and Epilogues, Which have been Published by Distinguished Wits, from the Time that Colley Cibber first came on the Stage, to the present Year (1778) (London).

Thelwall, John (1822), *The Poetical Recreations of the Champion and his literary correspondents; with a selection of Essays, literary and critical, which have appeared in 'The Champion' Newspaper* (London: Champion Press).

——— (1978, 1793), *The Peripatetic or, Sketches of the Heart, of Nature and Society, in a Series of Politico-Sentimental Journals, in Verse and Prose, of the Eccentric Excursions of Sylvanus Theophrastus*, Donald H. Reiman (ed.), 3 vols in 2 (repr. New York: Garland).

——— (1995a, 1795), 'The Present War a principal cause of the Starving Condition of the People'. – The first Lecture 'On the causes of the Dearness and Scarcity of Provisions', *The Tribune*, no. XVI, delivered Wednesday, April 29, in Claeys, 136–61.

——— (1995b, 1795), 'The Second Lecture on the Causes of the present Dearness and Scarcity of Provisions', *The Tribune*, no. XVII, delivered Friday, May 1, in Claeys, 162–81.

——— (1995c, 1795), 'A Warning Voice to the Violent of All Parties; with Reflections on the Events of the First Day of the present Session of Parliament; and an Enquiry whether Conciliatory or Coercive Measures are best calculated to allay Popular Ferments', *The Tribune*, no. XLVII, delivered Friday, Nov. 6, in Claeys, 314–27.

——— (1995d, 1796), *Sober Reflections on the Seditious and Inflammatory Letter of the Right Hon. Edmund Burke, To a Noble Lord*, in Claeys, 329–87.

——— (1995e, 1796), *The Rights of Nature, Against the Usurpations of Establishments*, in Claeys, 389–500.

——— (2001, 1793), *The Peripatetic*, Judith Thompson (ed.) (Detroit: Wayne State University).

Thiel, Udo (2005), 'Self-Consciousness and Personal Identity', in Knut Haakonssen (ed.), *The Cambridge History of Eighteenth-Century Philosophy* (Cambridge: Cambridge University Press), 286–318.

Thompson, Edward P. (1968), *The Making of the English Working Class* (Harmondsworth: Penguin).

Thompson, Judith (1998), 'John Thelwall and the Enfranchisement of Literature', in Tilottama Rajan and Julia M. Wright (eds), *Romanticism, History and the Possibilities of Genre: Re-forming literature, 1789–1837* (Cambridge: Cambridge University Press), 122–48.

———— (2001), 'Introduction', in Judith Thompson (ed.), *John Thelwall's* The Peripatetic (Detroit: Wayne State University), 11–61.

Thompson, Martyn P. (1987), *Ideas of Contract in English Political Thought in the Age of John Locke* (New York, London: Garland).

Tillyard, Stella (2005), 'Celebrity in 18th-Century London', *History Today* (June): 20–27.

Tobin, Beth Fowkes (1999), *Picturing Imperial Power: Colonial Subjects in Eighteenth-Century British Painting* (Durham: Duke University Press).

Todd, Janet (1986), *Sensibility: An Introduction* (London: Methuen).

Tosh, John (1999), 'The Old Adam and the New Man: Emerging Themes in the History of English Masculinities, 1750–1850', in Tim Hitchcock and Michèle Cohen (eds), *English Masculinities, 1660–1800* (Harlow: Longman), 217–38.

'The Trial of Ford Lord Grey of Werk, Robert Charnock, Anne Charnock, David Jones, Frances Jones, and Rebecca Jones, at the King's Bench, for a Misdemeanour, in Debauching the Lady Henriette, daughter of the Earl of Berkeley', Nov. 23, 1682' (1730), *A complete collection of state-trials, and proceedings for high treason, and other crimes and misdemeanours; from the reign of King Richard II. to the end of the reign of King George I*, 6 vols (London), 515–41.

Tufte, Edward R. (2003), *Envisioning Information* (Cheshire, CT: Graphic Press).

Tully, James (1988), 'Governing Conduct', in Edmund Leites (ed.), *Conscience and Casuistry in Early Modern Europe* (Cambridge: Cambridge University Press), 12–71.

Turner, Cheryl (1994), *Living by the Pen: Women Writers in the Eighteenth Century* (London: Routledge).

Van Sant, Ann Jessie (1993), *Eighteenth-Century Sensibility and the Novel: The Senses in Social Context* (Cambridge: Cambridge University Press).

Vanbrugh, John (1982, 1697), *The Provoked Wife* (Manchester: Manchester University Press).

Varisco, Daniel Martin (2007), *Reading Orientalism: Said and the Unsaid* (Seattle: University of Washington Press).

Vickery, Amanda (1993), 'Golden Age to Separate Spheres? A Review of the Categories and Chronology of English Women's History', *Historical Journal* 36: 383–414.

Wagner, Peter (1990), *Eros Revived: Erotica of the Enlightenment in England and America* (London: Paladin).

———— (1991), 'Hogarth's Graphic Palimpsests: Intermedial Adaptation of Popular Literature', *Word and Image* 7.4: 329–47.

———— (1994), 'Der Leser und Lesestoffe im graphischen Werk William Hogarths', in Paul Goetsch (ed.), *Lesen und Schreiben im 17. und 18. Jahrhundert: Studien zu ihrer Bewertung in Deutschland, England, Frankreich* (Tübingen: Narr), 223–41.

———— (1996), 'How to (Mis)read Hogarth – or Ekphrasis Galore', *1650–1850: Ideas, Aesthetics, and Inquiries in the Early Modern Era* 2: 203–40.

———— (1997), 'The Artist at Work: A (De)constructive View of Hogarth's *Beer Street*', in Frédéric Ogée (ed.), *The Dumb Show: Image and Society in the Works of William Hogarth* (Oxford: The Voltaire Foundation), 100–127.

———— (2001a), 'Introduction', in John Cleland, *Fanny Hill* (New York: Penguin), 7–32.

———— (2001b), 'Hogarthian Frames: The New Eighteenth-Century Aesthetics', in David Bindman, Frédéric Ogée, and Peter Wagner (eds), *Hogarth: Representing Nature's Machines* (Manchester: Manchester University Press), 23–46.

Wahrman, Dror (2004), *The Making of the Modern Self: Identity and Culture in Eighteenth-Century England* (New Haven: Yale University Press).

Wainwright, V.L. (1990), 'Lending to the Lord: Defoe's Rhetorical Design in *A Journal of the Plague Year*', *British Journal of Eighteenth-Century Studies* 13: 59–72.

Wallace, Anne D. (1993), *Walking, Literature, and English Culture: The Origins and Uses of Peripatetic in the Nineteenth Century* (Oxford: Clarendon).

Warraq, Ibn (2007), *Defending the West* (New York: Prometheus Books).

Watt, Ian (1987), *The Rise of the Novel: Studies in Defoe, Richardson and Fielding* (repr. London: Hogarth).

Weber, Harold (1996), *Paper Bullets: Print and Kingship under Charles II* (Lexington: University Press of Kentucky).

Weidle, Roland (2005), 'Negotiations of Personal Identity in Eighteenth-Century Domestic Tragedy: John Locke, George Lillo and Edward Moore', *Anglistik* 16.2: 35–48.

Weil, Rachel (1999), *Political Passions: Gender, the Family and Political Argument in England, 1680–1714* (Manchester: Manchester University Press).

Weimann, Robert (2000), *Author's Pen and Actor's Voice: Playing and Writing in Shakespeare's Theatre*, Helen Higbee and William West (eds) (Cambridge: Cambridge University Press).

West, Russell (2001), 'To the Unknown Reader: Constructing Absent Readership in the Eighteenth-Century Novel: Fielding, Sterne and Richardson', *Arbeiten aus Anglistik und Amerikanistik* 26.2: 105–23.

Wharam, Alan (1992), *The Treason Trials, 1794* (Leicester: Leicester University Press).

Wheatley, Henry B. and Peter Cunningham (1891), *London Past and Present*, 3 vols (London: John Murray).

Wheeler, Roxann (2000), *The Complexion of Race: Categories of Difference in Eighteenth-Century British Culture* (Philadelphia: University of Pennsylvania Press).

White, Thomas (1702), *A Little Book for Little Children: Wherein are set down Several Directions for Little Children*, 12th edn (London).

The Whole Proceedings against Robert Earl of Oxford and Earl of Mortimer (1715) (London).

Wiesenthal, Christine S. (1992), 'Representation and Experimentation in the Major Comedies of Richard Brinsley Sheridan', *Eighteenth-Century Studies* 25.3: 309–30.

Wilkinson, Tate (1790), *Memoirs of his own Life*, 4 vols (York).

Williams, Raymond (1977), *Marxism and Literature* (Oxford: Oxford University Press).

Wilson, Kathleen (1995), *The Sense of the People: Politics, Culture and Imperialism in England, 1715–1785* (Cambridge: Cambridge University Press).

Wind, Edgar (1938), 'The Revolution of History Painting', *Journal of the Warburg Institute* 2.1: 116–27.

Womersley, David (2005), 'Confessional Politics in Defoe's *Journal of the Plague Year*', in David Womersley, Paddy Bullard, and Abigail Williams (eds), *'Cultures of Whiggism': New Essays on English Literature and Culture in the Long Eighteenth Century* (Newark: University of Delaware Press), 237–56.

Wood, Gillen D'Arcy (2001), *The Shock of the Real: Romanticism and Visual Culture, 1760–1860* (New York: Palgrave).

Woodward, Josiah (1701), *Account of the Rise and Progress of the Religious Societies in the City of London, etc., and of their endeavours for reformation of manners* (London).

Wordsworth, William (1926, 1850), *The Prelude or Growth of a Poet's Mind*, Ernest de Selingcourt (ed.) (Oxford: Clarendon).

Wordsworth, William and Samuel Taylor Coleridge (1991, 1798, and 1800), *Lyrical Ballads. The text of the 1798 edition with the additional 1800 poems and the Prefaces*, R.L. Brett and A.R. Jones (eds) (London: Routledge).

Worth, Katharine (1992), *Sheridan and Goldsmith* (Houndmills: Macmillan).

Young, Edward (1759), *Conjectures on Original Composition. In a Letter to the Author of Sir Charles Grandison*, 2nd edn (London: A. Millar and R. and J. Dodsley).

Zaret, David (2000), *Origins of Democratic Culture: Printing, Petitions, and the Public Sphere in Early Modern England* (Princeton: Princeton University Press).

Zimmerman, Everett (1992), 'H.F.'s Meditations', in Paula R. Backscheider (ed.), *Daniel Defoe: A Journal of the Plague Year* (New York: Norton), 285–95.

Zipes, Jack (2006), *Fairy Tales and the Art of Subversion: The Classical Genre for Children and the Process of Civilization*, 2nd edn (New York: Routledge).

Zorn, Carsten (2007), 'Die Simpsons der Gesellschaft: Selbstbeschreibungen moderner Gesellschaft und die Populärkultur', in Christian Huck and Carsten Zorn (eds), *Das Populäre der Gesellschaft: Systemtheorie und Populärkultur* (Wiesbaden: VS Verlag), 73–96.

Index